NEW STUDIES IN BIBLICAL THEOLOGY 43

God's mediators

T0341701

NEW STUDIES IN BIBLICAL THEOLOGY 43

Series editor: D. A. Carson

God's mediators

A BIBLICAL THEOLOGY
OF PRIESTHOOD

Andrew S. Malone

APOLLOS

INTERVARSITY PRESS
DOWNERS GROVE, ILLINOIS 60515

APOLLOS (an imprint of Inter-Varsity Press, England)
36 Causton Street
London SW1P 4ST, England
Website: www.ivpbooks.com
Email: ivp@ivpbooks.com

InterVarsity Press, USA
P.O. Box 1400
Downers Grove, IL 60515, USA
Website: www.ivpress.com
Email: email@ivpress.com

InterVarsity Press®, USA, is the book-publishing division of InterVarsity Christian Fellowship/USA® and a member movement of the International Fellowship of Evangelical Students. Website: www.intervarsity.org.

Inter-Varsity Press, England, originated within the Inter-Varsity Fellowship, now the Universities and Colleges Christian Fellowship, a student movement connecting Christian Unions in universities and colleges throughout Great Britain, and a member movement of the International Fellowship of Evangelical Students. That historic association is maintained, and all senior IVP staff and committee members subscribe to the UCCF Basis of Faith. Website: www.uccf.org.uk.

Unless otherwise indicated, Scripture translations are the author's own. English versification is presumed, with Hebrew variations not indicated. Any italicization in Bible quotations has been added by the author.

Scripture quotations marked csb are taken from The Christian Standard Bible. Copyright © 2017 by Holman Bible Publishers. Used by permission. Christian Standard Bible®, and CSB® are federally registered trademarks of Holman Bible Publishers, all rights reserved.

Scripture quotations marked nirv are taken from New International Reader's Version (NIRV) Copyright © 1995, 1996, 1998, 2014 by Biblica, Inc.®. Used by permission. All rights reserved worldwide.

Scripture quotations marked niv are from the Holy Bible, New International Version (Anglicized edition). Copyright © 1979, 1984, 2011 by Biblica (formerly International Bible Society). Used by permission of Hodder & Stoughton Publishers, an Hachette UK company. All rights reserved. 'niv' is a registered trademark of Biblica (formerly International Bible Society). UK trademark number 1448790.

First published 2017

Set in Monotype Times New Roman
Typeset in Great Britain by CRB Associates, Potterhanworth, Lincolnshire

USA ISBN 978-0-8308-2644-5 (print)
USA ISBN 978-0-8308-8740-8 (digital)

UK ISBN 978-1-78359-527-3 (print)
UK ISBN 978-1-78359-528-0 (digital)

InterVarsity Press is committed to ecological stewardship and to the conservation of natural resources in all our operations. This book was printed using sustainably sourced paper.

British Library Cataloguing-in-Publication Data

A catalogue record for this book is available from the British Library.

Library of Congress Cataloging-in-Publication Data

A catalog record for this book is available from the Library of Congress.

P 25 24 23 22 21 20 19 18 17 16 15 14 13 12 11 10 9 8 7 6 5 4 3 2 1

Y 38 37 36 35 34 33 32 31 30 29 28 27 26 25 24 23 22 21 20 19 18 17

In honour of Peter Adam,
faithful servant of biblical theology and of God's priests

Contents

Series preface

New Studies in Biblical Theology is a series of monographs that address key issues in the discipline of biblical theology. Contributions to the series focus on one or more of three areas: (1) the nature and status of biblical theology, including its relations with other disciplines (e.g. historical theology, exegesis, systematic theology, historical criticism, narrative theology); (2) the articulation and exposition of the structure of thought of a particular biblical writer or corpus; and (3) the delineation of a biblical theme across all or part of the biblical corpora.

Above all, these monographs are creative attempts to help thinking Christians understand their Bibles better. The series aims simultaneously to instruct and to edify, to interact with the current literature, and to point the way ahead. In God's universe, mind and heart should not be divorced: in this series we will try not to separate what God has joined together. While the notes interact with the best of scholarly literature, the text is uncluttered with untransliterated Greek and Hebrew, and tries to avoid too much technical jargon. The volumes are written within the framework of confessional evangelicalism, but there is always an attempt at thoughtful engagement with the sweep of the relevant literature.

Although there are many studies of priesthood in the Old Testament, and quite a few that examine the development of that theme in the New Testament, not to mention dogmatic studies this side of the Reformation that tease out the implications of 'the priesthood of all believers', there is, as far as I know, no previous book-length *canonical* study of priesthood. Among the many strengths of Andrew Malone's impressive work, this book fills out both individual and corporate priesthood themes. On the one hand, it traces out the practices and theology of priests who serve in the wider community of the people of God, and on the other it traces out the ways in which the entire covenant community constitutes a corporate priesthood. It carefully surveys the voluminous biblical material on the Levitical priesthood, but it does not ignore how the Melchizedekian priesthood intersects with the Levitical priesthood in ways that make sense only where there is a sensitive biblical-theological reading of the data. Priesthood is a theme that not only runs through both Testaments; it is one of the controlling biblical-theological trajectories without which it is difficult to make much sense of the ministry, life, death, resurrection and ongoing exalted ministry of Jesus Christ.

D. A. Carson
Trinity Evangelical Divinity School

Author's preface

In his overview, Nicholas Haydock (2015: xv) laments that a canonical reading of Levitical priesthood remains inadequately explored. He rightly recognizes that such a whole-Bible approach will intersect with God's whole-Bible mission to the world. Others past and present have offered similar evaluations and I resonate with them. As we shall note in chapter 1, there are plenty of studies of *parts* of the whole. There are myriad investigations of the history of the Old Testament priests and a similar number focused on the New Testament's appropriation of such imagery for Jesus Christ. There is a growing number of studies of Israel's corporate priesthood, along with those concerned with what this means for the priesthood of God's new-covenant people.

Joining Haydock, my lament is not that these component parts have not been studied but that such studies are less frequently connected with each other. The result is that intersecting synergies are neither presented for readers' evaluation nor capitalized upon. A disinterest in connections is sometimes due to investigators' theological bases. Among those sharing a more conservative stance and a commitment to Scripture's relevance and connectedness, at least in most recent studies it is brevity that impedes some of this desired synthesis. I admire the overviews of Alex Cheung (1986), Richard Averbeck (1996) and Paul Ellingworth (2000) – but they total twenty-three pages between them. As another fledgling scholar aptly phrases it, 'While evangelical biblical theologians have given great attention to the temple, the next step is putting the priest in that temple and learning how the priestly types and prophecies inform the person and work of Jesus Christ' (Schrock 2013: 54, n. 6).

Motivation for the present project has been spurred by teaching several classes in recent years, especially as we have explored together books such as Exodus, Leviticus and Hebrews. I record here my gratitude to students who have encouraged me in various ways. In turn, we learn within a stimulating and variegated community of students and faculty, eager to understand and obey the Scriptures and to glorify God through this. I am grateful too to the leadership and governance structures of Ridley College for a generous sabbatical policy, from which this volume has benefited.

Gratitude belongs also beyond this immediate vocational context. Various scholars have generously offered input along the way. In particular, some or all of the manuscript has been read by Greg Goswell, Paul Barker, Peter Adam, Neville Carr, Lindsay Wilson and Matthew Emadi, whose various observations I appreciate. Insights from series editor Don Carson and Inter-Varsity Press commissioning editor Philip Duce have also improved the project. A number of small-group Bible studies and congregations have kindly trialled parts of the content and provided their own insights. All such believers, along with my daughters' enthusiastic interruptions, have sought to keep any academic thinking directed towards real-world application.

It is in such a real-world context that one can admire many before us who have explored – and obeyed – such priestly models. At risk of embarrassing him, I single out Peter Adam, who, in various combinations, has adored God as one of his believer-priests, spurred on other believers in their myriad ministries, cultivated individuals for formal church leadership and modelled it for them, directed students and researchers in their academic worship, contributed to the present NSBT series and, more than anyone I know, striven to promote the great high priesthood of Jesus to recent generations for whom the role and title threatens to be meaningless. Personally and corporately, I and many owe Peter a debt of thanks, one that is best repaid by our increased marvelling at God's work through our Great High Priest and by our obedient response as a royal priesthood among the nations.

Let us have gratitude, through which let us worship God acceptably with reverence and awe. (Heb. 12:28)

Andrew S. Malone

Abbreviations

AB	Anchor Bible
AcT	*Acta theologica*
AIL	Ancient Israel and its Literature
AnBib	Analecta biblica
ANE	ancient Near East(ern)
AOTC	Apollos Old Testament Commentary
ASV	American Standard Version
AUSS	*Andrews University Seminary Studies*
AV/KJV	Authorized Version / King James Version
AYB	Anchor Yale Bible
BBR	*Bulletin for Biblical Research*
BCOTWP	Baker Commentary on the Old Testament Wisdom and Psalms
BDAG	F. W. Danker, W. Bauer, W. F. Arndt and F. W. Gingrich, *Greek–English Lexicon of the New Testament and Other Early Christian Literature*, 3rd ed., Chicago: University of Chicago Press, 2000
BECNT	Baker Exegetical Commentary on the New Testament
BibInt	Biblical Interpretation Series
BJRL	*Bulletin of the John Rylands University Library of Manchester*
BJS	Brown Judaic Studies
BNTC	Black's New Testament Commentaries
BRev	*Bible Review*
BSac	*Bibliotheca sacra*
BST	The Bible Speaks Today
BT	*The Bible Translator*
BTB	*Biblical Theology Bulletin*
BZ	*Biblische Zeitschrift*
BZNW	Beihefte zur Zeitschrift für die neutestamentliche Wissenschaft
CBET	Contributions to Biblical Exegesis and Theology

CBQ	*Catholic Biblical Quarterly*
CEV	Contemporary English Version
Chm	*Churchman*
ConC	Concordia Commentary
CSB	Christian Standard Bible
CTJ	*Calvin Theological Journal*
CTR	*Criswell Theological Review*
CurBR	*Currents in Biblical Research*
DBI	*Dictionary of Biblical Imagery*, ed. L. Ryken, J. C. Wilhoit and T. Longman III, Downers Grove: InterVarsity Press; Leicester: Inter-Varsity Press, 1998
DJG	*Dictionary of Jesus and the Gospels*, ed. J. B. Green, J. K. Brown and N. Perrin, 2nd ed., Downers Grove: InterVarsity Press; Nottingham: Inter-Varsity Press, 2013
DNTB	*Dictionary of New Testament Background*, ed. C. A. Evans and S. E. Porter, Downers Grove: InterVarsity Press; Leicester: Inter-Varsity Press, 2000
DOTHB	*Dictionary of the Old Testament: Historical Books*, ed. B. T. Arnold and H. G. M. Williamson, Downers Grove: InterVarsity Press; Leicester: Inter-Varsity Press, 2005
DOTP	*Dictionary of the Old Testament: Pentateuch*, ed. T. D. Alexander and D. W. Baker, Downers Grove: InterVarsity Press; Leicester: Inter-Varsity Press, 2003
DOTPr	*Dictionary of the Old Testament: Prophets*, ed. M. J. Boda and J. G. McConville, Downers Grove: IVP Academic; Nottingham: Inter-Varsity Press, 2012
EBC²	*Expositor's Bible Commentary*, ed. T. Longman III and D. E. Garland, rev. ed., 13 vols., Grand Rapids: Zondervan, 2006–12
ECC	Eerdmans Critical Commentary
EDBT	*Evangelical Dictionary of Biblical Theology*, ed. W. A. Elwell, Grand Rapids: Baker, 1996
EGGNT	Exegetical Guide to the Greek New Testament
esp.	especially
ESV	English Standard Version

LIST OF ABBREVIATIONS

EvQ	*Evangelical Quarterly*
ExAud	*Ex auditu*
Gk	Greek
GNB	Good News Bible
GOTR	*Greek Orthodox Theological Review*
HCOT	Historical Commentary on the Old Testament
HCSB	Holman Christian Standard Bible
Hebr.	Hebrew
IBC	Interpretation: A Bible Commentary for Teaching and Preaching
ICC	International Critical Commentary
IEJ	*Israel Exploration Journal*
JBL	*Journal of Biblical Literature*
JETS	*Journal of the Evangelical Theological Society*
JHebS	*Journal of Hebrew Scriptures*
JJS	*Journal of Jewish Studies*
JPSTC	Jewish Publication Society Tanakh Commentary
JSHJ	*Journal for the Study of the Historical Jesus*
JSNT	*Journal for the Study of the New Testament*
JSNTSup	Journal for the Study of the New Testament: Supplement Series
JSOT	*Journal for the Study of the Old Testament*
JSOTSup	Journal for the Study of the Old Testament: Supplement Series
Lat.	Latin
LEB	Lexham English Bible
LHBOTS	The Library of Hebrew Bible / Old Testament Studies
LXX	Septuagint
MT	Masoretic Text
NAB	New American Bible
NAC	New American Commentary
NASB	New American Standard Bible
NBD³	*New Bible Dictionary*, ed. D. R. W. Wood, I. H. Marshall, J. D. Douglas and N. Hillyer, 3rd ed., Leicester: Inter-Varsity Press, 1996
NCV	New Century Version
NDBT	*New Dictionary of Biblical Theology*, ed. T. D. Alexander and B. S. Rosner, Leicester: Inter-Varsity Press, 2000
NEB	New English Bible

NET	New English Translation
NIBCNT	New International Biblical Commentary on the New Testament
NIBCOT	New International Biblical Commentary on the Old Testament
NICNT	New International Commentary on the New Testament
NICOT	New International Commentary on the Old Testament
NIDOTTE	*New International Dictionary of Old Testament Theology and Exegesis*, ed. W. A. VanGemeren, 5 vols., Grand Rapids: Zondervan, 1997
NIGTC	New International Greek Testament Commentary
NIRV	New International Reader's Version
NIV	New International Version
NIVAC	New International Version Application Commentary
NJPS	*Tanakh: The Holy Scriptures: The New JPS Translation According to the Traditional Hebrew Text*
NKJV	New King James Version
NLT	New Living Translation (1st ed. 1996; 2nd ed. 2004)
NovTSup	Supplements to Novum Testamentum
NRSV	New Revised Standard Version
NSBT	New Studies in Biblical Theology
NT	New Testament
NTAbh	Neutestamentliche Abhandlungen
OT	Old Testament
OTG	Old Testament Guides
OTL	Old Testament Library
par(s).	parallel(s)
PNTC	Pillar New Testament Commentary
PRSt	*Perspectives in Religious Studies*
PTR	*Princeton Theological Review*
REB	Revised English Bible
RSV	Revised Standard Version
RTR	*Reformed Theological Review*
SBJT	*Southern Baptist Journal of Theology*
SBLDS	Society of Biblical Literature Dissertation Series
SP	Sacra pagina
StBibLit	Studies in Biblical Literature

STDJ	Studies on the Texts of the Desert of Judah
STK	*Svensk teologisk kvartalskrift*
TBN	Themes in Biblical Narrative
TDNT	*Theological Dictionary of the New Testament*, ed. G. Kittel and G. Friedrich, tr. G. W. Bromiley, 10 vols., Grand Rapids: Eerdmans, 1964–76
Them	*Themelios*
THOTC	Two Horizons Old Testament Commentary
TLOT	*Theological Lexicon of the Old Testament*, ed. E. Jenni with C. Westermann, tr. M. E. Biddle, 3 vols., Peabody: Hendrickson, 1997
TOTC	Tyndale Old Testament Commentaries
TS	*Theological Studies*
VE	*Vox evangelica*
VT	*Vetus Testamentum*
VTSup	Supplements to Vetus Testamentum
WBC	Word Biblical Commentary
WTJ	*Westminster Theological Journal*
WUNT	Wissenschaftliche Untersuchungen zum Neuen Testament
ZABR	*Zeitschrift für altorientalische und biblische Rechtgeschichte*
ZAW	*Zeitschrift für die alttestamentliche Wissenschaft*
ZECNT	Zondervan Exegetical Commentary on the New Testament

Chapter One

Orientation

Why a book about priests? To some it is a blasé topic and to others potentially inflammatory. Are we venturing into a domain that will incur disinterest or disdain? We can readily spotlight some of the different personal, academic and pastoral contexts in which a biblical theology of priesthood should prove fruitful.

Perspectives on priesthood

Personal perspectives

All the formative decades of my own life were spent in churches with a congregationalist structure, mostly Baptist. A 'priest' was some guy from another denomination who dressed up and led his church in liturgy (and often using a book other than the Bible). Natural suspicion of anything different suggested that here was someone leading a crowd who did not quite worship God in the 'right' way.

Traditions with a tendency towards flatter leadership structures can indeed view priests as somehow inappropriate. There might be a general nagging doubt largely based on ignorance or uncertainty about what these traditions espouse. Sometimes there is a firm commitment to the unique priesthood of Christ and the general priesthood of all believers, which suggests that a layer of consecrated leadership usurps something of divine prerogatives on the one hand while depriving church members of their identity and ministry on the other.

I now work and worship in a more episcopal context, formally Anglican. It seems to me that there is a great variety of views on what the ordained priesthood means, among clergy as well as church members. In general, the more hierarchical a denomination's ecclesiastical structure, the more one finds that certain elements of a service are reserved for the right person, and that person is typically the one called the local 'priest'. In some traditions this extends to gradations of sacred space where only the right people might venture, at the right times and with the right demeanour (and perhaps the right vestments).

This is a simplistic and subjective outline. Of course I misperceived many things in my younger formative years. As I move into my older formative years, I recognize that various alternatives lie between the extremes sketched here. Such variety is also found *within* traditions. Some Anglican parishes are relatively relaxed on most matters, while some Baptist congregations fiercely guard the administration of the Lord's Supper.

If I had to characterize a key issue here, it would be that all such traditions are unsure of what to do with some of the priests in Scripture. Some of the Bible's priests are just what 'we' expect them to be – and others are too alien or too difficult. So we focus on passages and doctrines with which we feel secure, and we relativize or disregard those with which we disagree or that we cannot accommodate. Although this book has little to say directly about contemporary church leadership, we must develop facility in the biblical language of 'priest' so that we might be equipped to gauge how that term and concept may or may not be relevant today.

A biblical theology of priesthood forces us to engage with all the priests in Scripture, those with whom we are familiar and those who feel like long-lost (or perhaps disinherited) relatives. A biblical theology of priesthood drives us to be more thorough Bible readers.

Academic perspectives

Academia might be construed to include anything written down, not least in a series with the word 'Studies' in its title. The following pages indeed are cast in relatively scholarly tones.

To one dominant academic perspective, the priests of the Bible have proven to be a historical conundrum. The historical-critical method, which has dominated many echelons of biblical scholarship over the last century or two, tries to determine when Israel's priesthood *really* came to prominence. (Such historical explorations abound. Aelred Cody felt that his 1969 survey of continental scholarship was bordering on unnecessary.) What consensus exists leans towards a date during Israel's monarchy if not towards or after the monarchy's termination. The priesthood finally gained sufficient power that it could rewrite – or perhaps even compose for the first time – the earlier histories and doctrines of the nation and could ensure that the priesthood was cast in a desirable light. Again this is a simplification, but it means that some scholars end up commenting on their reconstruction of the history *behind* the text. The words of the Bible are the presenting symptoms of some underlying reality that has to be coaxed from between the lines. It has been complained that such reconstructions can be sufficiently distant from the canonical message that they furnish 'little relevance for a *theology* of priesthood' (Wells 2000: 100; italics throughout this volume are original, unless otherwise indicated). Even to those with a more conservative view of Scripture, the Bible presents a number of academic curiosities. If the Pentateuch insists that there is to be one high priest at any given time, how do we interpret the preponderance of plurals in the Gospels and Acts? If Israel's priests are to be drawn from the tribe of Levi, what do we make of the ascription of priesthood to Jesus from the tribe of Judah? And how *do* we progress towards a priesthood of all believers when few believers are from Levi's line and the vast majority have no Jewish background at all?

A biblical theology of priesthood urges us to engage with the written texts of the Bible, especially as they are presented in the final canon and even when they appear to develop and change as that canon unfolds. A biblical theology of priesthood makes us more accurate exegetes of Scripture.

Pastoral perspectives

Whether or not we agree with having priests in Christian denominations, God's design for priests and priesthood is profoundly pastoral. A biblical priest can be comprehended in the same way that we might use the word 'pastor' today. As we will see, God's priests have been commissioned to aid worshippers in serving the one true God acceptably and pleasingly, and even to bring unbelievers into relationship with him.

I have already hinted at the priesthood of Jesus Christ. The threefold office of 'prophet, priest and king' remains popular in many confessional circles – yet many proponents cannot articulate much about the second title. Jesus' priesthood will certainly occupy a healthy proportion of the coming pages. Wading through chapters of often unfamiliar and excruciating detail in books like Exodus and Leviticus and Numbers does not excite many modern Christians, but it is a helpful way to grow in appreciation for the person and work of Jesus. It is not only a helpful way, but a way that is appropriate and that ultimately is ordained by God.

A biblical theology of priesthood engages the needs of God's frail people in a range of ways, not least in bringing us to magnify our understanding and proclamation of the birth, earthly ministry, death, resurrection, ascension and ongoing heavenly ministry of the Lord

Jesus Christ. A biblical theology of priesthood fuels our doxology and evangelism!

Biblical theology: an outline

What is this biblical theology of which we speak? To the uninitiated, it may simply imply that one's theology is derived from the Bible. Rather, it is a more formal discipline that has been rekindled over the past several decades and is now (again) a thriving industry in itself. One can find whole books devoted to exploring its goals and methods, from slim overviews (J. M. Hamilton 2014a) through to weighty tomes (Scobie 2003). Individual books study individual topics (as per many in the present NSBT series) and dictionaries collate series of summaries (e.g. *EDBT*; *NDBT*).

Scholars can explore such matters elsewhere but may be interested to discern my own approach. What I record in the next few paragraphs is more a lay introduction, written for readers who may find unfamiliar the surprise twists and turns that a biblical theology can entail.

A helpful illustration

The notion of a tapestry helpfully illustrates biblical theology. When one looks at a finished masterpiece, one can notice patches of dominant colour. One whole section may be blue. Perhaps that remains the primary place or the only place where blue occurs. Another colour might return repeatedly across the work; a section of red towards the left might recur once, twice or many times as we scan towards the right. The isolated colours and the recurring ones both contribute to the overall presentation.

Biblical theology is especially concerned with the colours that recur or appear to recur. The isolated patches are, of course, important in themselves, and they are indispensable in the weaver's result. For example, biographers of Jesus dare not downplay the one or two Bible passages that identify him as a craftsman (traditionally 'carpenter', Mark 6:3; cf. Matt. 13:55) or the single claim that he started his public ministry aged 'about' 30 years old (Luke 3:23). But biblical theology investigates those threads that recur more often. Conservative interpreters accept the Bible as written under the inspired guidance of a single Author and expect to see similar themes repeat themselves consistently throughout the masterpiece. In the opening chapters of Scripture, God punishes Cain for murdering Abel and likewise shields Cain against any capital retaliation (Gen. 4:1–16); God's concern for human life is repeated after the flood (9:5–6); even those ignorant of the Bible know the commandment 'Thou shalt not murder' (Exod. 20:13; Deut. 5:17); and the Old Testament is full of condemnations of those who flout this expectation. That same expectation – indeed, the very same command – is affirmed by Jesus and his apostles (e.g. Mark 10:19; Rom. 13:9; Jas 2:11), and the closing chapters of the Bible continue to despise murderers (Rev. 21:8; 22:15). We can confidently discern God's attitude towards intentional, unwarranted life-taking.

It is not too difficult to allow that divine expectations or habits might make minor course adjustments as the story unfolds. Our weaver might introduce a similar hue of the same colour or highlight it with a complementing shade. Jesus famously condemns murder *and* amplifies God's concern to also include anger (Matt. 5:21–22); here in the Sermon on the Mount he likewise strengthens God's dissatisfaction with adultery, divorce, oath-taking, retaliation, and so on.

Conservative interpreters wanting to hold the canon together under God's inspiration are usually far more challenged where God appears to change his mind or his mode of operation. Although they were mistaken, the earliest Christians were surprised that God would welcome Gentiles into his kingdom without first requiring them to become Jewish (esp. Acts 11:1–18; 15:1–35 and the wider section in which Luke narrates this). Readers looking for consistency expect that the Holy Spirit might work with and dwell within God's followers in exactly the same way in both the Old Testament and the New, but biblical theology can demonstrate that this is almost certainly not the case (see the convincing thesis of J. M. Hamilton 2006, with Hamilton's impact précised in Malone 2014). As weavers apparently do, an early thread is ended and is replaced by another that is noticeably or even startlingly different.

That God might vary his response on some matters brings to light an important difference between biblical theology and systematic theology (cf. Carson 2000). The latter tends more to discern a once-off stance on a given topic, scrutinizing the metaphorical tapestry once it has been completed. Biblical theology remains alert to variations that occur as the whole is being produced, as if one were studying a series of time-lapse photographs while the weaver's shuttle is still at work. In coming chapters we ourselves will trace the story of the Bible as it unfolds, looking as much at progressive developments as at any finished portrait.

Some relevant language

Like any other discipline, theology has its own vocational vocabulary to describe such matters. The only structural terms that I want to introduce here are paired and flow smoothly from the tapestry illustration. Many topics in Scripture show a great deal of consistency or 'continuity'. Others are sufficiently different that we should rightly speak of 'discontinuity'.

Again, this is a crude binary distinction and, at least with discontinuity, it is rarely a matter of complete reversal. A white thread is rarely replaced with a black one. So we do well to think about and speak about *degrees* of continuity and discontinuity. This produces plenty of tension among believers and among scholars as we wrestle with these different degrees, these shades of grey as it were. Essays and books abound on any and every issue; good examples and relevant terminology are provided by scholars such as Craig Blomberg (2000) and John Feinberg (1988).

Biblical theology of priesthood: a sketch

Exploring the theme of priesthood across the canon yields both continuities and discontinuities. I outline here something of my findings. This is to illustrate further my approach to biblical theology, to sketch a big-picture map of where we are going, and perhaps to facilitate time-poor readers who seek to locate their favourite threads. It is also an opportunity to preview some of the key language I employ in our exploration.

It seems to me that the Bible speaks broadly of two kinds of priests, and I break my study into part I and part II. The two categories are interrelated and we need to investigate their intersection as well.

The first kind of priest is the sort who gets singled out within a community, just as happens in some church denominations today. These are the individuals who would record 'religious worker' as their vocation on a census. Part I surveys these religious workers. How did a workforce of priests arise? What did God expect of them? How did they fare in their responsibilities in the Old Testament (chapters 2–4)? The Israelite priests continued to operate into the New Testament, yet we also find that the biblical authors started to think of *Jesus* as one of these religious workers – and ultimately as the *replacement* of all earthly priests. How do the Old Testament precursors help us to understand better this presentation of Jesus and his work (chapter 5)?

Part II observes that, at the same time as a select group of Israelites were appointed as individual religious workers (albeit as part of a team of specialists), God commissioned the whole Israelite people as a corporate, national priesthood. The Bible's language for this is 'a kingdom of priests' or 'a priestly kingdom'. What did this mean for the nation, and how should we see the intersection between individual priests and this corporate priesthood (chapter 6)? And, just as the notion of individual priests was transferred to Jesus and even transformed by him, the New Testament transfers the corporate responsibilities of national Israel to God's international church comprised of Jews and Gentiles. What can modern believers grasp of God's intentions and mission for his church today (chapter 7)?

In effect, we are making two passes across the tapestry of Scripture, the first time tracing the continuities and discontinuities of one category of thread (individual priests) and the second time inspecting the consistencies and changes of the second category (corporate priesthood). Unlike a systematic snapshot, our time-lapse analyses demonstrate significant transformations within both categories. Part II builds on some of the details and language of part I, and so it is commensurately shorter. Chapter 8 offers some brief reflections on how our overall biblical theology ought to influence the way that we comprehend and proclaim Jesus and his priesthood (the fruit of part I) and to enhance the identity and mission of the church (the results of part II).

Strengths and weaknesses

This big-picture map already suggests that there will be a number of outcomes of our investigation. Again, I unashamedly tout my hopes that investigating a biblical theology of priesthood will result in greater praise of the triune God and his global mission, as we better appreciate both Jesus' work and our own. This content might afford some additional, passing bases for the place of 'priests' in contemporary church identity and leadership.

There are also a number of corresponding weaknesses. Some shortcomings will be of my own making and others are welcome to correct and refine and extend them. Even where the Scripture and author indexes might look lengthy, there are all too many passages and scholarly lines of enquiry (scholarly threads!) that have not been explored exhaustively. I will have left uncommented someone's favourite grammatical construction and ignored someone else's

7

preferred monograph. Where constraints of length and of sanity have required a choice, I intend to have erred a little more towards breadth rather than depth. I am greatly indebted to the myriad investigators who have gone before me and, while I hope to provide a healthy cross-section of the breadth *and* depth available at the scholarly level, I am all too conscious of the many works untouched or engaged only superficially. I readily apologize for any concepts and nuances that I may have misconstrued or missed altogether.

As noted in the author's preface, there are many studies of one or more of the four areas of investigation sketched above. There are fewer that combine all four threads, and these threads' collocation here is intended to provide an introduction to each separately and to explore how they work together to enhance our understanding. As such, my investigation has the flavour of a survey, in some ways like a high-level web page. We have opportunity to delve into finer details on some topics, but other topics leave only a (hypothetically) hyperlinked scholarly reference to be explored or a nagging lacuna for someone else to fill. Hopefully the web page itself functions as a passable collation of relevant issues. To change the metaphor, the survey is something like a table of contents, cataloguing some of the various investigations that have gone before. Its contribution is as much in its collation and sifting of existing ideas as in seeking to pioneer new territory, and hence it is more heavily documented than some in the NSBT series.

Terminology

The biblical terms

Hebrew and Greek terms have been introduced sparsely and only when they enhance our understanding of a passage.

Conveniently, the primary terms with which we are concerned are hardly difficult to navigate. There is really only one Hebrew word for 'priest' (*kōhēn*), although there are obvious cognates such as 'high priest' and 'priesthood'. There is much dispute about the derivation of the term, but we can talk confidently about 'priests' and let the Bible give texture to its use of the word. Similarly, the Greek of the New Testament (and also of the Greek translation of the OT, the Septuagint) revolves around one term (*hiereus*) and its cognates.

For completeness, while the same terms are used continuously throughout each testament, God's priests are not always serving in the same physical location. We shall encounter the tabernacle constructed by Moses and the Israelites (much of Exodus). After the move into Canaan and capture of Jerusalem, a temple was prepared by David and built by Solomon (narrated in Samuel, Kings and especially Chronicles) and thus often titled 'Solomon's Temple'. It was destroyed at the fall of Jerusalem in 586 BC, and then replaced after Israel's release from Babylonian exile (administered by Zerubbabel, under the watchful eye of leaders such as Ezra and the prophets Haggai and Zechariah); this 'Second Temple' was still the centre of Jewish cultic ritual at the time of Jesus. Refurbished by Herod the Great, and thus sometimes also known as 'Herod's Temple', it would stand until the next sacking of Jerusalem in AD 70. Other activities of godly priests might be glimpsed prior to the tabernacle, and there are plenty of priests serving other gods in other locations.

The English terms

As I lament in chapter 8, the biblical terms are actually easier to engage than is the English language of 'priest(hood)'. Part of that has to do with the linguistic and theological etymology of the English words. Further, readers of all cultural backgrounds and ecclesiastical traditions will have their own existing perception of 'priest'. There are times when that existing perception correlates well with the biblical portrait, but at other times 'priest' (as we each comprehend it) may not be the best fit.

We might admire studies that can sustain original-language terms. We could wade through the Bible – twice – speaking purely of *kōhănîm* and *hiereis* (the plural forms of *kōhēn* and *hiereus*). But that is less accessible for some, and it is a misplaced zeal to think that we can undo the longstanding use of 'priest'. In keeping with convention, I continue to use the word 'priest'. We must, however, remain alert to whatever connotations we bring to that term.

A conceptual term

Apart from the language of 'priest(hood)', one is hard pressed to find a discussion of the topic that does not invoke the English concept of 'mediator' and/or 'mediation'. I happily continue in that vein.

The language of 'mediator' is sometimes prone to misinterpretation. It is sometimes (mis)used by limiting its sense to the mediating of *communication*, as if a priest is a courier who shuttles missives back and forth between two negotiating parties. The biblical priests and priesthoods do have an important role in such communicative mediation. But they are much more than that. At the least, we find that the priest himself is a *representative* of each party as he speaks on behalf of one to the other. The priest is more an authorized and recognized ambassador than a background courier. The image comes to a head in the Greek term for 'mediator' (*mesitēs*; there is not much in the way of a Hebrew equivalent). It moves into the realm of reconciliation and assurances and guarantees. One flagship lexicon (BDAG, 634) gives as its primary definition, 'one who mediates betw[een] two parties to remove a disagreement or reach a common goal, *mediator, arbitrator*'. This is certainly the case with Jesus' mediation between God and humanity. We should remain attuned to possibilities of this sense in other contexts of priests and priesthood. William Propp (2006: 527) helpfully reminds us that 'One Latin term for priest, *pontifex*, etymologically means "bridge-maker"' and suggests that 'this would be a most appropriate description for Aaron the Great Priest'.

We might hear the word 'priest' and conjure up an image of an archaic shaman beseeching the gods through rituals and liturgies and sacrifices. We might leap to something not wildly dissimilar in some of today's denominations. We do well also to recall famous political leaders who bring warring factions to the negotiating table and who oversee the hammering out of a peace accord.

A blank slate

Beyond the overarching sense of mediating, scholars quickly catalogue from their preferred texts their favourite activities concerning biblical priests. We could construct composite lists that include elements such as teaching, tending, serving, judging, proclaiming and blessing. The Bible itself, near the beginning and the end of the Hebrew order of the canon, provides its own summaries (e.g. Lev. 10:10–11; 1 Chr. 23:13; cf. Deut. 33:8–10). Although some such preferencing is probably unavoidable, let us attempt to work through the Bible and discover those activities and lists for ourselves. In that sense, the ensuing presentation is as much expositional and synthetic as it is analytical and thesis driven. It aids us to see the data laid out, the questions raised and explored, and to trace the threads of Scripture for ourselves. This will augment and refine our existing knowledge, reinforce or reshape our theological frameworks, and make us better expositors of the texts and their consequences for God's holy people.

Part I
God's individual priests

Chapter Two

The Aaronic priesthood begins

Priests and priestly activities are mentioned before the nation of Israel is formally established at Mount Sinai in the middle of the book of Exodus. Yet we can evaluate those prior mentions by starting with the priesthood instituted at Sinai. In this chapter we survey the midlands of the Pentateuch and the foundational expectations of Old Testament priests, and we find that priests participate in a range of activities with the central focus of facilitating proximity between God and humanity.

The Sinai context

Modern readers of the Bible are often shaped by the action genres so prevalent in contemporary films, television shows and novels. We become used to moving from one set-piece highlight to the next while waiting, perhaps impatiently, through any unavoidable character development or dialogue. Formal studies of biblical books can favour structures based on action and movement, even when alternative organizing principles are viable.[1]

It is thus necessary to remember that a third of the Pentateuch narrates events while Israel is stationary at Sinai (and another quarter

---

[1] A geographical structure is common not least for the books we are about to scrutinize. Exodus is often presented as the stories of Israel in and escaping from Egypt (chs. 1 – 13/14), travelling in the wilderness (chs. 13/14 – 18) and camped at Sinai (chs. 19 – 40); so Durham 1987. V. P. Hamilton (2011: xxiii) notes the preponderance of 'locomotive verbs' in Exodus. Yet the uncertainties about where to end the Egypt/exodus section and about when Israel arrives at Sinai suggest that these locations are not the primary focus of the author/redactor. I am thus more sympathetic to interpretations that focus on content rather than location, such as rescue from Egypt (chs. 1 – 15/18), giving of the law (chs. 15/19 – 24), and the tabernacle (chs. 25 – 40); so Enns 2000; cf. Wenham 2003: 58; Garrett 2014: 138–139. Likewise, the traditional geographical interpretation of Numbers (e.g. Wenham 1981; 1997) is now heavily challenged by insights into generational transition (Olson 1985; 1996; adapted by Ashley 1993; R. D. Cole 2000). NT narratives face the same tension, with Acts traditionally interpreted geographically (e.g. Witherington 1998; Keener 2012–15) but with Luke's literary markers given increasing credence (esp. Longenecker 2007).

while camped on the plains of Moab). The exodus generation arrives by Exodus 18:5 and does not set out again until Numbers 10:11. The intervening five dozen chapters cover only a small splinter of time: barely eleven months. The nation of Israel is formally founded and the law given (Exod. 19 – 24), and we hear all too soon of their idolatrous rebellion with the golden calf and the renewal of the covenant (Exod. 32 – 34). Apart from related explorations of the law (esp. Lev. 17 – 27) more than three dozen chapters are focused squarely on the design and building of the tabernacle and its furniture and on the personnel and rituals required for its operation and transport (Exod. 25 – Lev. 16; Num. 1 – 10). Later chapters of the Pentateuch contribute further to these elements (e.g. Num. 15 – 19).

We should not underestimate the significance of the tabernacle or the successive instantiations of the temple that would come to replace it. It serves as the proverbial 'slice of heaven' – a geospatial representation of God's presence among his people. To pick up the political imagery glimpsed in my previous chapter, the tabernacle is God's embassy, wherein his local representatives function and where he describes himself as dwelling among his people.

And so we turn to consider what this Sinai material in Exodus through to Numbers has to say about the tabernacle personnel. We work in detail through what is said expressly about the high priest, about other priests, and also about their assistants the Levites.

A reminder of terminology

Each of these three categories of tabernacle personnel can be described in various ways. The interrelationship between them can sometimes also be a trap to those unfamiliar with them. What is summarized here is revisited in more detail later in this chapter.

The Levites comprise one of the tribes of Israel, named after the third of Jacob's twelve sons (Gen. 29:34). The adjective 'Levitical' especially describes them once the members of their tribe are assigned to sacral duties. When Moses is sent again to confront Pharaoh, the Exodus narrative interjects a partial family tree of Jacob's descendants (Exod. 6:13–27). Following the list of the first two of the twelve sons (along with their offspring) the third branch – Levi's – dominates the remainder of the genealogy. Here readers learn two immediately relevant facts. First, Levi had three sons: Gershon, Kohath and Merari. In due course the Levites and their tabernacle responsibilities come to be classified according to these three clans. The second discovery is that Aaron and Moses, apparently born in that order, are among the descendants of Levi.[2] Exodus 6:23 introduces us to Aaron's wife and four sons. It is only the members of Aaron's family who qualify to be priests. In turn, it is only the current head of Aaron's family who serves as the high priest among other priests. What we have here is an increasingly narrow subset of personnel. To revisit these in reverse order, we find that (1) Aaron (and whichever individual succeeds him as family head) is the high priest. No other member of Aaron's family holds that position while the current high priest lives. (2) Only Aaron's descendants can be tabernacle priests. Not even Aaron's brother, Moses, is a priest in the same sense. (3) It is only members of the tribe of Levi who can serve as Levites in the tabernacle (and there are other constraints as well). Other Israelites, such as the descendants of Reuben and Simeon, are welcome in the tabernacle and temple but may not undertake Levitical duties.

Related terminology can also be confusing. The senior priest is variously known as 'the high/great priest' or 'the chief/head priest' or 'the anointed priest', and most often just 'the priest' (Duguid 1994: 59). Leviticus 21:10 brings together several such terms in describing 'the priest, the one greater/higher than his brothers, on whose head has been poured the oil of anointing and who has been ordained to wear the garments'. Although such terms are interchangeable, I shall tend to follow the one found more frequently and almost always translated in English texts as 'the high priest'.[3]

The Bible often refers generically to 'the priests', clearly indicating authorized members of Aaron's family. Additional adjectives can be employed. Scripture uses the fuller phrase 'the priests, the sons of Aaron' and equally frequently identifies 'the Levitical priests'. Scholars use such biblical phrases and often fairly abbreviate the former to speak of 'the Aaronic priest(hood)' (cf. 2 Chr. 35:14 NIV).

---

[2] V. P. Hamilton (2011: 106) notes that the five occurrences of 'Aaron and Moses', rather than the seventy-eight uses of 'Moses and Aaron', appear in genealogies (Exod. 6:20; Num. 3:1; 26:59; 1 Chr. 6:3; 23:13). Hamilton also observes (108–109) that, while the narratives here and in Num. 3 move quickly to describe God's instructions to Moses, both genealogies take time to spell out *Aaron's* descendants; some importance is preserved for the Aaronides even when not the immediate focus of a passage.

[3] Standard lexicons outline the terminology used and their references. The points here are helpfully collocated by Jenson (1997: 601). We ought also to recognize that we are applying the term 'high priest' retrospectively; the formal title is not recorded until Num. 35:25 (Duke 2003: 647).

Such phrases are interchangeable because, although not all *Levites* belong to Aaron's family, any Levitical *priest* ought to be descended from Aaron.

The Aaronic priesthood

Although it is simple enough and attractive to synthesize categories that align with our own modern concerns, Scripture supplies an excellent agenda for us. As much as any systematic textbook, the Bible itself concentrates discussions of the Aaronic priesthood in several major blocks within the chapters set at Sinai:

- Within its larger section prescribing and describing the construction of the tabernacle and its furnishings (Exod. 25 – 40), Exodus 28 – 29 focuses directly on the priests, their dress code and their commissioning.
- Leviticus 1 – 7 outlines the sacrifices that the priests oversee.
- Leviticus 8 – 10 deals with the formal ordination of the priests.
- The remainder of Leviticus is concerned with various aspects of Israelite behaviour, for which the priesthood has substantial responsibility.
- Other priestly responsibilities are found in subsequent books, not least the opening chapters of the adjacent book of Numbers.

As we work through this general order, we follow Scripture's agenda. In turn this leverages the sense and contexts that develop when ancient and modern readers experience the Pentateuch in canonical order.

What gives rise to the priesthood?

Although there is little mention of priests in Exodus 19 – 27, these opening chapters at Sinai introduce a new intensity in the relationship between God and his elect nation Israel. They lay the theological groundwork for the need to have Aaronic priests at all.

Having 'saved' his people from slavery in Egypt (Exod. 14:30) through the well-known plagues and exodus, God summons Moses to offer Israel a new status (19:3–6). The bulk of Exodus 19 recounts the careful preparations for and events of this nation-founding theophany. (We return in chapter 3 to the intriguing mention of priests in 19:22, 24, and in chapter 6 to the commission of Israel to be 'a kingdom of priests' in 19:6.) The law is then given and the covenant ratified (Exod. 20 – 23, 24).

There are of course many important elements in these chapters and many commensurate studies of them (e.g. Moberly 1983; Niehaus 1995). Without diminishing the significance of the intervening chapters, it seems to me that it is the first and last of these chapters (Exod. 19, 24) that most readily explain the rest of God's revelation at Sinai concerning the tabernacle with its personnel and operations (Exod. 25 – Num. 10). Both Exodus 19 and 24 revolve around the nearer presence of God among his people and require brief further inspection.

Exodus 19 demonstrates the grand privilege that Israel experiences as Yahweh draws near to commission it as 'my personal treasure', hand-picked from among all the peoples of the whole earth (19:5).[4] The people are agreeable and have three days to prepare for God's coming descent to endorse Moses as his spokesman (19:7–15). Narrated in the latter half of the chapter, the theophany itself is a frightful event – a full multisensory encounter with God. The Israelites see lightning and a thick cloud, and hear thunder and (even before leaving their camp) 'the sound of a very loud trumpet' (19:16). Moses then leads them out of the camp 'to meet God' (19:17; cf. 3:18; 5:3)! They experience fire and smoke and earthquake: standard theophany elements (19:18–19; cf. 20:18; Isa. 6:4; Amos 9:1).

Later reflections on this event focus on the Israelites' terrified response. They demur from any further direct experience and thrust Moses forward as their proxy (Exod. 20:18–21; Deut. 5:22–27) – an appropriate fear that God commends (Deut. 5:28–30). Moses is thus the sole remaining go-between, an English description that recognizes that he operates bidirectionally. (The paraphrastic NIRV actually uses the term 'go-between' where Moses and Jesus are described in the NT as mediators, Gal. 3:19–20; 1 Tim. 2:5; Heb. 8:6; 9:15; 12:24.) Moses is sent by the people to stand in their stead (Exod. 20:19; Deut. 5:27) and God is pleased to communicate back through Moses his instructions to them (Deut. 5:31; cf. Exod. 20:22). This two-way role is instructive for our conception of priests.

Equally instructive is the very notion of being in God's presence. The people retreat, foisting the responsibility upon Moses. Yet, at the completion of the law-giving through Moses, seventy-four leaders are summoned into God's presence (Exod. 24:1–2), including three to be

---

[4] For a similar image, Carpenter (1997: 224): 'Israel will become the "crown jewel" among all the nations.' We explore in ch. 6 the imagery of 19:5–6, the more exclusive translation ('*instead of* all the peoples') and the purpose of Israel's (s)election.

named shortly as priests: Aaron, Nadab and Abihu. Moses alone draws nearer to God, but all seventy-four feast safely in his presence (24:9–11). Indeed, the text says – twice – that they 'see' God, though it gives no further description of him but only of his surrounds (cf. Isa. 6; Rev. 4) and overtly observes that God did not smite them on this occasion (a threat all too readily expected; e.g. Gen. 32:30; Lev. 16:2; Judg. 13:22; Isa. 6:5). Safe approach to God will become an important element of priestly service.[5] The next section of Exodus begins with three chapters on the construction of the tabernacle (Exod. 25 – 27). There are a great many studies of this portable temple and the more permanent versions built later. The tabernacle/temple is absolutely central to the biblical story and warrants its own attention. For our purposes, we can afford only the briefest summary here, though in coming chapters we shall glimpse these buildings in the background of most priestly activities.[6]

Physically, the tabernacle comprises an outer courtyard surrounding a central tent. This central tent is subdivided unevenly into two areas, the first ('the Holy Place') leading into the second ('the Most Holy Place' or 'the Holy of Holies'). Exodus 25 – 27 introduces the materials and dimensions for the structures and the items of furniture that populate and operate in the different areas.

Conceptually, the tabernacle represents a concentration of God's presence in creation. Although such theology is developed in subsequent biblical books, an executive summary is already foregrounded in the present chapters of Exodus. God instructs Moses to solicit materials from the Israelites. (Even in such mundane matters Moses functions as an intermediary. In 25:2 God solicits offerings 'for me', but they are collected by Moses.) While God prescribes specific resources, their overarching purpose is announced: the people 'will make for me a holy place (= a sanctuary) and I will dwell in their midst' (25:8). The next verse labels this structure a 'tabernacle', which itself is merely Latin for 'tent' just as the Hebrew noun connotes. Our religiose English can obscure three important points here. The first is

---

[5] Exod. 19:21 implies that the nation might have successfully sighted God, though the text there makes no claim that this occurred. Others dismiss the possibility of meeting God visually in the way 24:9–11 describes. I argue in Malone 2007 for the plausibility of seeing God; expanded in Malone 2015, e.g. ch. 2.

[6] See e.g. the thick volume of Beale 2004. To some extent, my present volume aspires to be a twin to his, concerned with the personnel of the tabernacle/temple and with developments and extensions under the new covenant; it could potentially be subtitled *Priesthood and the Church's Mission*. In this respect, note now the brief study of Haydock 2015, the synthesis of Anizor and Voss 2016, and the general theme of Lister 2015.

the simple linguistic connection within 25:8–9: God is planning 'to dwell' (*šākan*) in a 'dwelling' (*miškān*). Second, the various nouns are largely synonymous: God's 'dwelling' is a 'tent' described as a 'sanctuary'. Certainly the latter communicates something special, holy, sacred – and ensuing verses will highlight some opulent elements. But architecturally God's residence is nothing different from any other Bedouin's. Third, we must not overlook the equally simple but startling fact that the transcendent deity plans to localize his presence and encamp among a nation of humans.[7] Moses is thus primed to articulate God's construction blueprints. God himself is adamant that Moses' builders are to follow *God's* specifications (25:9). The intricate details which new-covenant believers can blithely gloss over, sometimes with eyes glazed over, are divinely designed! Moreover, evangelical interpreters are swift to observe that God does not merely show Moses some schematic but the real dwelling of God that Moses is to emulate (cf. Heb. 8:1–5; Acts 7:44) (e.g. Beale 2004: 295; V. P. Hamilton 2011: 455).

And the very first item to be constructed portrays God's throne or, more precisely, the footstool serving his heavenly throne. The ark of the covenant is where God will meet and speak with Moses, who, again, will convey God's instructions to Israel (Exod. 25:22). It is thus 'the focus of the entire enterprise' (Sarna 1991: 159). This focus on the ark also distinguishes Moses more as God's ongoing messenger than as the exclusive kind of temple builder that other ANE accounts might emphasize; whether through their representative or even directly, the ark is the place where God will meet *all* the Israelites (29:43) (Utzschneider 2014: 274, 285). One even wonders if God intended any link between the name of the first priest, Aaron (*'ahărōn*), and the 'ark' (*hā'ārōn*) at the focus of Aaron's ministry.

The remainder of the tabernacle complex is equally fascinating but need not consume our attention. From this central presence of God, the tabernacle expands in (conceptually) concentric circles. The ark is to be placed in the innermost room of the sanctuary tent. As one moves closer to God's presence above the ark, one must be more suited

---

[7] This very point will form the crescendo of the prologue of John's Gospel. Just as God plans to dwell among his people in a dwelling/tent (Gk *skēnē*; Exod. 25:8–9), and we shortly find the completed tent/tabernacle filled with God's glory (Gk *doxa*; 40:34–35), so John 1:14 marvels at Jesus' incarnation: 'the Word became flesh and dwelt [*skēnoō*] among us, and we have seen his glory [*doxa*]'! (Although Exod. 25:8 LXX lacks the expected *skēnoō*, its choice of *ophthēsomai* – 'and *I will be seen* among them' – is itself arresting.)

19

to meet him. The converse also holds: the outer room, then the tabernacle courtyard, then the Israelite camp surrounding the tabernacle complex, and finally the rest of the world represent decreasingly holy, and thus increasingly safe, regions. It is this progression of 'graded holiness' that occupies the priests, who care for the tabernacle and its Israelite worshippers for as long as God – who is elsewhere described as 'a consuming fire' (Exod. 24:17; Deut. 4:24; 9:3; Ps. 97:3; Heb. 12:29) – chooses to dwell in their midst.[8]

Who becomes a priest?

The concentric bands of graded holiness correspond to the levels of access privilege that are appropriate to different members of the Israelite community. While the language of 'holiness' may conjure up for contemporary readers images of pious behaviour, such ethical living is the result of holiness rather than its cause. Old Testament scholars persistently correct the popular interpretation and observe that holiness is effectively a *status* (e.g. Wells 2000: 55–57; Gentry 2008: 47–48; Abernethy 2016: 18–19). Being more holy marks someone or something as more like God or more suited to being in God's presence. It is from this proximity to God that we derive secondary senses such as 'set apart' or 'upright'.

God thus prescribes who is deemed 'holy/sacred' enough to draw closer to him. On the scale of graded holiness for tabernacle access to God, the priests are at the top of the list with the high priest holding the highest rank. John Scholer (1991: 15) adroitly summarizes that 'The feature most characteristic of the priest was his holiness . . . The distinguishing trait of the high priest . . . was his greater degree of holiness.' In God's dwelling, God specifies the guest list.

God's guests can readily be viewed as those who attend to him and to his dwelling (esp. Leithart 1999). From Exodus 27:20–21, the instructions for tabernacle appurtenances start to include something of their operation. Here we are told that oil should be sourced for the lampstand (previously designed at 25:31–40) so that 'Aaron with his sons shall tend it, from evening until morning before Yahweh.'[9]

---

[8] 'Graded holiness' is the focus of Jenson 1992. His subtitle further clarifies this as *A Key to the Priestly Conception of the World*, and he articulates a 'Holiness Spectrum' running from Very Holy → Holy → Clean → Unclean → Very Unclean.

[9] A new division starting at 27:20, based precisely on more operational instructions, has been championed by Milgrom (1991: 236–237) and continues to gain acceptance (e.g. Meyers 2008: 17–18; V. P. Hamilton 2011: 453). A link between lampstands and high-priestly vestments also helps to clarify the imagery of Rev. 1:12–16 (esp. Winkle 2012: 293–298).

It is at this very point that God's instructions to Moses turn to describe in more detail the selection, attire and consecration of Aaron and his sons (Exod. 28 – 29). Aaron is the primary focus here, with his four sons more his assistants than his equals. Just as 28:2–5 is concerned almost exclusively with Aaron's unique clothing, so the preceding verbs and prepositions (27:21; 28:1) are singular, focused on Aaron's role (V. P. Hamilton 2011: 480, 482). This itself reminds us that, while Moses' instructions turn swiftly to consider this wardrobe, the very first command (28:1) is one that sets aside Aaron and his family ('bring [them] near to you . . . from among the Israelites') with the express purpose 'to be a priest for me'.[10]

Aaron's sons are introduced alongside him – Nadab and Abihu, Eleazar and Ithamar. The four regularly appear in these two pairs. Exodus has already introduced them in the Levitical genealogy (6:23), with the older pair overtly participating in the covenant ratification meal on Mount Sinai (24:1, 9). After they are named here in 28:1, however, frequent mention throughout Exodus is made only of Aaron and 'his sons' (with only Ithamar earning unique mention by name in 38:21). Leviticus similarly refers to the priestly family as 'Aaron and his sons', though it also often clarifies its concern with 'Aaron's sons, the priests', which again suggests a delineation of work between high priest and other priests. Even throughout their ordination (Lev. 8) they remain 'Aaron and his sons'. And Aaron's first day on the job (Lev. 9) is clearly focused on his special actions, with 'his sons' assisting him. The four sons are named in Leviticus only when Nadab and Abihu flout some priestly privilege and die (Lev. 10:1–2), and Eleazar and Ithamar are recognized as 'Aaron's remaining sons' (10:6, 12, 16). Individual responsibilities fall by name to Eleazar and Ithamar and their descendants only in subsequent books. Aaron, the high priest, enjoys most of the spotlight most of the time.

What do priests wear?

Apparently clothing maketh the man. Having introduced Aaron and his attendant sons, and even before prescribing their commissioning or their task list, Exodus 28 moves straight to detail the high priest's dress code. Moses is instructed to 'make garments of holiness for

---

[10] Most English translations render the suffixed infinitive construct in 28:1, 3, 4 (*lĕkahănô*) as subjective and plural: 'for *them* to serve as priests'. Both grammar and context tend towards Aaron as its singular object: 'to make *him* a priest' (V. P. Hamilton 2011: 482; cf. Houtman 2000: 472).

Aaron your brother' (28:2), a task for which he is provided with divinely empowered assistants.[11] That same verse spells out the garments' purpose. Some Bible readers might quibble over the nuance of the clothing itself (do 'sacred vestments' [NRSV] sound more liturgical than 'holy garments' [ESV]?), but translating their purpose is far more significant. At stake is the question of whether they benefit more the high priest ('to give him dignity and honour' [NIV], 'for glorious adornment of Aaron' [NRSV, NAB]) or those around him ('for glory and for beauty' [ESV, NASB]). Of course the two are linked, but the translation options invite us to delve further, and the latter inference seems better. As we have already started to observe, the adjective 'holy (garments)' or 'sacred (vestments)' concerns something or someone related to God; these clothes distinguish the high priest from those around him as someone closer to God. Nor is any individual specified in the purpose terms; it is unclear whether the dignity/glory and honour/ beauty belong to the high priest or describe his clothes. Perhaps there is an element of both, as in the paraphrastic NIRV: 'When he is wearing them, people will honor him. They will have respect for him.' Gordon Wenham (1979: 138, 139) concurs with this kind of sociological function:

> A uniform enables the rest of society to identify immediately figures of authority, and to pay them appropriate respect . . . In a religion the principal doctrine of which was the holiness of God, the high priest, who mediated atonement between God and man, was an extremely important person. His glorious clothing symbolized the significance of his office.

Moreover, although Wenham proceeds to suggest that we can probably no longer identify some of the specific symbolism involved, scholars

---

[11] The instruction in 28:2 is addressed directly to Moses: '*You* will make'. When 'Solomon offered' 144,000 sacrifices (1 Kgs 8:62), the context clarifies that the syntactically singular task was accomplished with assistance. Likewise the next verse in Exodus explains that Moses is to recruit 'everyone wise of heart whom I have filled with a spirit of wisdom, and *they* will make . . .'. Similar passages have tabernacle artisans 'filled with the Spirit of God' (Exod. 31:3; 35:31; cf. 35:35; 1 Kgs 7:14). Though Exod. 28:3 is sometimes added to this list (e.g. Wood 1976: 42–43), it is regularly overlooked or disregarded by others promoting pneumatological inspiration (e.g. J. M. Hamilton 2006: 27, n. 8, though perhaps recognized indirectly at p. 200; Stuart 2006: 605–606 contrast 650–652; G. A. Cole 2007: 124–125; V. P. Hamilton 2011: 482–483 contrast 520–522, 600–601).

are increasingly confident that the high priest's uniform is modelled on and communicates the same kinds of messages as the tabernacle itself. Gregory Beale's study of the temple (with the tabernacle as its near-identical precursor) argues that the colouring and tripartite symbolism of both clothing and building communicate God's grandeur, graded from more common through to exquisite brightness (Beale 2004: 39–43; cf. Enns 2000: 530). Crispin Fletcher-Louis even collates evidence that the high priest could be seen *as* God (2006: 159–160; cf. Propp 2006: 526). The 'glory' and 'beauty' expressed in the high priest's vestments are *God's*, on display in the splendour of both the building and his chief human representative.[12]

The coming verses reinforce this interpretation. We are assured that the couturiers are divinely empowered (28:3) and use materials that are also prescribed for the tabernacle itself (28:5). The *purpose* of Aaron's 'holy' (*qōdeš*) garments is specified in the two concluding phrases of 28:3; both are important. Primarily, the clothes distinguish him as closer to God. Like the adjective, the verb here belongs to the 'holy(ness)' word group that we have started to appreciate, one of the most foundational to any priestly identity and function. Readers of all traditions will recognize the plethora of foreign terms and English derivatives that render the verb here (*qādaš*): Aaron is to be 'set apart', 'consecrated', 'sanctified', 'recognized as (or made) holy'. The second purpose affirms the clause already seen in 28:1: the garments, presumably along with the eye-catching way they distinguish Aaron from others, will facilitate his 'be[ing] a priest for me'.

Verses 4–5 list some (though not all) of the garments that the rest of the chapter will spell out along with their materials. The chapter then proceeds to outline the construction of the high-priestly ephod, gemstone-inlaid breastpiece, a blue robe on which to mount these, a linen turban with an engraved golden emblem, a linen tunic and an embroidered sash. Various studies exist of each item, its symbolism and possible ancient equivalents (in addition to commentaries; e.g. Rooke 2009). But the biblical narrator offers sporadic comments that themselves are sufficient to glimpse further insights into the role of some items:

---

[12] Beale touches elsewhere upon the priestly garments, such as noting the significance attached in ANE cultures to the receiving or changing of clothes (2004: 30) and seeing the high priest's superlative outfit as representing the most holy element of threefold sacred space (32–33). Beale's point is captured succinctly by Chester (2016: 142): 'the word "glory" is only used in Exodus of the LORD, with the significant exception of Aaron's garments'.

- The ephod (28:6–14) includes a stone on each shoulder, six names of Israelite tribes engraved on each. They expressly serve as 'reminder stones for the Israelites: Aaron will carry their names before Yahweh . . . as a reminder' (28:12). The high priest comes before God on behalf of all Israel.[13]
- The description of the breastpiece (28:15–30) opens and closes with comments concerning decision-making. Although the precise mechanism is unknown, as is the role of the mysterious Urim and Thummim, we find here the expectation that the high priest communicates God's decisions to his people. We certainly read of this happening in subsequent generations (esp. Num. 27:21). Like the ephod to which it attaches, the breastpiece bears twelve inscribed gemstones 'as a continual reminder before Yahweh' (Exod. 28:29).
- The symbolism of the robe fits well with wider temple imagery (28:31–35) (e.g. Beale 2004: 39–40). But a function is narrated expressly: the attached bells are audible as Aaron enters God's presence and subsequently exits (28:35). The ominous corollary 'and he will not die' reprises the awe-full privilege and responsibility that the high priest bears in gaining close access to God.
- A turban is specified in passing, primarily as the material against which the golden rosette is displayed (28:36–38). The shape or nature of the floral emblem is unclear but, again, key descriptors and a function are specified. It is engraved with 'Holy to Yahweh', and it would be consistent with the chapter that this designates the high priest. Verse 38, 'turgidly formulated and not altogether intelligible in its details' (Hostetter 1997: 785), suggests that Aaron's role – twice marked by his continual bearing of this rosette upon his forehead – alleviates the guilt of Israelite worshippers and renders them or their gifts acceptable before God. We have already noted that Aaron's grand garments mark him as 'holy' (*qōdeš, qādaš*; 28:2–3). The rosette's engraving inscribes this very title upon him: 'Holy to Yahweh' (*qōdeš layhwh*; 28:36). Indeed, issues of holiness are at the heart of this verse's description of the high priest and his actions on behalf of Israel's worship, with forms of *qdš* used thrice in 28:38 alone. Parallel passages thrice elucidate the rosette as a 'holy crown' (29:6; 39:30; Lev. 8:9), both words being significant. The rosette and its engraving may

---

[13] While my translation of *zikkārôn* as 'reminder' may sound more colloquial and less formal than the common 'remembrance' or 'memorial', it conveys the more active role as the high priest brings the names of *living* tribes into God's sight; cf. Allen 1997: 1105.

actually title not just the high priest but *all* God's holy people (Durham 1987: 388–389). Thus the high priest, often rather literally, stands in for the nation with his headwear reminding God of the nation's God-given, God-approaching status.

It will be important later in our investigation to observe the number of *royal* elements here. Davies (2004: 157) opens his survey of the vestments precisely by summarizing that 'The depiction of the priest in his vestments can only be described as regal in character.'[14] Only now do the instructions broaden to the outfit of Aaron's sons as well. The high priest's uniform is rounded out with a tunic, turban and sash (28:39) and leads tidily into a description of what Aaron's sons will wear. Their uniform and function are clearly derivative of Aaron's. For them are constructed tunics, sashes and (different) headwear (28:40). These serve the same purpose as does Aaron's adornment: exactly the same phrasing for Aaron in 28:3 now has his sons also bedecked 'for glory and for beauty'.

The remainder of Exodus 28 resumes the treating of the priests collectively. Moses is to dress them, anoint them, ordain them (see below) and 'consecrate/sanctify them' (28:41). Reflecting the clothing and ministry previously described for Aaron alone, summarized in 28:1–5, so equipped all five 'will be priests for me'. Further, they are supplied with lengthy underpants. The text explains that these will prevent guilt and death when they enter the tabernacle or approach the altar as part of their service (28:42–43), though we have to infer from elsewhere (esp. 20:26) why underwear serves such a protective function.

Despite the paragraphing of nearly every English Bible, the last line of the chapter may refer back to the chapter as a whole (so NIV; Stuart 2006: 618). The 'perpetual instruction' would concern the individual treatment of Aaron and each descendant who succeeds him as high priest.

It may be that the absence of reference to footwear indicates that the priests served barefoot. Victor Hamilton (2011: 494) certainly notes the chief examples of Moses (3:5) and Joshua (Josh. 5:15), who were obliged to remove their shoes in Yahweh's presence.[15]

---

[14] With 'holy crown', Rooke (2000: 19) tantalizingly suggests that 'holy' might be primary and might highlight 'the priestly aspects of the monarchy rather than . . . supposed royal aspects of the priesthood'.

[15] It is such instructions to Moses and Joshua, coupled with an angelic figure, that fuel the intrigue concerning the mysterious 'Angel of the Lord'; see e.g. Malone 2011; 2015: 81–142.

In summary, we find already that a select individual is marked as holy (is 'consecrated') in order to approach God's presence on behalf of God's people, assisted by priestly members of his family. The high priest especially is vested in such a way as to draw attention to this role, in the eyes of other Israelites if not also in God's sight. Douglas Stuart (2006: 604) captures well a number of issues we have seen and to which we shall return:

> Vestments signified authority in the ancient world . . . Because Israel was begun as a theocracy rather than a monarchy, the sort of vestments that conferred dignity and authority that a king might have worn in other cultures were worn by God's high priest in Israel as a way of confirming the high priest's role as representative of Yahweh for purposes of worship.

How are priests commissioned?

Having prepared Moses to vest, anoint, ordain and consecrate Aaron and his sons to serve as priests, summarized in 28:41, Exodus 29 turns to detail what must be done 'to consecrate them to be priests for me' (29:1). Where chapter 28 focuses on the high priest's matchless uniform, most of the events in chapter 29 treat high priest and priest alike – though a hierarchy remains. Like a modern recipe, the new chapter begins with a list of required ingredients before proceeding to outline what happens with them. While the loaves and sacrificial animals are important, most contemporary interest resides in the similar verbs (and sometimes similar vestments) that are appropriated in a variety of commissioning services today.

Food, animals and ordination candidates are to be assembled at the entrance of the tabernacle, where the priests are washed (29:1–4). Then Aaron is outfitted with his special clothes. This appears to be in logical order of getting dressed, culminating in the turban and its rosette, here described as 'the holy crown' (29:5–6). With the spotlight now on Aaron's head, he is anointed with anointing oil (29:7). The other priests are then also dressed, and all five are sashed (29:8–9). These uniforms, and presumably the ministries they authorize, are then described as 'a priesthood' for a perpetual instruction.

We now find the first of the more liturgical verbs: the last clause of 29:9 instructs Moses to 'ordain' Aaron and his sons (see commentaries and lexicons such as Delcor 1997 for the idiom 'to fill the hand'). It is extremely unclear whether this verse summarizes what has already occurred (so ESV, NASB) or what is to follow (esp. NIV). While 29:29–30 notes the importance of the priestly garments for ordination (and anointing), other verses such as 29:35–37 clarify that ordination involves the myriad events that can require several *days*. It is thus safe to assume, if only from these summaries near the start and end of the chapter, that 'ordination' here comprises these many activities. A series of sacrifices ensues. Among many details several stand out, not least because of repeated elements and their overt association with the priests. Each of the three animals sacrificed has the priests lay their hands on its head (29:10, 15, 19). The first is a sin offering, suggesting that Aaron and his sons are purified from their own sins. The second is a burnt offering, a pleasing gift of food to God. The third is the most dramatic: the second ram's blood is placed on the extremities of Aaron and his sons, and then sprinkled on Aaron and his garments and on his sons and their garments. It is at this point that Aaron, along with his clothes and his sons and their clothes, is considered 'to be holy/consecrated' (*qādaš*; 29:21).[16]

Coming verses formally title this third sacrifice 'the ram of ordination' and, along with the various breads prepared earlier, further sacrificial ceremonies continue. Their significance for our study is found in 29:27–28. Parts of the ordination ram are 'set apart' (*qādaš*), and 29:28a calls this a 'contribution' (*tĕrûmâ*) that is provided 'to Aaron and to his sons . . . from the Israelites'. In near-identical syntax, 29:28b further clarifies that this 'contribution [*tĕrûmâ*] from the Israelites will be . . . a contribution [*tĕrûmâ*] to Yahweh'. Here, as elsewhere, we find the priesthood standing in for God among his people.

Further events of the seven-day ordination ceremony are outlined. There is brief comment on the succession of high priests and repetition of key terms such as 'ordination' and 'consecration' and 'anointing' (and the introduction of the verb 'to make atonement'). The most frequent word group remains 'holy' (*qdš*): Aaron's garments are 'sacred', for ministering in 'the holy place' (29:29–30); parts of the ordination ram are 'consecrated' and cooked in a 'sacred' spot (29:27, 31), though only the priests may eat of this sacrifice that has ordained and 'consecrated' them because it is 'holy' (29:33), and leftovers are similarly 'holy' (29:34); the altar is also 'consecrated', which makes

---

[16] My phrasing here reflects the apparent vestiges of Aaron's pre-eminence. This final verb, with its four subjects, is still *singular*; so too the final preposition locating these attendant subjects 'with *him*'. The threefold placing or pressing of hands on the sacrificial animals' heads is similar. While in the middle sacrifice '*they* place' their hands, the verb is singular for the first and third, a sense expressed judiciously by V. P. Hamilton (2011: 495): 'Aaron, and his sons too, shall lean their hands . . .'

27

things touching it 'holy' (29:36–37 [×5]). I have preserved here the English terms commonly used in Bibles to demonstrate the array of synonyms.

Until this point in proceedings, Moses functions as the master of ceremonies. As we shall see later, Moses himself behaves like a high priest before (and sometimes even after) Aaron's formal commissioning.

The commissioning of the priests is concluded with summary verses concerning the daily operation of the tabernacle, along with its purposes and its personnel. There God will 'meet with you to speak to you' (29:42). The first 'you' is plural and the second singular, and it seems uncertain whether both pronouns refer to Moses alone or to a wider audience. Certainly the following verse recognizes that God will meet with the Israelites. God's presence in the tabernacle means that 'it will be consecrated by my glory' (29:43). Any misperceptions of the passive sense are dispelled immediately as God takes direct responsibility: 'I will consecrate the tent of meeting and the altar; and Aaron and his sons I will consecrate to be priests for me' (29:44).

This statement concludes the immediate chapters on the designation of a high priest and his assistants. Yet two more verses remind the reader of the whole point of having priests to serve in God's consecrated tent. 'I will dwell in the midst of the Israelites, and I will be their God' (29:45). The final verse likewise repeats God's desire to 'dwell' (*šākan*) among them; not only does this summarize the purpose of the tabernacle (25:8) but God confirms here that this was the purpose of the entire exodus rescue (29:46)!

What does a priest do (part 1: in Exodus)?

Exodus 30 – 31

With a grand image of Yahweh and his tabernacle in Israel's midst and something of the high priest's role therein, it is tempting to turn to Leviticus to see the priesthood in action. Carol Meyers correctly observes that the pending, 'descriptive' chapters of Exodus 35 – 40 dedicate far less attention to the priests than do the 'prescriptive' chapters 25 – 31, towards the end of which we are moving (Meyers 2005: 225; 2008: 14, though she confuses one of her labels). Yet the remainder of Exodus is also important. There continue to be hints at the persons and purposes of the priesthood. Even should the limelight be toned down or focused elsewhere, the remainder of Exodus sets a vital context in which the priest-heavy content of Leviticus must be understood. Exodus is the historical context in which early Israelites would be versed as they contemplated the priesthood. It is also the literary context through which later readers, ourselves included, travel to subsequent books in the canon.

After a more functional or operational introduction to the tabernacle and its priests, we now catch glimpses of the priests at work as the remaining furniture is described. The incense altar placed just outside the Most Holy Place, along with the lampstand previously outlined, is one of Aaron's daily responsibilities and also requires annual atonement (30:7–10). Both activities prefigure important events later prescribed in Leviticus.

The bronze basin in the outer courtyard, called a bronze 'laver' by prior generations, is expressly for the use of the priests. Whether entering into the Holy Place or exiting to the courtyard altar they are to wash their hands and feet 'so they will not die' (30:17–21).

A formula is dictated for 'sacred' anointing oil that will be used to dedicate the tabernacle and its furniture (30:22–33). Like the priests, every item is to be 'consecrated', making them 'especially holy' (as CSB renders the cumulative compound *qōdeš qādāšîm* in 30:29). Indeed, the paragraph repeats the need to anoint Aaron and his sons, consecrating them 'to be priests for me'. Unsurprisingly, the oil that marks out both the tabernacle and its personnel is itself 'sacred' and should be treated as 'sacred'. The same is prescribed for the incense when its formula is provided (30:34–38). The anointing oil, the special incense and the incense altar are each overtly associated with the ark of the covenant – the centrepiece of the tabernacle complex, introduced first (25:10–22) and as the place where God meets with his human representative to communicate to his people (25:22).

Even the final, shorter instructions in Exodus 31 remain on theme. In one of the more overt pneumatological passages in the Old Testament, we hear that the temple artisans are 'filled with the Spirit of God' to facilitate their crafts (31:1–6). As said the summary at 29:42–44, it is God himself who consecrates his dwelling place, marking it off as unparalleled and fit for God. And the carefully placed warning about the Sabbath (31:12–18, paired with 35:1–3) not only twice affirms the Sabbath as 'holy' but introduces it as a sign to help the Israelites acknowledge God as the one who makes them holy, 'who consecrates you' (*qādaš*; 31:13).

As already suggested, the remainder of Exodus has less to say directly about the Aaronic priesthood. Nonetheless, these chapters give us some brief insights into the context in which the priesthood is birthed and prepare us for the priestly emphases of Leviticus. We should first recall the Levitical genealogy in Exodus 6. While it initially appears to be an unwarranted interjection in the story of Moses' rescue of Israel, it is wedged between Moses' near-identical complaints that he is unsuited to speak for God (6:10–12, 28–30). The narrator makes clear that Aaron and thence his successors are part of God's communication plans (6:26–27; 7:1–2).[17]

Exodus 32 – 34

The golden calf of Exodus 32 is among the better known incidents in the book. With or without its aftermath, Israel's idolatry at Sinai is easily studied in isolation without any regard for the surrounding thirteen chapters and their formalization of the cultic system. So how does Exodus 32 – 34 fit within Exodus 25 – 40 and the book as a whole? We might propose two areas in which to invest our thoughts briefly. Each is significant in itself, though this present survey can touch but lightly upon them.

First, the most obvious connection and contrast concerns correct worship of Israel's God. Even while Moses is on Mount Sinai receiving the stone tablets and the specifications for God's dwelling, his people propose an alternative. It is traditionally assumed that the Israelites construct for themselves other gods altogether (e.g. 32:4) (e.g. Moberly 2008: 48). This is a shocking betrayal given their recent pledges of allegiance to Yahweh and to his expectations of them (19:8; 24:1–11). It is equally tragic – and even more relevant to the immediate context – if we merit the suggestion that Israel has broken more the second commandment than the first. God's people here might continue to worship *Yahweh* but impatiently construct their own golden footstool for him, along with corrupt forms of altar and feast (e.g. Sarna 1991: 203–204; Enns 2000: 568–571; V. P. Hamilton 2011: 529–534).[18] This does not explain some of our historical questions: If Moses is still on the mountain, how much of God's tabernacle design and planned priesthood are the Israelites privy to? But, whether the Israelites are

---

[17] Thus V. P. Hamilton (2011: 105–110, following Walsh 2001: 71–73) varies from many commentators and translators in blocking together 6:10–30. One of the few to analyse the role of the genealogy in any depth is Marx (1995), who resolves that 'This genealogy and the framework in which it is set allow P to highlight the setting apart of the Levites and to emphasize the specific role of the high priest, established by Yahweh to be the vehicle of his saving intervention for his people' (335, my tr.).

[18] One pressing challenge is whether *'ĕlōhîm*, accompanied by plural verbs and demonstratives (32:1, 4, 8, 23), means 'gods' or 'God' or 'a god'. The singular sense is supported by NASB, HCSB, NAB, NJPS, with the CEV capturing the whole hypothesis: 'Make us *an image of* a god' (32:1).

intentionally or unintentionally corrupting their worship of Yahweh or are arbitrarily chasing other god(s), the narrative of Exodus carefully juxtaposes God's measured plans with Israel's impromptu surrogate.[19] Second, the result of this alternative attempt at worship threatens God's presence among his people. The nature of God's presence may also be a contributing cause of the incident. Even while God is detailing the sanctuary in which he will dwell among them (esp. 25:8) his people are manipulating their own imitation. God will be met when and where and how *he* chooses. He subsequently threatens to not join them on their journey; that his presence would portend danger (33:3 repeated at 33:5) forebodes that he will no longer graciously alleviate their sin. Moses' ensuing negotiations, including cameos of the prototype 'tent of meeting' and Moses' face-to-face intimacy with God (33:7–11), bring God to reinstate his presence and to pronounce his forgiving nature.[20] God also reiterates his demand to be worshipped exclusively and something of his covenant expectations.

After these challenges to the worship and the presence of God, the narrative returns to God's correct treatment. Nor is it purely about the realization of architecture. The resumptive narrative is prefaced with quite some detail about Moses' mediatorial function: his intimate proximity to God allows him to speak for God and even physically affects the skin of his face (34:29–35). There is also a brief reminder about the 'holy' Sabbath (35:1–3) before the details of the building of the tabernacle. Moreover, a reader's valuation of the tabernacle – with the entailed dwelling and consecration and election and forgiveness – rises sharply when contrasted with Israel's stumbling and near-fatal attempt at a facsimile (cf. Stuart 2006: 659–660). Perhaps there is also a contrast presented for Aaron; the man designated to be the primary mediator between God and Israel clearly has not yet learned of or appreciated the gravity of his nominated role.

Exodus 35 – 40
Indeed the ensuing chapters of Exodus narrate the successful and enthusiastic construction of the tabernacle. This is not the place to

---

[19] An important extension of this issue is explored by Herring (2012), who suggests that Moses' glowing visage in 34:29–35 marks him as '*the extension and manifestation of the divine presence*' and the calf as the people's attempt to fill Moses' absence with another tangible representation. My gratitude to Patrick Senn for this reference.

[20] Yahweh's self-revelation in Exod. 34:6–7 forms a core strand in the biblical-theology tome of J. M. Hamilton 2010 (e.g. 133–137).

analyse in detail any differences between design (chs. 25 – 31) and execution (chs. 35 – 40). But one or two matters influence our study of the Aaronic priesthood.

The construction phase begins with Moses summarizing the entire complex and the contributions required, not unlike the verbal equivalent of an architect's model (35:4–19). We notice first that there is only the briefest glimpse, right at the end, of any human staffing (35:19). Familiar with architectural models and artists' impressions of a proposed residential or retail complex, we might easily dismiss a human figure or two as a last-minute attempt at realism or an indicator of scale. But we shall see in our next chapter that there are significant parallels between the construction of the tabernacle and the creation of the universe narrated in Genesis. There the personnel, who are increasingly recognized as priestly figures, are introduced last as an indication that preparations are complete and that everything is operational. This is also the order repeated in the closing chapters of Exodus: of Moses' summary here, of the actual manufacturing described in ensuing chapters, of the narrator's digest of what is produced (39:32–43), and even of the detailed implementation in the final chapter of Exodus. We should also notice that some of the language becomes repetitive and formulaic, including that concerning the temple personnel. As we have already observed in various ways, this language reinforces the primacy of Aaron's individual role. Exodus remains concerned with 'Aaron the priest' (31:10; 35:19; 38:21; 39:41; language that continues into Leviticus and Numbers), clearly pre-eminent among his assistant sons. There remains the sense of a single primary mediator.

And so the elements of the tabernacle are fashioned. Contributions flood in (and generosity eventually has to be restrained!); skills are volunteered; leading artisans are divinely inspired. In some detail we read of the careful construction of the buildings, the ark and other furniture, and various accoutrements. Despite the detail, the specifications here are perfunctory and focused very much on physical dimensions and compositions; any eventual functionality, as narrated in the prescriptive chapters, is noticeably absent.

Only as we reach the closing chapters do more operational matters creep in. Exodus 39 moves to itemize the crafting of 'garments for serving in the Holy Place' (39:1); again the focus is on 'garments for Aaron'. Exodus 39:1–31 takes almost as much space to recount their manufacture as was devoted to their original design in Exodus 28, and seven times it is punctuated with the refrain 'just as Yahweh had commanded Moses' (39:1, 5, 7, 21, 26, 29, 31). Without at all intimating any disobedience in earlier chapters (see similar sentiments at 35:4, 10; 36:1; 38:22, which comprise both the introduction and summary to chs. 35 – 38) one gets the sense that, when it comes to the priestly elements, the narrator is working even harder to show full compliance by repeating this 'quality-control clause' (Durham 1987: 493). And this compliance is confirmed and highlighted as we move to the two final summations. In 39:32–43, everything is brought before Moses. Both the start and end of this pericope highlight that 'the Israelites had constructed according to everything that Yahweh had commanded Moses – thus they constructed (all the work)' (39:32 ≈ 39:42). The same sentiment, already itself with a rather redundant clause, is repeated yet again in the final verse: Moses inspects all their craftsmanship and – 'behold' – everything complies and Moses blesses them (39:43).[21]

The erecting of the tabernacle in Exodus 40 recapitulates many of the points we have already surveyed. God directs proceedings through Moses (40:1). The ark is the centrepiece, yet 'shielded' (40:3 NIV, NET), with the remaining elements described concentrically away from this Most Holy Place. The entirety is anointed for consecration/holiness; forms of *qdš* occur five times in 40:9–11. Aaron is summoned, washed, vested, anointed and consecrated so that 'he will be a priest for me', as are his sons (40:12–15). Perhaps for the first time Aaron's sons receive their own overt commission ('and *they* will be priests for me') though even here their anointing is derivative ('just as . . . their father'). As at 29:9, here the Aaronic family is set aside perpetually.

Like the previous chapters as a whole, Exodus 40 is divided into prescriptive and descriptive sections (40:1–15, 16–33). We now read, in equal detail, that Moses complied with these instructions: erecting the structure, arranging and shielding the ark, and organizing the rest of the temple furniture. These eighteen verses begin with the assurance that 'Moses did according to everything that Yahweh had commanded him – thus he did' (40:16) and are regularly punctuated with the

---

[21] V. P. Hamilton (2011: 613) notes the rare syntax surrounding '(Moses) saw . . . and behold' here in 39:43, finding parallels only in Gen. 1:31 and 6:12. As we shall see in my next chapter, the parallel with the completion of creation – also concerned with 'all the craftsmanship that was constructed' and accompanied by blessing (Gen. 2:1–3) – is significant and probably intentional (cf. Enns 2000: 550; Dozeman 2009: 761–762). I use the ≈ symbol to indicate passages that share close parallels but are not strictly identical.

compliance formula 'as Yahweh had commanded Moses' (40:19, 21, 23, 25, 27, 29, 32). Such repetition is impossible to miss when some seventeen iterations are found in Exodus 39 – 40 after only two or three occurrences earlier in the book (V. P. Hamilton 2011: 617). As 39:42–43 seems to echo the completion of creation, 40:33 triumphantly summarizes, 'So Moses completed the craftsmanship.' As at creation and at Sinai (esp. 24:15–18), God's localized presence on earth is facilitated. The last paragraph of Exodus narrates the arrival of the cloud above the tabernacle and the glory of the Lord filling it, a point narrated twice (40:34–35). Although God's glory can be withstood on some occasions,[22] here it is so intense that Moses himself cannot enter. The narrator closes the book by noting that the movements of the cloud dictate the transience of the Israelites and the tabernacle because of God's presence represented there.

What does a priest do (part 2: in Leviticus)?

When Exodus ends, it is unclear if Moses is barred permanently from the tabernacle. Some think so, but further entry and divine encounters are narrated (esp. Num. 7:89; cf. 1:1; 12:8; 17:1–9) just as God had promised Moses when dictating the design of the tabernacle and ark (esp. Exod. 25:22).[23] Though admittedly we do not hear how far he penetrated, Moses' next entry into the tabernacle is in the company of Aaron (Lev. 9:23). This question of tabernacle entry introduces a superb entrée to the book of Leviticus.[24]

At least the first half of Leviticus is concerned with how the priesthood regulates the proximity of the Israelites and the holy God dwelling in their midst. Broadly speaking, the sacrifices detailed in Leviticus 1 – 7 render an Israelite increasingly holy and suitable to draw closer towards the centre of the camp and God's presence there (classically Wenham 1979: 25–29; cf. 1996). The graded holiness against which an Israelite is measured is substantially spelled out in chapters 11 – 15, clarifying in a paradigmatic fashion what makes one

---

[22] e.g. Exod. 16:7, 10; Lev. 9:6, 23; Num. 16:19, 42; 20:6; Deut. 5:24; Ps. 63:2. While it is sometimes allowed that God's glory might be manifested to special leaders like Moses, most of these occurrences involve all Israel.

[23] V. P. Hamilton (2011: 620) clearly intimates that nowhere in the Pentateuch does Moses ever again enter so closely into God's presence. Note, though, that Hamilton's informant (Milgrom 1991: 134–138) is focused only on the Priestly source, addressing only part of the Pentateuch.

[24] The recapitulation of Exod. 40:34–38 in Num. 9:15–23 further suggests that the intervening material, including all of Leviticus, serves as an operating manual for the tabernacle (Milgrom 1991: 139).

more clean or more unclean. Fully a quarter of the Old Testament's uses of the noun 'priest' (*kōhēn*) are found in Leviticus, with the vast majority (85%) concentrated in these twelve chapters (Lev. 1 – 7, 11 – 15).

It is significant then that the intervening chapters, Leviticus 8 – 10, are concerned with the ordination of the priests and with a prominent object lesson concerning inappropriate access to God's presence. Without any disrespect to the importance of the sections that frame them, it is chapters 8 – 10 that earn our attention here. Indeed, while many of the prescriptions of Exodus are fulfilled within Exodus, instructions there for ordination come to pass only here in Leviticus.

Reprising the language of Exodus 29 (e.g. Milgrom 1991: 545–549), Leviticus 8 recounts the ordination of 'Aaron and his sons'. Although this locution sounds collective, and the chapter largely treats the priests together, it probably once again accentuates the high priest. Having looked at the relevant verbs and verses such as 8:12–13, John Hartley (1992: 110) concludes that 'Thus it appears that strictly speaking Aaron's anointing was of a higher order than that of his sons. Therefore, the term "the anointed priest," as in Lev 4:2–12 specifically refers to the high priest (cf. 21:10).' The same accentuation continues in Leviticus 9. At the end of the ordination week, it is Aaron who completes the extensive ritual. His sons barely appear and only in the way that theatre assistants aid the master surgeon.

More significant is the *purpose* of Aaron's work in Leviticus 9. Moses' opening instructions are clear on two points. First, while these sacrifices are manipulated by Aaron and though he has to deal first with his own status, the primary offering comes from the Israelites as a whole. The instructions are communicated to Aaron in the presence of all the elders (9:1), the Israelites collectively supply the requisite animals before their whole assembly (9:3–5), and the major sacrifices are made 'for the people' (9:7, 15, 18). In turn, the people are the primary beneficiaries on this day, receiving blessings from Aaron and Moses (9:22–23). Moses' second point highlights an even more astounding outcome. These sacrifices, brought by the people and offered by Aaron, facilitate the glory of the Lord appearing to all the people. This is the stated climax of the ritual (9:23–24). It is also promised in advance: 9:6 is a command addressed from God to the Israelites in the plural, with God's appearance as the purpose. Sometimes the connotations of 'glory' are deprecated so as to water down this dramatic outcome. But Moses has already promised through Aaron that the express purpose of these sacrifices is 'because today

Yahweh [himself] will appear to you' (9:4)! This does not demand that the people experience a full, unattenuated sighting of God – but neither is the language of 9:4 diluted by any euphemism or symbol intermediate of God's presence.

Here, already, on the first day that the tabernacle becomes operational, we find the gamut of sacrifices from chapters 1 to 7 employed (Hartley 1992: 122). *And the purpose of such sacrifices is on display. When God (via his priest) instructs the people concerning sacrifice, and then the people (via their priest) bring those offerings before God, God willingly and substantially and safely rendezvouses with his people.* Although there are other highlights elsewhere, one wonders if Leviticus 9 showcases the cultic system at its zenith. We can confidently assert that, at God's initiative, such a system has been ripening since Exodus 25. More broadly, we can follow traces of God's desire to meet with his people further back to Exodus 19, Exodus 3, Genesis 12, Genesis 3 or even Genesis 1 and 2 (such traces are examined in our next chapter). It may be no exaggeration to propose that the achievements of Leviticus 9 have been unparalleled since Eden and will not be matched again (if they are at all) until Solomon's dedication of the temple in 1 Kings 8.

Whether we are children with a new toy or adults with a new device, things are often never better than when we first unwrap something from its box. So it is with the priesthood. The text gives no indication how much time occurs before the shine starts to fade, and the fault here lies not with the product but with operator error. Certainly the narrator moves immediately, in the very next verses, to demonstrate that rendezvousing with the living God is as hazardous as it is rewarding. Leviticus 10 narrates how Aaron's two apparently eldest sons fail to follow the instructions. We are not told the precise details of their breach. The fire they bring before Yahweh is 'unauthorized', a term further explained as something (whether a substance or gesture or location or timing) 'which he had not commanded them' (10:1). Their fiery end is further explained in 10:3 where God insists that, *concerning proximity to himself*, the issue is his 'holiness' (*qdš*) and his 'honour/glory' (*kbd*).

The rest of the chapter remains instructive. As the dead priests' cousins carry them away, Aaron and his two surviving sons are not to abandon their consecrated state or their place (10:4–7). Juxtaposed here are further instructions about ongoing purity. Just as nudity has the potential to offend God (e.g. Exod. 20:26; 28:42–43), inebriation on the job can also prove fatal (Lev. 10:8–9). Moreover, perhaps illustrated by remaining sober, the priests are here adjured to remain alert to broader issues that foster death. They are to 'differentiate' (*bdl*) between the holy and the common, the unclean and the clean; and they are to teach the Israelites all the commands given by God through Moses (10:10–11).[25] Although our survey must progress, we must acknowledge the centrality of these verses. Studies such as Jacob Milgrom's trace the Aaronic priesthood's success (and otherwise) with this commission, as will we in chapter 4. Conscious also of the teaching command here, Milgrom (1991: 615) hardly overstates the importance of Leviticus 10:10–11 when he asserts that 'The making of distinctions *(lĕhabdîl)* is the essence of the priestly function.'

The remainder of Leviticus 10 wraps up the focused concentration on the priests themselves and is not what we might expect. Evading a detailed explanation, we might note several features in passing. First, the priesthood represents the wider people. Aaron and his family eat a portion of what the Israelites have brought before God (10:12–15). Such food remains graded in its holiness: some is sufficiently holy that it must be consumed within the tabernacle precincts, while some may be taken away to a '[ceremonially] clean' location. And there remains the threat that the priests may arouse God's anger if such strictures are not observed. Yet even here God remains aware of human frailty, and Aaron's non-compliance with the letter of the law is excused because of his concern for the spirit of the law (10:16–20). Indeed, any erring on Aaron's part reflects his concern to avoid replicating his sons' disrespect of graded holiness and to act appropriately in God's eyes (Wenham 1979: 160).[26]

These three chapters, Leviticus 8 – 10, underscore the centrality of holiness. God's holiness is reflected in the tabernacle complex and its rituals and personnel – and in its operational outcome. In his exposition of Leviticus, overtly titled *Holiness to the LORD*, one of Allen Ross's summaries (2002: 238) is laden with English synonyms: 'Those

---

[25] The syntax connecting v. 9 with vv. 10–11 (cf. NASB, NIV, NJPS, NET) has significance beyond any link between sobriety and inculcating holiness. A connection would confirm that the infinitive constructs of vv. 10–11 ('to distinguish', 'to teach') are the purview of both Aaron and '[his] sons with [him]' (v. 9). The significance of these instructions is heightened by the observation that here alone in Leviticus does God address Aaron without Moses (cf. 11:1; 13:1; 14:33; 15:1) (Hartley 1992: 134–135).

[26] Although not necessarily agreed or convincing, a chiastic structure for Lev. 10 is sometimes proposed (e.g. Hartley 1992: 129–132; intimated by Sklar 2013: 156). If this is intentional, it both contrasts Aaron's cautious respect with his sons' hauteur and further concentrates attention on the instructions of 10:8–11.

who lead the congregation in spiritual service must be fully consecrated to the LORD . . . Those set aside for service to the holy God must sanctify the LORD before the people by how they conduct themselves in ministry.'

Nor should we miss the theme as the rest of Leviticus unfolds. Clean and unclean distinctions are elaborated in chapters 11 – 15 with their rationale summarized in 11:44–47. They are particularly concerned with the people's 'consecration' because of God's 'holiness' (*qdš* repeatedly; 11:44–45) and hence the need to 'differentiate' (*bdl*) food categories (11:47). The holy God's sacred people are to embody the consecrated priests' teaching. And the priests are the arbiters of cleanliness and the practitioners of sacrifice: they gauge someone's suitability to draw close to God and facilitate steps towards readiness. The central roles of the Day of Atonement and the high priest in Leviticus 16 are explored below. Then the latter half of Leviticus continues to call God's people to reflect their sacred/holy status in the way they live, to which we return in part II.

Of course much more could be explored regarding the place of priests in Leviticus, but we have seen sufficient to illuminate the developing picture. God wishes to dwell among humanity, and to do so safely he requires that his people be prepared. The Aaronic priesthood mediates between God and his chosen people in all the senses of that English verb. The priests *communicate* the standards of holiness that God expects and *facilitate* this holiness through the sacrificial system. The result is the successful *reconciliation* of humanity to God, no matter how partial and fleeting that contact is under the old covenant and how much greater contact is envisaged and effected under the new covenant.

In this respect, we realize that the priests are not called to be active instead of the people. Rather, the priests' task is to cultivate and motivate the people to action *themselves*. Milgrom (1991: 617–618) catalogues how each tranche of instructions in Leviticus is addressed as well to the people for their benefit (e.g. 1:2; 7:38; 15:31; 16:29–31; 21:24). Priestly mediation remains crucial, but it is never an end in itself. While God almost invariably communicates in secondhand fashion, his goal is to be as direct as possible. God's interactions with the priesthood are not for the sake of those priests; neither is the people's contact with the priest an end in itself. The priest is in every way an intermediary. The priest's own goal is to bring God and people together and, as far as they remain estranged, he aims to be as translucent as possible as he mirrors the two parties to each other.

What does a priest do (part 3: in Numbers)?

Whether or not the book of Numbers is best explained by geography, its opening chapters remain set at Mount Sinai and are concerned with the operation of the tabernacle in the midst of the Israelite camp. It is no surprise, then, to find further instructions here for God's priests. The last sentences of Exodus narrate the initial and glorious erecting of the tabernacle. Yet even at that point we readers are reminded that this is a portable palace for a mobile God. Of course that is what the Hebrew terms connote, despite Western conceptions of a 'tabernacle' sometimes envisaging something more permanent than a mere transient 'tent'.[27]

Where Exodus and Leviticus highlight narrower priestly responsibilities, from the opening chapter of Numbers the spotlight broadens to the rest of Levi's tribe. The Levites are singled out for special care of the tabernacle (see below) and Aaron's priestly family is, of course, a select subset of this tribe. Consistent with the model of graded holiness, the Levites camp just outside the tabernacle courtyard, one step closer to God than the other Israelites (Num. 2:17). The priestly family camps in an even more prominent place, at the tabernacle's entrance (3:38). The verse spells out the purpose of this arrangement for Moses and Aaron and his sons in both positive and negative fashion. The priests' presence at the tabernacle entrance is emphatic: 'protecting the protection of the Holy Place, for the protection of the Israelites'. Should they fail in their prophylactic role, 'the unauthorized person who approaches will be put to death'. Similar instructions for the Levites in 1:53 give the same two perspectives, negative and positive (cf. 8:19). This setup reinforces the image of a king ensconced in the midst of his entourage (cf. 1 Sam. 26:5).

Like any mobile community – including an army – the encampment travels frequently. Here we discover the primary work of the Levites and fresh responsibilities for the priests. Relocation takes place at God's behest and the dramatic theophany at Sinai has already migrated from mountain to tabernacle. God is on the move; the

---

[27] Many other promising parallels concerning portable palaces could be explored further. For example, Beale tidily distils the key findings of Homan (2000) that the tabernacle's layout, central furnishings and movements – and thus perhaps its functions – bear close resemblances to 'mobile Egyptian military tent camps' (Beale 2004: 64). As we shall see shortly, Beale and others argue that the tabernacle itself is a visual microcosm of God's entire creation.

GOD'S MEDIATORS

tabernacle remains as hazardous as was Sinai (e.g. Exod. 19:10–25; 20:18–21). Although the Levites do the work of carefully transporting God's portable palace (see below), it remains the priests' responsibility to oversee the process. Put crudely, Aaron is the chief executive of the whole venture, assisted by his sons, who in turn subcontract the bulk of the labour to their Levite cousins. Aaron's singular leadership is sufficiently clear that the Levites are commissioned to serve *him* and to ensure *his* responsibilities are met (esp. Num. 3:5–9). In turn, the work of the Levites in their three major divisions is overseen by the Aaronic priests (3:32; 4:16, 27–28, 33; 7:8).[28] As with many modern executives or specialists, the important work in Numbers remains the purview of the priests: they carefully package the holy 'hazardous materials' before entrusting them to the Levite couriers (esp. 4:1–20). Although the outcome is a different kind of activity, the paradigm for the priests and the status of their work remains the same as elsewhere in the Sinai narrative. One needs to be holier the closer one gets to God, and this now includes the furnishings of his portable palace.

One final addition to the priests' work is that they direct the nation's movements as well as the tabernacle's. Of course God is the primary leader: the details of the cloud's setting out and settling down is repeatedly explained as the motivation to move the tabernacle and thus Israel's camp (Exod. 40:34–38; Num. 9:15–23); this is overtly described throughout the Numbers account as 'the command of Yahweh'; and, while Moses is connected with the silver trumpets, it is ultimately Aaron's sons who marshal the people for civic and military matters (Num. 10:8).[29]

Numbers contains other references to Aaron and his sons, but their priestly work continues in the vein already established in the previous books and need not detain us. We return in chapter 4 to inspect what happens once the people depart from Sinai and the priesthood

[28] Virtually the only detailed mention of priestly work during the 'descriptive' construction of the tabernacle in Exod. 35 – 40 is a preview of this kind of oversight of Levitical assistants (Exod. 38:21).

[29] Deeper inspection of the cultic system should consider the significance of the phrase *šāmar mišmeret* (classically Milgrom 1970: 8–16). Here in Num. 9:19 it might be rendered 'the Israelites *obeyed the obedience of* Yahweh' (cf. 9:23; Lev. 8:35; 18:30; 22:9). The same phrase is translated above as the priests '*protecting the protection of* the Holy Place' (Num. 3:38; cf. 1:53; 3:7–8, 28, 32; 8:26; 18:3–5; 31:30, 47). The noun is admittedly vague. Dependent on the term it qualifies, it can indeed mean obeying some kind of charge (cf. Gen. 26:5; Block 2012: 275). But given that the many uses in Numbers beyond 9:19, 23 are concerned with 'guard duty' (e.g. Ashley 1993: 49, 69, 78, 91, etc.) we might wonder if the change of subject and object in 9:19, 23 really alters much the sense that the setting up of camp remains focused on the tabernacle and its protection.

begins operating 'on the road', seven weeks after the assembling of the tabernacle.

The high priest

Throughout our study of the Aaronic priests, and even in recent paragraphs concerning Numbers, we cannot help but notice how they function as assistants of the high priest. The Levites, too, serve the priests and even the high priest directly (esp. Num. 3:5–9). We have thus already surveyed many of Aaron's own responsibilities. Yet there remain a few elements that apply exclusively to this chief of the family, to which we now turn.

Who becomes high priest?

At the incumbent's death, the high priesthood appears to pass to the next oldest male of the Aaronide family. With Aaron's death choreographed in advance, we read of the careful and public transfer of the high priest's grand vestments to his son, Eleazar (Num. 20:22–29). We might also observe that, despite surviving his sons' misdemeanour in Leviticus 10, Aaron's untimely death is due to a failure to promote God's holiness (*qādaš*; 20:12). In turn, after Eleazar's death (Josh. 24:33) we find his son Phinehas leading Israelite worship before the ark (Judg. 20:26–28). In the Levitical genealogy already studied, three generations of high priests are named in anticipation (Exod. 6:23–25), and postexilic genealogies are equally concerned to trace Levitical and high-priestly lineages back to Mosaic times (e.g. Ezra 7; 1 Chr. 6). Something of the patrilineal model is glimpsed in Exodus 29:29–30 and Leviticus 16:32.[30]

Of course, the ideal is not always met. In coming centuries potential variations to the patrilineal model arise, and it is ultimately abandoned in intertestamental times.

What does a high priest do?

We have already noted that the high priest is, on most occasions, *the* priest. The question might be correspondingly phrased 'What does an assistant priest *not* do?'

---

[30] Each heir apparent makes prominent appearances before his accession (e.g. Num. 25; Josh. 22) though cause and effect is less clear. While this might indicate some kind of apprenticeship (R. D. Cole 2000: 338), it may equally reflect a narrator's anticipatory character inclusion. Passages like Num. 3:4 and 1 Chr. 24:2 suggest that Nadab and Abihu had no sons to complicate the succession planning.

I have recently mentioned Leviticus 16. The Day of Atonement rituals arguably form the most prominent and exclusive responsibility of the high priest. Worthy of extensive study in itself (e.g. Hartley 2003; Hieke and Nicklas 2012) we can but rehearse the occasion in broad brushstrokes.

This annual event purifies the tabernacle complex from the previous year's accumulated sins (and hence some, such as Milgrom, refer to 'the Day of Purgation'). The key human actor on this occasion is the high priest, who dons an array of outfits and offers a series of sacrifices that resets each part of the system (esp. 16:33). This sequential resetting facilitates another year's sacrifices – and the ongoing presence of God among his people. Such comprehensive maintenance requires the high priest to enter even into the Most Holy Place, albeit extensively washed, humbly attired and with his own sins first atoned for (esp. 16:11–17). Indeed, the whole chapter opens with a two-part warning (16:1, 2). The narrator frames this as an instruction linked with Nadab and Abihu's fatal approach before God. God himself outlines the ceremony's events in terms of how Aaron can safely approach the ark and God's presence. The danger and concomitant privilege are palpable: 'For I will appear in the cloud over the atonement cover' (NIV)! Many of the instructions that follow in Leviticus 16 are cast precisely in terms of these annual enhanced access privileges.[31]

The eminence of the high priest is also regularly noted with regard to Israel's judicial system. In particular, the protective banishment of an inadvertent manslaughterer expires when the high priest does. Mark Rooker (2000: 140) tidily captures both definitive roles: 'The high priest held a unique position with great responsibility (see Lev 16), and his importance is illustrated by the fact that his death marked the end of a historical epoch (Num 35:25, 28, 32).' Others observe additional examples where the high priest appears to dictate the fate of the nation, especially concerning sin (e.g. Cheung 1986: 267).

Two further factors are easy to miss but worth remembering (Duke 2003: 653–654). In passing we read that the high-priestly breastpiece

---

[31] Further, we have noted the importance of being vested at the start of one's ministry, as with the ordination of Aaron and his sons (Lev. 8:5–13), the transfer of high priesthood from Aaron to Eleazar (Num. 20:22–29), and the visionary recommissioning of the high priest Joshua (Zech. 3). Perhaps the high priest's authority is freshly renewed as he resumes his regalia after venturing into God's presence (Lev. 16:24). The more common explanation is that the washing and changing here is to *downgrade* the holiness contracted from God (Milgrom 1991: 1048–1049; Hartley 1992: 241–242).

houses the mysterious Urim and Thummim (Exod. 28:15, 29–30). The breastpiece's design receives inordinate space and is described overtly as the 'breastpiece for making decisions' (NIV, CSB). With the embedded Urim and Thummim, we are assured that 'Aaron continually carries the decision-making of the Israelites over his heart in the presence of Yahweh.' In turn, it would seem that such divination was utilized especially as God's people headed into war. The arrangement seems to be generalized when Joshua is commissioned to lead Israel's conquest; the high priest, Eleazar, will furnish 'the decision of the Urim in the presence of Yahweh' (Num. 27:15–23). A later incident is facilitated by the subsequent high priest, Phinehas (Judg. 20:26–28). It appears to be standard practice that the high priest commends the Israelite army to battle, reminding them that God himself goes with them to fight (Deut. 20:1–4). Rodney Duke also infers fairly from the overt presence on the battlefield, once of Phinehas (Num. 31:6) and repeatedly of the ark, that priests were part of Israel's manoeuvres. Certainly later texts confirm a priestly presence (e.g. Num. 10:8–10; Josh. 6:1–21; 2 Chr. 13:12, 14). As such, the priesthood further aligns with or represents God's own presence.[32]

What about Moses?

Sharp thinkers recognize that, while the high priesthood is inaugurated with Aaron and carried on by his descendants, Aaron himself is consecrated by Moses. We then recall that Moses has conducted various other priestly roles, especially before Aaron's ordination and especially with respect to mediatorial practices between God and humanity. Moses even joins the priests in sleeping at the entrance of the tabernacle. Where might we fit him into the hierarchy?

A classic study remains Milgrom's excursus (1991: 555–558). He acknowledges Moses' behaviours but identifies them more as a kingly role than a priestly one. Indeed, we explore later how regal and sacerdotal roles can blur together, as well as a little more of Moses' behaviour. Milgrom notes additional limits: some priestly prerogatives are expressly denied Moses. Ultimately, Milgrom wisely admits that Moses is a special case, commissioned by God to kick-start a new institution.

That said, we must not disregard the many examples of Moses' behaviour that accord with what will become more institutionalized

---

[32] One weakness with the final parallel drawn here is that there seems little evidence that the *high* priest – the individual most representative of God – ventured into battle. In Num. 31, Phinehas has not yet succeeded his father, Eleazar.

in the high priesthood. There are many instances of Moses' inter-mediation that are continued with Aaron and his successors.

The Levites

There is much to be debated over the identity of the Levites, especially their relationship to the Aaronic priesthood. However, our concern here is with their initial function – and with brevity.[33] The observations above have already summarized the traditional responsibilities of the remainder of Levi's tribe who are not members of Aaron's priestly family. These residual Levites assist the priests in service of the tabernacle (and these Levites, like the priests, are recompensed by the wider Israelite community). Scholars readily acknowledge the work of Milgrom (e.g. 1970), which highlights the Levites' 'guard duty' and 'porterage'. The two terms (*mišmeret, 'ăbōdâ*) are especially concentrated as the Levites are commissioned in Numbers 3 – 4.[34]

For our purposes, the Levites simply represent one more gradation of sacred space and personnel. It is significant that we cannot really describe them as 'sacred' personnel; the *qdš* word group applies to the Levites only in the late writings of Chronicles and, even then, on a small number of special occasions after the centralization of worship in Jerusalem (1 Chr. 15:11–15; 2 Chr. 23:1–10; 29:1–36; 30:13–17). Indeed, in the four decades of wilderness wandering, Numbers focuses almost entirely on the Korahite rebellion and the confirmation of the distinctions between priests, Levites and people (Num. 16 – 18) (Keil and Delitzsch 1996, 1: 650). The solitary narrative has Korah and his non-Levite allies protesting at God's hierarchy. The wording of their complaint against Moses and Aaron is pointed: 'There is too much [authority] for you, because all the community – all of them – are "holy" [*qādôš*] yet Yahweh is in their midst. So why do you exalt yourselves above the assembly of Yahweh?' (16:3). And the remaining

---

[33] D. A. Hubbard (1996) helpfully rehearses the major interpretative issues concerning historical identity and reconstruction. His article also evinces how such issues consume many reference works as with Garrett 2003, structured around 'the problem of the Levites'. This is a key motivation for producing the present volume in a manner less focused on historical matters. The Levites are not particularly crucial to our study; at most they might add to the number of legitimate priests.

[34] That the tabernacle and its high priest represent God is further strengthened by the probability that the Levites are to 'protect his (Aaron's) protection' (as well as the whole community and the contents of the tabernacle) (3:7–8) (cf. ESV, Ashley 1993: 78–79). Indeed, such protection may be accomplished *by* their '*ăbōdâ* (service/porterage).

confrontation is precisely about who qualifies as 'holy' (*qādôš*): who is God's, whom 'he will bring near to himself' (16:4–7)! The Levites are 'differentiated' (*bdl*) from the wider community – but not as much differentiated as the priests (16:9–10, 40). With their level of holiness somewhere in between priesthood and laity, one's perceptions of the Levites depend on one's frame of reference. Compared with everyday Israelites, the Levites appear and function very similarly to the priests (e.g. Wells 2000: 115–119). Compared with the priests, the Levites appear less holy and more 'lay' (e.g. Jenson 1992: 130–135).

Summarizing the Aaronic priesthood

Although it risks adding new material in a closing summary, the Aaronic priesthood is tidily captured by the *qrb* word group. God is concerned with who should – and who should not – dare to approach him. Priests may be found 'near' to God (*qārēb*; Ezek. 40:46; 45:4) but others will find such proximity fatal (Num. 1:51; 3:10, 38; 17:13; 18:7). The verbal form regularly appears in discussion of the safety of 'drawing near' (e.g. Exod. 3:5; Lev. 9:5; 16:1; 21:17–18; Num. 16:5, 9–10; 18:3–4, 22; 27:5; Josh. 3:4; 1 Sam. 14:36; Ps. 65:4; Ezek. 44:15–16; Zeph. 3:2). An even greater volume of the hiphil form describes the bringing of an offering (cf. Kühlewein 1997: 1166), with the nominal cognate (*qorbān*) a key umbrella term for 'offerings'; such language is especially concentrated in the priestly material narrated around Mount Sinai. To anticipate a discussion later in chapter 6, it is not only priests who can draw near. While this is true, and the priests more regularly draw nearer to God, they also facilitate the successful drawing near of each Israelite worshipper (frequently in Lev. 1 – 3) and sometimes *all* Israelites may approach God (e.g. Exod. 16:9; Lev. 9:5; Deut. 4:11; Ps. 65:4).[35]

Nor is graded access to God a stratified end in itself, as if it were some formal caste system to privilege some permanently and relegate others. Those who draw progressively closer to God – cleaner Israelites, Levites, priests and ultimately the high priest – do so on behalf of and in solidarity with the entire nation. Some come to experience, however partially, what God desires for all. In turn, God commonly chooses those who are closest to him to communicate with his people

---

[35] While other forms (*qārôb*, *qirbâ*) equally capture the sentiment, they are rarer in describing proximity to God (e.g. Lev. 10:3; Deut. 4:7; Pss 73:28; 119:151; 145:18; 148:14; Isa. 55:6; 58:2; Ezek. 43:19). The first and last of these examples are most relevant to priestly behaviour.

and to regulate their proximity. Duke's summary (2003: 654) captures well the two-way role of priests and the terminology surrounding them:

> Only the priests, who were specially sanctified, could step carefully into that gap and mediate between the divine and human realms. Through their instructions and rituals, the priests warned Israel how its waywardness, intentional and unintentional, polluted God's dwelling and hindered God's presence in their covenant relationship . . . God had provided the means of removing the pollution, of purifying the unclean person and of restoring the divinely intended order. It was through the priesthood that this message of grace was mediated.

Within such summaries, we find intermingled a range of priestly privileges and responsibilities. There are hints that the priests represent the people before God, especially when the high priest 'bears' in his breastpiece the twelve inscribed gemstones 'as a continual reminder before Yahweh' (Exod. 28:29). More frequently, we find the priests representing God to the people, especially in instructing them about God's expectations (esp. Lev. 10:10–11). A range of other activities are arguably concerned less with representation and more with reconciliation, whether that be in assisting the Israelites to bring correct worship, purging the cultic system of accumulated sins on the Day of Atonement or pronouncing blessings over the people. The majority of a priest's task is to facilitate the reduction of the gap between God and humanity, regardless of which party initiates the move. Different interpreters may highlight certain elements in preference to others, but we must be aware of the smorgasbord of options from which they might select.

Both halves of the book of Exodus conclude with God's glory in a cloudy theophany among his people (Durham 1987: 501; V. P. Hamilton 2011: 620). Yet, where Sinai was a fixed geological formation, God has commissioned his own portable throne and palace. Having carefully marshalled and instructed concentric circles of sentinels, God is ready to move out in the midst of his people and into the midst of his world.

Chapter Three

Biblical antecedents to the Aaronic priesthood

Surrounded by concentric layers of honour guard, God is enthroned between the cherubim above the ark in his portable dwelling. From there he rules his people and leads them in warfare. Yet before we explore what happens as they mobilize forth from Mount Sinai we can consider the biblical antecedents to the recently instituted Aaronic priesthood.

In doing this, we are recognizing that the Sinai narrative is not the first we read of priestly language or behaviour. Both are already found in Genesis and the earlier chapters of Exodus. It aids our cumulative study to explore the wider, universal notions behind Israel's vocational priests. Cue the roiling harp music and chronological caption as the flashback begins . . .

Creation and priesthood

While we could continue working backwards through Exodus to Genesis and then backwards through Genesis, it sets a solid foundation (and shields our minds from too much temporal distortion) if we return to the beginning of the biblical narrative and work forward from there. We find that the opening chapters of Scripture already furnish a significant starting point for perceiving priesthood: the Aaronic priests did not spring into existence as a brand new venture to surprise Israel. Working from the beginning of the Bible is also a standard approach for many biblical-theology models; students starting out in the discipline marvel that Genesis 1 – 3 seems to contribute something to virtually every biblical-theology thread.

In what may be a rare consensus concerning Genesis 1 – 2, the last few decades have seen wide acceptance of the idea that the descriptions of creation are shaped by concerns for sacred space. In particular, the garden of Eden is presented as the sanctuary within which God dwells locally, and the sanctuary is considered complete when the deity's representative 'image' is installed.[1] Because the first-named humans were God's original individual representatives and also the apparent total of humanity, they contribute to our understanding both of vocational priests (here in part I) and of priestly expectations of corporate laity (later in part II). Any sacral roles at creation are thus significant for our whole study. Our evaluation is aided by working through a series of issues, and a flurry of footnotes illustrates the depths to which some of the issues could be further mined.

Is sacred space a valid model of creation?

There is great momentum for seeing parallels between the cosmos and Israel's sacred buildings. Studies such as Gregory Beale's demonstrate such parallels (e.g. 2004: 29–66) narrowing from the wider world of the general public, through an intermediate special region, and ultimately into God's holy presence. Such a gradation is still crudely approximated in any modern world view that distinguishes between the earthly realm 'down here' and the supernatural realm 'up there'.

Sacred space can be paralleled in several senses. Beale shows how Israel's cultic architecture depicts the whole cosmos. There are also obvious links between Israel's sanctuary and God's own immediate realm. Fascinating questions remain about how all these realities interact (cf. Exod. 25:9, 40; Heb. 8:2, 5). The chain of logic is usually distilled: (1) God dwells in his heavenly temple; (2) something of this is imitated in the cosmos he creates; (3) Israel's cultic architecture thus reflects one or both of these antecedents. Such multivalence leaves open some ambiguities. For example, does the outer courtyard of the tabernacle represent the clean Israelites adopted as God's people or does it symbolize the entire created realm? Are both true in different applications of a sliding metaphorical scale?

Alongside many obvious parallels, some are incomplete or uncertain. This means that the adoption of Eden as sacred space has been widespread but not wholesale. This is demonstrated by noting

---

[1] Influential investigations, citing further sources and ANE parallels, include Wenham 1986, the extensive writings of Walton (e.g. 2001: 147–152, 180–188; 2003a; 2003b; 2009: 72–92; 2011; 2015a: 104–127), Beale 2004: 66–80 (cf. 2005: 7–12 ≈ 2011: 617–622) and the 'comprehensive summary' of Davidson 2015. The reach of the idea is illustrated in recent works such as Alexander 2008: 20–31; 2012: 122–125; Gentry and Wellum 2012: 209–216; Beale and Kim 2014; Lints 2015: 43–56; L. M. Morales 2015: 39–74; Anizor and Voss 2016: 28–30; and Hays 2016: 20–27.

that even within the Old Testament faculty of one prominent theological institution (Wheaton College) dissension remains. John Walton (see n. 1) is a leading spokesman for the functional parallels and a transparent influence on Beale (formerly also at Wheaton). Yet colleague Daniel Block remains resistant to many of the parallels and their corollaries. Block's restraint invites caution in our assessments, even though he admits that views such as Walton's constitute 'an overwhelming current of scholarly opinion' (Block 2013: 3).

For our immediate purposes, Block allows that the earthly sanctuary buildings are modelled after the cosmos (developments 2→3 above) and that sacred space is a broadly accurate category for the description of creation. With this much agreed, we can explore with confidence the possible interpretations of Eden as sacred space if not more precisely as the central sanctuary.[2]

Is Eden a garden sanctuary?

While much could be fruitfully explored here, our primary concern is whether it is appropriate to read Genesis 2 as portraying sacred space in a way analogous to Israel's later tabernacle and temples. If so, we can then ask what might be detected about priesthood in what is narrated about Adam and Eve. These issues of infrastructure and personnel are closely intertwined, with scholars' conclusions about one of them influencing the other. My division here into two topics is rather administrative and artificial. Indeed, it is sometimes the latter question that is more decisive; we return to the question of priestly personnel only after mapping out Eden's terrain.

One's spatial conception of Eden strongly predisposes one to accept or reject any sacerdotal role for the garden and its human inhabitants. So it is worth recognizing that schematic precision is elusive. Strong opinions are based on minimal evidence. Even a précis here demonstrates the lack of clarity available for weighty conclusions. The question turns on how we understand the terms

---

[2] Block (2014: 298) rejects the interpretation that 'God created the cosmos, and even the garden of Eden, as a temple.' He does, though, allow multiple links between Eden and the tabernacle (including the key verse, Gen. 2:15, which we scrutinize shortly) and describes the design of the tabernacle (and thence the temple) 'as a microcosm of the heavenly residence of God . . . as a microcosm of Eden' (304; cf. 308, 310–311). His more detailed study primarily protests what the word 'temple' connotes and the validity of reading later Edenic–temple links back into Genesis. In short, the garden is clearly sacred space (2013: 17, 22) even if it is best not to infer functionality from later buildings.

'garden' and 'Eden' and their relationship in the familiar phrase 'garden *of* Eden'.[3]

Eden identifies a region associated with the garden. At its first mentions we learn that God plants a garden 'in' Eden and that a river 'proceeds from' Eden to irrigate the garden (Gen. 2:8, 10). These distinctions suggest that we do well to interpret the familiar phrase as 'the garden *located in* Eden' or 'the garden *named after* Eden'. While the Bible very occasionally treats the two synonymously (Ezek. 28:13), as does common parlance, there is little reason to completely collapse the distinction between the two and think of a 'garden *identified as* Eden'.[4]

A distinction between garden and Eden then adds possibilities for thinking about sacred space. The traditional model focuses on the first preposition (Gen. 2:8) and sees the garden as a subset located 'within' Eden. Eden is presumed to be within the wider world. This gives rise to figure 3.1.[5]

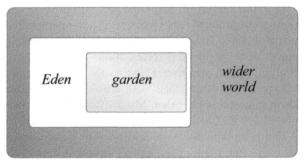

Figure 3.1

However, building more on the second preposition (2:10) renders plausible an alternative sense of being 'adjacent to' Eden (Walton 2003b: 202; Beale 2004: 74–75). This could be suggestively represented as per figure 3.2.

[3] I proceed by assuming, as do most conservative interpreters, that there is something geographical and spatial about these terms. If they are purely symbolic, some of the following concerns evaporate, though the question of the relationship between the symbolic terms remains.

[4] Common usage presumes here an appositional construct, as does Block's description (2013: 11, n. 41) of Eden as a 'toponym'. I am alert that such constructs exist (Malone 2015: 97–101) but we must ask whether one obtains here.

[5] A similar diagram is offered by Block (2013: 17 = 2014: 299), who adds the rivers described in 2:10–14. Block assumes it is Eden that is 'eastwards' from the reader's perspective (2:8), though it may well be that the garden is towards the east of Eden (Sailhamer 2008: 75).

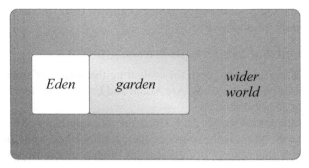

Figure 3.2

Drawn here expressly akin to schematic plans of the tabernacle, such a model corresponds to the graded holiness we have already surveyed. Beale carefully equates each of the elements in such a diagram with the corresponding zones of the tabernacle.[6]

Whichever might be the more accurate representation, the immediate relevance of such musings concerns where we might locate the man whom God places. Even more relevant – and less explored – is where we might picture God himself. Both man and God are described as being in the garden (2:8; 3:8), but it is unclear whether God is found at other times in or around Eden. Certainly figure 3.2 is attractive, identifying humanity's original responsibilities as tending the holy place adjacent to God's own presence and mediating between God and the wider world. Yet such a blueprint is surmised as much from later biblical texts as from Genesis. It also diverges from the tabernacle model when, prior to the fall, God is found walking in the garden rather than being constrained to the Most Holy Place.[7]

Apart from many suggestive parallels related to design and function, it is the role of personnel in the garden and sanctuary that most

---

[6] To a lesser extent, so also does Walton (2001: 182 ≈ 2003b: 205). In an attempt to accomplish something similar with the former, more traditional diagram, Davidson (2015: 73) describes the narrowing spheres of (the wider world →) the Eden territory → the garden therein → 'the middle of the garden' with its two significant trees (2:9). Most see the trees as integrated furnishings of the general garden, often with the tree of life prefiguring the sanctuary's lampstand, rather than as delimiting a separate, more holy zone within the garden as Davidson proposes.

[7] Only briefly does Walton address the silence of Genesis on tabernacle parallels (2001: 183 ≈ 2011: 186, n. 182), asserting that sanctuary imagery was sufficiently familiar to both the author and audience. Proponents of both interpretations are unhelpfully silent on the crucial first preposition ('in' [*bĕ*] Eden), though Block (2013: 16–17) comes closest to identifying how crucial to the debate is the preposition and any diagrams we derive from it.

highlights any possible equivalence. Thus we turn to consider the vocation of Adam and Eve.

Do Adam and Eve serve as priests?

This is a key question, both for evaluating the nature of the garden and for our particular study. Are Adam and Eve relevant to a biblical theology of priesthood?[8] The fulcrum is Genesis 2:15. Humanity is commissioned 'to work and to keep'. What is the object of their actions? And what are they to do with this object? Both questions influence how we interpret God's commission.

The answer to the first question is largely agreed, even though it is difficult to demonstrate. Delving into the Hebrew construction opens a grammatical can of worms. The commission is 'to work *it* and to keep *it*'. Everyone is content that both occurrences of 'it' behave identically – but what is 'it'? Most presume it to be a pronoun referring to the 'garden' (e.g. Walton 2001: 172; 2015a: 105), though the question remains why a feminine pronoun is used with a masculine antecedent. Walton does not engage the possibility that the pronoun corresponds with the feminine 'ground' found in the garden, as overtly expressed in 2:5, 'to work the ground' (V. P. Hamilton 1990: 171, n. 1). But Walton's overall stance is preserved, if not strengthened, by most others who favour *no* direct object or who accept feminine 'Eden' as the antecedent (see Mathews 1996: 209, n. 96; cf. Wenham 1987: 47).[9]

Walton acknowledges that our interpretation is guided better by the verbs themselves than by their object. These verbs might better determine whether 'garden' denotes 'land to be tilled or sacred space to be cared for' (Walton 2015b: 240). Some commentators promulgate without question the traditional notion that these are agricultural verbs (e.g. V. P. Hamilton 1990: 171; Hartley 2000: 60). Even some who are familiar with the cultic parallels make nothing further of them (e.g. Mathews 1996: 52, 208–210; McKeown 2008: 249–251, 261, 355) or overtly reject them (Block 2013: 10–12). All such agricultural options leave us with a humanity that *gardens* in God's (sacred) space.

---

[8] I speak of Adam and Eve together. The initial descriptions of the garden and God's commissions appear to concern only 'the man' (2:5–17), with his female counterpart not yet fashioned. But Davidson (2015: 72, n. 21) rightly notes that both she and the serpent readily understand her to be bound by those same commissions: note the plural terms in 3:1–5.

[9] Though heralding the same outcome, Walton's cited source further muddies the waters. Hendel (1998: 44) reaches the antecedent 'garden' by reading the affixed Hebrew *h* as masculine (-*ô*) rather than feminine (-*â*).

In investigating further, Walton admits that the first verb ('work' ['*ābad*]) is too broad to be definitive, so we are reliant on the sense of the second ('keep' [*šāmar*]).[10] He is right that *šāmar* occurs regularly in liturgical and sanctuary contexts with the sense of guarding or protecting. Less helpful is his insistence that Eden offers no people or animals that, in the verb's agrarian sense, need to be guarded against (Walton 2001: 173 = 2003b: 206); a primary priestly duty is to protect God's sanctuary from things such as 'the unclean creature lurking on the perimeter of the Garden' (Beale 2004: 69), a protective task at which Adam and Eve fail! The stronger arguments from proponents such as Walton are that (1) the collocation of the two verbs is particularly prominent in tabernacle settings (esp. Num. 3:7–8); (2) the ensuing commands in Genesis demonstrate concern more with 'guarding' God's expectations than with gardening; (3) the wider descriptions of Genesis 1 – 2 already lean in directions related to sacred space. I find such conclusions fascinating and, overall, persuasive. But it is these latter lines of argumentation that are more defensible and that should be reinforced. Helpful too is the warning that focusing on an agricultural interpretation can devolve into an insular 'serving and preserving' role for humanity that ignores the mandate, here and elsewhere, to organize the wider world (Walton 2001: 186–187). God's workers are to be more proactive than reactive.[11]

Given that both verbs can apply in both domains, we may not be able to be any more precise. We might ask whether it is the botanical vocation or the priestly role that is to the fore. Kenneth Mathews (1996: 209, n. 96) judges any priestly connotations to be secondary inferences and favours the earthier application. Others insist that priestly work is primary, without denying that part of this work is horticultural (unsurprisingly, Beale 2004: 68; Walton 2015a: 107–108). We need not, and perhaps cannot, resolve this issue with any further precision. It is sufficient that a good many interpreters allow that there is some degree, at least secondary if not primary, to which Adam and Eve are commissioned as priests.

---

[10] For example, '*ābad* readily applies to physical gardening (e.g. 3:23; 4:2, 12). Indeed, it is fairly protested that the nearest occurrence of 'to work the ground' has appeared just previously; 2:5 sets up the need, which is met in 2:15 (Averbeck 2015: 229).

[11] Again, we must not underestimate how much our geospatial visualization influences our interpretation and the central role of prepositions in this. Beale's argument (2004: 69; cf. fig. 3.2) pictures the serpent encroaching from outside the garden ('who then enters'), while Block (2013: 11) pictures the serpent already within.

What do Adam and Eve do as priests?

The extent to which Adam and Eve serve as priests depends on how we answer the various questions above. If we follow Walton to the extent that Genesis offers an almost entirely functional description of God's sacral workers in God's sacred space, their priestly role is substantial and significant. (If we should prefer something a little more cautious, some of the following suggestions may be diluted.) And of course if we sense a priestly context here, our wider conception of priesthood will be shaped by the behaviours we witness in the garden.

Walton (2001: 185) rightly considers some implications of priesthood:

> The verbs *'abad* ('serve') and *šmr* ('keep') do not indicate what people are to do to provide for themselves but what they are to do for God. This may have involved some landscaping and pruning, but that is not the point. Adam's duty in the garden is to maintain it as sacred space, not as a food cupboard. It is a high privilege to serve in the sacred precinct. He is to preserve its holiness and its character, just as priests did for the temple or tabernacle.

It is unspecified how Adam is to preserve holiness, though the examples above of obeying God's expectations and excluding uncleanness are sensible starting points.

Many factors may drive readers to retreat to the more familiar interpretation: our lack of familiarity with Old Testament priests, difficulties with extrapolating priestly insights and applications here, an aversion to priesthood language and concepts altogether, or the more obvious and stimulating applications related to physical labour. Few of our contemporaries today actually 'work the ground' (2:5, 15), but our imaginations are much more capable of linking this instruction with other blue-collar and white-collar vocations than with clerical-collar work, as we might simplistically take the alternative to be. One motivation for my present volume is to outline more of the Bible's assumptions about priestly work. I trust it will aid in thinking about what various priestly mandates for individuals and groups might look like as we translate from the ancient millennia narrated in Scripture into myriad twenty-first-century applications.

While such applications are concentrated primarily in my later chapters, we can anticipate glimpses of them here. What does Genesis

1 – 3 suggest to us about human responsibilities before God if 2:15 is more about priestly service than physical labour? (Of course these chapters contribute to a vast range of other topics such as cosmology, zoology, anthropology, human relationships and humanity's fall into sin. Each of these has implications for personal and vocational behaviour as well.)

Simplistically, we could sample the two central entries in the position description of Aaronic priests that we have already perused (Lev. 10:10–11). Vocational priests are to distinguish the gradations of holiness in God's world so as to keep apart the holy and the unclean, especially in terms of the sacred spaces radiating outwards from the tabernacle. Already we have seen that this accords well with the notion of 'working and guarding' the holier areas of God's creation (Gen. 2:15), at least prior to the fall. We shall need to give careful thought to what constitutes God's sacred spaces today, when it is especially now God's holy *people* in whom he dwells (e.g. Rom. 8:9–11; 1 Cor. 3:16–17; Eph. 2:19–22). Priests are also expected to teach God's people all that he expects of them. Contemporary application of this appears obvious – though we must work hard at identifying and appropriating 'all the commandments that Yahweh spoke to the Israelites through Moses' (Lev. 10:11). There is insufficient evidence for the sometimes popular claim that God taught Adam and Eve about blood sacrifice and that they in turn taught this to their sons (Gen. 3:21; 4:2–5) (e.g. Reymond 2002: 534; Davidson 2015: 76–79). Nonetheless, apart from the fact that this is not (yet) 'a commandment spoken through Moses', the hypothesized elements would correspond well with the kinds of teaching activity and holiness content expected of God's priests.

Conversely, it may be that there is little application to find in Genesis independently of the Aaronic priesthood. Some later priestly responsibilities were unnecessary when, prior to the fall, the garden sanctuary facilitated God's presence without requiring any expiatory function (cf. Davidson 2015: 68–69). It may be that certain priestly responsibilities that we can barely glimpse were surrendered or corrupted in the fall (cf. Strong 1907: 725). Much of what Adam and Eve should have been may only be recognized when the Aaronic equivalent is reintroduced and then developed through the remainder of Scripture, along with the redevelopment of sacred space as a quality contained within and among believing Christians (cf. Walton 2001: 192–201; Beale 2004: 395–402). This is our own quest in coming chapters. The description in Genesis may also be indistinguishable from that in

Leviticus if the former is intentionally cast in the language or ideals of the latter.[12]

More complex avenues of investigation also present themselves. Glimpses of priestly vocation may remain when we study the concept of humanity created in the 'image' and 'likeness' of God (Gen. 1:26–28).[13] A prominent statue with a bilingual inscription has led some to see that these two descriptors might not be completely synonymous. Rather, one might describe the statue's function as bearing the 'image' of its deity towards humanity and the other descriptor as representing the 'likeness' of humanity before deity (Garr 2000; Middleton 2005: 106–107; Block 2010: 127–128). This is certainly an attractive parallel to my working hypothesis of priests as intermediaries who stand as two-way representatives between two parties: humanity would function as God's 'image' towards others and yet the 'likeness' of humanity before God. Of course, we must admit that this Mesopotamian statue – set up by a pagan human in his own likeness – may have limited application to humanity made in Yahweh's image. More promising is the claim that statues like this occurred throughout the Mesopotamian region and with images of various deities (Walton 2011: 80–81). So we can be confident that at least one-way representation would have been understood by readers of Genesis.

Equally difficult to navigate is the balance between priestly and regal roles that are invoked when exploring the topic of God's image. Most studies identify the *royal* parallels (e.g. Dempster 2003: 59–62) and all are agreed that humanity is granted a share in God's ruling of the cosmos. Just as Adam and Eve serve as the prototypical man and woman *and* as husband and wife, so their regal and priestly activities are intertwined and challenging to untangle. Michael Morales (2015: 233) exemplifies this when he insists that 'the commission bestowed upon Adam entailed that his kingship would be in the service of his priestly office, namely that he would rule and subdue for the sake of gathering all creation to the Creator's footstool in worship'. Indeed, we shall see progressively that distinguishing between royal and sacerdotal duties is more a modern invention. It is only some perspectives

---

[12] Some readers may struggle with the issues of textual updating (on which see e.g. Grisanti 2001; Malone 2016). Yet it is conservative views of the Pentateuch that favour a cohesive document penned by a single author *several centuries after the events narrated in Genesis and in the light of all that had occurred since.* So Averbeck (1997a: 341): 'Genesis was almost certainly written after Exod-Lev.'

[13] The connection between image and priest is strongly advocated by Kline (1980: 35–56), though his attention and details are ultimately invested elsewhere.

of ANE accounts – though a substantial swathe of Old Testament narrative – that treat kings and priests as distinct. Richard Middleton (2014: 44) makes the enticing but unsupported claim that when priests, like kings, were seen as mediating the presence of deities, these priests were described as the 'image' of those gods. Other quips linking 'priest' and 'image' are found in passing (e.g. Horton 2011: 400–401). Moreover, such human roles work only in contradistinction to one another; it is harder to determine distinct priestly behaviour if 'In sum, a priest is what a human person ought to be' (*DBI* 663).

This brings us full circle. If there is any link between God's making humanity in his image and likeness (Gen. 1:26–28) and his commission to work and to keep the garden (2:15), we may catch a clearer sense of this latter task. Only with a fuller grasp of God's priests might we be better poised to evaluate the tantalizing hints from the opening chapters of Scripture.

Patriarchs and priesthood

We are not, however, left with nothing to say betwixt Genesis 3 and Exodus 19 with its Sinai narrative. Just as God moves to start restoring glimpses of sacred space and fresh but diminished echoes of divine–human communion, so we spy scraplets of priestly behaviour. Yet we should not linger long in these chapters, for they merely reinforce what we have already studied in the major bookends encasing them.

Among others, Beale argues cogently that we cannot study priests in isolation. Adam and Eve were created for a royal role as much as a priestly one (esp. Gen. 1:26–28). And their dominion entailed extending the order that defined the sacred space of God's garden until it encompassed the whole earth. Yes, such an interpretation can challenge some romantic notions of the garden, but I suspect this tells us more about our doctrinal traditions than about our exegesis. The entire thesis of Beale's tome (2004) is that biblical and human histories witness this expansion of God's rule, from creation to new creation, from the garden to the ends of the earth. God's rule over a central sliver of sacred space, despite the threat of sin, is re-established in concentric radii as God – through priestly individuals and his priestly people – stakes ever wider claims.[14]

---

[14] Acknowledging Beale, the biblical theology of J. M. Hamilton (2010) spends 600 pages demonstrating universal recognition of God's glory as the centre of the biblical story. 'Just as Adam was to rule and subdue, the nation [of Israel] was to extend its

Beale develops the familiar themes of God's commission to humanity, most notably 'be fruitful and multiply' (1:28), and notes how these recur throughout Genesis and beyond. More strikingly and rarely found elsewhere, he traces how sanctuary themes prevail at each repetition. Each patriarch has God appear to him, pitches a tent ('tabernacle'), on a mountain, builds an altar and worships God, often near Bethel ('House of God'). Beale (2004: 96) marvels that 'The combination of these five elements occurs elsewhere in the Old Testament only in describing Israel's tabernacle or temple!' He thus sees the patriarchs' behaviour as the fledgling steps of sacred space expanding beyond the garden. He also notes how sacred space is independent of a specialist building.[15]

This observation evidently helps us better appreciate the religion of the patriarchs. Alongside comparative studies of other nomadic ancients, we can identify themes that remain important throughout Christian Scripture. Equally significant is that Beale's data establishes a nexus between the garden and Sinai narratives (Gen. 1 – 4; Exod. 19 – Num. 10), connecting themes from both. Where Beale is concerned to look forward and see where these echoes of the garden develop in the remainder of Scripture, we can also look backward from Sinai and find further evidence that the garden – its structure and purpose and commissions – is not unrelated to later models of Israelite worship. Any lingering doubts about the veracity of identifying the garden as sacred space can be further soothed.

Patriarchal priestly behaviours

Where Beale focuses on the 'where' of patriarchal worship, we might briefly consider 'what' their priestly behaviour comprised.

The first of Beale's five categories is easy to overlook, yet it is arguably the primary connection between Eden and Sinai. Just as God seeks Adam and Eve while 'walking about' in the garden (Gen. 3:8 NLT), his presence is the climax of the covenant blessings: 'I will set my tabernacle among you, and I will not reject you. I will walk about among you and be your God, and you will be my people'

(note 14 *cont.*) border until the glory of God covered the land as the waters cover the sea (Num. 14:21; Isa. 11:9; Hab. 2:14)' (50).

[15] Esp. Beale 2004: 94–99, with his wider chapter (ch. 3). He summarizes that chapter elsewhere, and particularly the pattern highlighted here (Beale 2005 ≈ 2011, ch. 19). Beale's approach is echoed and extended by Schrock 2013 (esp. 53–93), showing the priestly typology grounded in Adam, Noah and Abraham.

(Lev. 26:11–12).[16] So it is no surprise, and is a strongly persistent theme, that God should manifest himself to the patriarchs. The niphal form of the verb *rā'â* is widely recognized as the regular technical term for narrating theophanies, and from this single verb form alone we can confirm appearances to Abraham, Isaac and Jacob (Gen. 12:7; 17:1; 18:1; 26:2, 24; 35:1, 9; 48:3). Even in the patriarchal period God is present with his people and in a way consistent with the vocational priesthood he later institutes.[17]

Moreover, Augustine Pagolu (1998: 54) suggests that other patriarchal cultic practices are *responses* to God's self-revelation – precisely as is the case at Mount Sinai. He expressly lists the building of altars and the offering of sacrifices. Beale explores some of Pagolu's other contributions that intersect with sacred space. Issues of both 'where' and 'what' develop some encouraging consistency throughout the Pentateuch.[18]

We might digress momentarily to acknowledge Job. The patriarchal figure is clearly concerned to keep his ten children aligned with God:

> Whenever a round of banqueting was over, Job would send for his children and purify [*qdš*] them, rising early in the morning to offer burnt offerings for all of them. For Job thought, 'Perhaps my children have sinned, having cursed God in their hearts.' This was Job's regular practice. (Job 1:5 CSB)

Likewise, at the end of the book Job prays for his wayward friends – if not somehow else ratifies their burnt offerings (42:7–9). Samuel Ballentine (2002) compiles such indications and sends us to others who concur that 'Job, like Abraham, plays the part of the perfect priest' (Habel 1985: 88; cf. 28, 529).

Beale's final point concerns the prominence of 'house' language and is also worth a moment's thought. That Abraham and Jacob are

---

[16] Building a biblical theology of *The Tabernacling Presence of God*, Booth (influenced by Beale) draws such connections. See e.g. Booth 2015: 16, 45; Beale 2004: 66, 111.

[17] For additional theophany recipients and terms, see e.g. Malone 2015: 35–37. We should especially note Exod. 24:9–11. At the climax of the Sinai covenant, Moses and Aaron, Nadab and Abihu (and seventy other elders) are invited close enough to see God. Two verbs for 'seeing' (*rā'â*, *ḥāzâ*) reinforce this privilege, and the overt inclusion of Aaron's eldest sons anticipates their pending election as priests (Exod. 6:23; 28:1).

[18] Our focus on continuities does not deny various discontinuities. Pagolu thus devotes a chapter (ch. 4) to Jacob's apparently unique enthusiasm for raising sacred pillars (esp. Gen. 28:18–22), even though such pillars are later largely condemned (e.g. Exod. 23:24; 34:13; Lev. 26:1; Deut. 16:22).

connected with the phrase 'house of God' and eponymous 'Bethel' (esp. Gen. 28:16–19), is helpful when such a phrase is used, at least by later authors, occasionally of the tabernacle (Josh. 6:24; 9:23; Judg. 18:31; 19:18; 1 Sam. 1:7, 24; 3:15) and several hundred times of the temple (after some anticipatory uses, particularly starting from David's proposal in 2 Sam. 7:5–7). Most of these points are showcased in Genesis 35:1–15, a passage underutilized by Beale. Instructed by God, Jacob commands his household to prepare as they ascend the mountainous region upon returning to Bethel.[19] The terms are cultic, especially Jacob's call to 'purify' themselves; the verb (*ṭāhēr*) is found only here before its heavy concentration in Leviticus 11 – 16 and in later, primarily cultic, contexts. Moreover, as Jacob Milgrom has argued (1991: 965–966), such purification and the washing or changing of clothing is the regular precursor to a theophany. Though he is responding to God's self-revelation, it is unclear whether Jacob expects to meet with God. But the narrative certainly highlights both Jacob's prior encounter with God and the very name 'Bethel'. Jacob's cultic behaviour includes obediently building an altar, and he indeed experiences a theophany 'again'.

Further encouraged by overt arboreal mentions on many similar occasions, Beale (2004: 102) is confident that such 'patriarchal shrines both recalled the original temple in Eden and anticipated the tabernacle and temple'. Though we are granted few insights into the priestly behaviours of the patriarchs, we do find them offering sacrifices, building reminders of God's presence, and leading worship ('calling on the name of the LORD'). And we certainly find them encountering God's presence directly! We might wonder if other patriarchal behaviours, such as multiplying in descendants and cultivating flocks (esp. Gen. 29 – 30) and interceding for others (e.g. 18:22–33; 20:7, 17), should also be linked with priestly roles.[20]

---

[19] This must surely include a topographical ascent (V. P. Hamilton 1995: 374) even though, drawing on a similar physical 'going up' to Jerusalem, Wenham (1994: 323) hears here additional cultic overtones. See Dumbrell 2002: 57–58 for the idea and sources that a mountain (or ziggurat) formed a natural nexus betwixt heaven and earth.

[20] Jacob's fruitfulness is even more significant if 29:31 – 30:43 forms the centre of this eleven-chapter *tôlĕdôt*. The concentric structure proposed by a past generation (esp. Fishbane 1975) remains influential (e.g. Wenham 1994: 168–170; Mathews 2005: 376–379; McKeown 2008: 238–239). We see later that royal themes (e.g. 17:6, 16) may also be relevant to priesthood.

Priests on the way to Sinai

The 'formal account' (*tôlĕdôt*) of Jacob's family finds them migrating to Egypt. As the biblical narrative transitions from Genesis to Exodus, and even as God rescues his people from ensuing slavery and brings them to himself at Mount Sinai, we find scattered mentions of foreign and Israelite priests. Each of them in incremental fashion contributes to our understanding of the formalized, vocational priesthood to be instituted shortly. Such connections would likely have been drawn by the first readers of the Pentateuch, who would already have been abundantly familiar with the operation of Israel's cultic system.

Foreign priests

As the story unfolds, we discover that the Israelites have no monopoly on priests. Joseph marries the daughter of Potiphera, almost universally seen as a priest of Ra serving at On (Heliopolis). Potiphera's role or lineage is significant enough to record thrice (Gen. 41:45, 50; 46:20) and we read elsewhere of Egyptian priests (47:22, 26). The commonality of such priests throughout surrounding nations is illustrated here by the fact that Genesis simply uses the regular Hebrew term for 'priest(s)'. While the narrative records special remuneration habits applicable in Egypt, it needs to add nothing about priestly roles in society.

Harder to assess is Moses' father-in-law, 'the priest of Midian' (Exod. 2:16; 3:1; 18:1). We first meet him with the name Reuel (2:18). That name contains a theophoric element (*'ēl*, 'god') and the narrative here and in Exodus 18 casts him as an ally of Moses (Paul Hughes 2003). He is commonly seen as coming to follow Israel's God (18:8–12); he certainly behaves like an Israelite priest, offering a range of sacrifices and eating 'in the presence of God' with the Aaronide elders, and perhaps evocatively doing so 'in the tent' (Fretheim 1991: 196). He also offers Moses some sage advice (18:13–27), though there is no indication that there is anything priestly about this additional content or process. Of greater relevance is the fact that we find here that Moses is 'to be [an advocate] for the people before God', especially in terms of teaching and judicial decisions (18:19–20).[21]

---

[21] It is not certain we should equate Reuel and Jethro as the same individual. Durham (1987: 22) rightly balances the 'unexplained confusion in the transmission of the name . . . with no doubt about his priestly role'.

The lessons of Melchizedek

The brief earlier cameo by Melchizedek (Gen. 14:18–20) is as enigmatic as Reuel/Jethro. The text overtly describes Melchizedek as both 'king of Salem' and 'priest of God Most High'.[22] As with subsequent foreign priests, this first titled 'priest' in Scripture earns no further explanation. Melchizedek's blessings of Abram and of God, along with his receiving of Abram's tithe, presuppose a priestly function not detailed until later. Indeed, any priestly matters here are secondary. The text prioritizes Melchizedek's regal standing and embeds this encounter as a contrast to the king of Sodom's 'cool, if not surly, reception of Abram' (Wenham 1987: 321). We must thus be careful about overloading this mysterious individual who aligns himself with Abram's own God (cf. 14:22). Nonetheless, there are several relevant themes of Genesis and of priesthood that intersect and propel our discussion.

The blessing of Abraham – and of the wider nations through him – is of course a core theme of Genesis (esp. 12:1–3). And, where Aaronic priests and Levites will acquire a role of pronouncing such blessings (esp. Num. 6:22–27), only here in Genesis do we find an overt priestly blessing (Mathews 2005: 149). In turn, this evokes the connection between blessing and the (priestly?) mandate to fill the earth (e.g. Gen. 1:28; 9:1; 12:1–3; 17:16; 22:17–18; 26:3–4, 24; 28:1–4, 13–14). Similarly, the mention of Abram's tithe to Melchizedek resonates with later Israelite practices; the 'tithe' (*ma'ăśēr*) occurs only here before such payments are mandated to priests (Lev. 27:30–33) and to Levites (Num. 18:21–29). The verbal cognate (*'āśar*) is found once before Deuteronomy – at the climax of Jacob's behaving very much as a patriarchal priest (Gen. 28:22).

Priests and kings

Resonance does not guarantee complete equivalence, but it seems clear that ancient Melchizedek is painted in priestly terms familiar to later readers in Moses' era and beyond. Equally significant is that such earlier priests are barely distinguished from *royal* roles. We have just seen that Melchizedek is cast as much as a king as a priest. And, while familiarity with the Israelite cult (and with modern Christian

---

[22] Usually obscured in major English translations, the Hebrew construction suggests '*a* priest' (so CSB, NASB, NJPS) rather than an exclusive position. See Stuart (2006: 108, n. 12), concomitantly arguing for a definite '*the* priest of Midian' in Exodus.

parlance) may infer religious overtones, 'tithes' were foremost a civil tax due to kings and their delegates (e.g. 1 Sam. 8:15, 17). By analogy, these tithes were sometimes seen as paid to a human *king* as the priestly representative of a nation's deities (Averbeck 1997c on both points). The priest-king Melchizedek thus opens our eyes to myriad other ways in which the two roles intersect. Granted, priest and king were largely separated once Israel gained a monarch, but the link between priest and king was closely knit in surrounding nations (Paul 1997: 935). There is every reason to see connections forged even in Israel's own perceptions and especially prior to the formalization of national identity (Exod. 19) and the institution of the monarchy (1 Sam. 8). A small sampling of widespread evidence is illustrative:

- Yet another verb of Genesis 2:15 is relevant. God 'put/placed' the man in the garden. But the verb employed may be more than synonymous with 2:8; it may intentionally intimate notions of 'rest', just as God himself rested at the completion of creation (2:1–3) (Beale 2004: 69–70).[23]
- We have repeatedly observed the genealogy of Exodus 6:14–25 concerned with the Levitical line. Yet Aaron's wife – and thence his priestly sons – is granted also a noble, *Judahite* heritage; 'this marriage betokens the interrelationship of the priesthood and royalty, for Nahshon was the ancestor of King David' (Sarna 1991: 35).
- It is not difficult to find interpreters identifying the high priest's robe (Exod. 28:2, 40) as a symbol of 'royal' dignity and beauty (e.g. Block 2014: 24), especially when the term for 'robe' is otherwise used largely of royal figures (1 Sam. 18:4; 24:4, 11; 2 Sam. 13:18; 1 Chr. 15:27).
- We have already noted that surrounding cultures did not distinguish priests from rulers. Joseph's priestly in-laws – and thence Joseph's sons who play a prominent role among the twelve tribes (in a convoluted dance with Levi no less) – can be praised as 'the elite of Egyptian nobility' (Sarna 1989: 288).

---

[23] Drawn from Ross 1988: 124, this is part of Beale's own argument that 'Adam should always best be referred to as a "priest-king"' (2004: 70). While highly attractive, we must concede the fragility of the data. The verbs for 'rest' (*nûaḥ*, *šābat*) are linked semantically but not lexically, with lexical parallels available only in much later OT writings. Moreover, lexicons consistently recognize two different hiphil forms of *nûaḥ* and classify Gen. 2:15 in the second, less relevant, category.

- Although the introduction of a formal Israelite monarchy is not explored until my next chapter, we can anticipate that Israel's king could claim the role (and even title) of Israel's high priest (Rooke 1998; Merrill 1993).

Already we want to be wary of simplistic reductionism. It is true that there is a *general* division of labour:

> In Israel's organizational structure there is a separation of the royal and the priestly office. The first office is reserved for descendants of David (of the line of Judah) and the second for the descendants of Aaron (of the line of Levi). (Paul 1997: 935; cf. Mathews 2005: 155)

But we might rejoin that such a distinction obviously applies only after the introduction of the monarchy and that these general boundaries are neither rigidly imposed nor observed. Again, this anticipates my next chapter, which finds further non-Aaronic individuals behaving as priests, and part II, which demonstrates all of God's people commissioned corporately for such behaviour. That is, we are beginning to discover that some of the boundaries concerning the Levitical tribe and the Aaronide family may not be rigidly impermeable.

Other early priests

If Scripture already hints that every priesthood is not rigidly exclusively Aaronide, the glimpsing of other priests becomes a little less confronting. Already in Reuel/Jethro and Melchizedek we have seen non-Israelite priests offering worship to Israel's God. There are hints of other Israelites serving a similar function, at least prior to the formalizations at Sinai.

Certainly as the leader of the people, Moses can be found undertaking responsibilities that would shortly be defined as priestly. Moses builds altars after the defeat of Amalek and for the covenant ratification ceremony (Exod. 17:15; 24:4–8). Indeed, further altars are regulated by the Sinai covenant and overtly linked with God's presence and blessing (20:24–25), and we see them built by variegated leaders after the institutional priesthood begins (e.g. Josh. 8:30–35; 22:9–34; Judg. 6:24–27; 1 Sam. 7:17; 14:35; 2 Sam. 24:25; 1 Kgs 18:30–39).[24] It

---

[24] For such references, see e.g. Averbeck (1997b), who also tackles the tension introduced by centralized worship/altar in Deut. 12. Some altars appear to be completely lay initiatives (Judg. 13:19–20; 21:4).

is true that the only direct scriptural attribution of Moses as priest is made in Psalm 99:6 and that interpreters sometimes demur on the grounds that the title can apply to more than the strict Aaronide priesthood (so Levine 1989: 49). We should observe, though, that the psalm does nothing to discourage such a classification. Moreover, where the epistle to the Hebrews repeatedly employs the rhetorical compare-and-contrast technique called *synkrisis*, the instant the preacher declares his core thesis of Jesus as 'a merciful and faithful high priest in service to God' (Heb. 2:17–18) he introduces faithful Moses as a favourable exemplar (3:1–2) (Witherington 2007: 163). So there is neither surprise nor offence in discovering the title '(high) priest' assigned to Moses by Second Temple authors and modern scholars.[25]

We thus find Moses speaking and operating alongside the high priest: regularly alongside Aaron (e.g. Num. 3:38–39; 4:34–49; 14:5; 16:3), with Eleazar (26:1–3; 31:51–54) and with all the priests (Deut. 27:9). This does not rule out asymmetrical behaviour between Moses and the high priest (e.g. Num. 16:46–50; 31:6, 41) but such asymmetry does not completely preclude Moses from priestly actions. Indeed, Psalm 99:6 counts Moses alongside Aaron as one of Yahweh's 'priests'. The same verse adds Samuel as another who 'called on [Yahweh's] name' (cf. Jer. 15:1). We return to Samuel's significance in my next

---

[25] A small sample suffices. Lane (1991: liv–lv) lists Philo, *On the Life of Moses* 2.66–186; *Who Is the Heir?* 182; *On Rewards and Punishments* 53, 56. Nongbri (2010: 694) draws attention to Strabo, *Geography* 16.2.35. Milgrom's investigation (1991: 555–558) catalogues rabbinic supporters; Milgrom himself allows Moses as 'the interim priest' (as does Hartley 1992: 113, 116) and otherwise notes that Moses' priestly behaviour may be linked to his royal-like position. Gage and Carpenter (2014: 16–17) offer some textual hints from Exodus, especially that Exod. 2 may be structured around Moses' competing *priestly* heritages. Gray (1925: 205) identifies Moses as 'the first of the Hebrew priests', and Wells 2000 is effusive:

> The special identity [of a priest] involves special responsibilities . . . and more generally to negotiate the special relationship between Yhwh and the people. Thus he is the focus of Yhwh's holy presence with Israel and of Israel's identity before God. Moses is the ultimate priest, the channel for encounter with Yhwh . . . Although the Pentateuch never describes Moses as a priest, he is clearly presented fulfilling many of the functions of a priest; indeed he 'fills in' when Aaron fails (Exod. 32–34). He is the ultimate mediator between Yhwh and Israel . . . (123, 127; cf. 105–107, 109–113)

The grammar of Ps. 99:6 remains debated, with the prepositional prefix ('*among/as* his priests') being used to include or exclude Moses (see options in Tate 1990: 527; Goldingay 2008: 130). The favourable comparison of Heb. 2:17 – 3:2 invites further exploration, especially when it cites Num. 12:7, which is itself the chiastic centre of Yahweh's poem praising Moses' unprecedented access.

chapter, where we discover that he himself and his ministry may further ratify non-Aaronide priests. Indeed, it would be foolish to consider Moses' priesthood only where the word 'priest' is associated with him. Where we have been investigating priesthood under the rubric of 'mediator', we remain alert to the many examples of Moses behaving in relevant ways. The 'mediator' (*mesitēs*) described in Galatians 3:19–20 is almost certainly Moses, as many paraphrases overtly identify (NLT, NCV, CEV; with 'go-between' in NIRV, GNB). To the extent that they are priestly prerogatives, we see Moses teaching the people God's ways, guarding his graded holiness, entering God's presence (in ways even more intimate than a high priest's, e.g. Num. 12:6–8), offering cultic and civic judgments, pronouncing blessings, interceding for wayward Israel, and ordaining the next high priest. Again, not every element is exclusively the work of a priest or a high priest, but their juxtaposition on Moses' *curriculum vitae* reinforces our impressions and Wells's language of Moses as a priest.

Moses may have enjoyed a number of assistants prior to the demarcation of the Aaronic priesthood. As the people gather at Sinai, the behaviour of 'the priests' as well as of the people is mandated (Exod. 19:22, 24). At the ratification ceremony thereafter, 'young Israelites' assist Moses with various sacrifices (24:5). Of course these terms might simply connote general assistants (e.g. V. P. Hamilton 2011: 310). However, given clear hints that Exodus is addressed to readers at least four decades after these events (esp. 16:34–36), it is probable that the language here is 'proleptic' and applied to 'those destined to be priests' in the coming days and chapters (Sprinkle 1994: 20–21). Such textual updating (see n. 12 above) addresses the readership of the label rather than the audience of the referents, and so these phrases hardly guarantee that there are additional priests here in Exodus to accommodate.

Summary

The flashback studying the lead-up to the formal inauguration of the Aaronic priesthood at Mount Sinai interacts with and reinforces my prior chapter's study of that institution.

It is unclear how much we can describe the first humans as the first priests. There is certainly evidence that this is likely and that it could be explored even further, and also a likelihood that they functioned in ways consistent with later priestly behaviour. We can readily find links with service, blessing, teaching, sacred space and holy living. But these are expected from all God's people to some extent, so it is difficult to determine if there is anything distinctively vocational initiated here.

Certainly we find the patriarchs continuing some of these practices. Again, it is uncertain how much this reflects special individual behaviour and how much is a general corporate expectation of God's chosen people. Nonetheless, the notion of vocational priests who offer sacrifices and lead worship hardly arrives in Exodus as a novel concept among the Israelites.

Debate over the nature of God's people and God's 'image' has introduced the issue of leadership. Where lay readers and biblical scholars alike can segregate God's priests from God's kings, already Genesis and Exodus suggest that a crisp delineation may be unwarranted. The same overlap is found even as we turn to the ensuing history of Israel and the formal introduction of kingship.

Chapter Four

Old Testament prospects

Tracing a biblical-theology thread is often done from start to finish, Genesis through to Revelation. That fits well with our linear minds and with linear biblical history. Yet we know also that our comprehension of past events is influenced by intervening experiences and contemporary language. The events of the book of Exodus have been completed when its author sits down to compile them, and even most first-time readers know in advance many of the outcomes. So, although strictly anachronistic spoilers, there is nothing untoward about 'flashforward' elaboration of the high-priestly succession (Exod. 6:14–25), mention of '[the ark/tablets of] the testimony' before their actual provision at Sinai (16:34), disclosure that forty years pass until the Israelites escape the wilderness for Canaan (16:35), and probably even proleptic labelling of those who would shortly be known formally as 'priests' (19:22, 24).[1]

Likewise, few readers can approach the Old Testament without knowing something of how that earlier part of the wider story turns out. Our ears ring with Jesus' condemnation of the priests (and scribes and Pharisees and others) of his day. Jesus' passion predictions include 'the chief priests' (Mark 8:31; 10:33; pars.), and we know this is indeed how things turn out (11:18; 14:1, 43, 53–65; 15:1–11, 31). Peter likewise faces danger equal to Jesus' while in the courtyard of Caiaphas (14:54, 66–72). And that is before we progress to the persecution of the earliest believers in Acts (esp. Acts 4 – 5; 9; 23 – 26). We are conditioned to think of God's priests, at least by this later point of biblical history, as the bad guys.

So how did matters reach this point? Indeed, how fair is it to stereotype the religious fervour of the Second Temple period in a negative light? The present chapter builds on the foundations that we have found in Genesis, Exodus and Leviticus and meanders through the remainder of the Old Testament. Certainly the scene is set. Just as Adam and Eve may have done, and as the patriarchs did, the Aaronic priesthood is poised ready to lead their wider family in appropriate

---

[1] For further examples beyond Exodus, see Malone 2015: 151–163; 2016.

worship of the Holy One of Israel. They will guard Yahweh's holiness, and guide his people towards him at appropriate times and through ordained means, teaching the people about such expectations. Their physical care for the tabernacle complex is matched by their spiritual maintenance of it, especially the high priest's purging of accumulated sins on the Day of Atonement. It seems that the priests may bring the people's prayers before God, and pronounce blessings upon them in Yahweh's name. Yet, if things are so promisingly poised as the Israelites set out from Sinai, what happens on the way to the New Testament and its apparent condemnation of the temple and its priesthood?

The remainder of the Pentateuch

It is easy to find evidence for our prejudged conclusions to the Old Testament. Even as the Aaronic priesthood is formally prescribed and consecrated at Mount Sinai, there is evidence that God's human mediators are frail and prone to failure; the wedging of the golden calf incident in the midst of Exodus 25 – 40 is an ominous indicator. Yet even in these very instances of catastrophic failure we catch glimpses of successful mediation between God and sinful humanity. We should thus be attuned to both negative and positive examples as we survey Israel's fate from Sinai to their arrival at the borders of Canaan.

The golden calf revisited

Interestingly, the language of 'priest(hood)' dries up during the golden calf incident. The heavy concentration in Exodus 28 – 31 and 35 – 40 withers to silence as Aaron stands before a false god(s) or an unauthorized representation of Yahweh in the intervening chapters.[2] Whether or not Moses has yet announced Aaron's designated prominence in the forthcoming cultic system, readers have heard God's designs and thus witness Aaron stripped of any theological dignity.

Despite concern for the whole wayward people, Moses focuses his accusation singularly on Aaron (32:21). It is not our place here to surmise Aaron's motives. Even if, historically, there be any truth

---

[2] Admittedly there are but two references to the *khn* word group between 31:10 and 38:21, both in 35:19. But the recognized palistrophic structure of Exod. 25 – 40 (e.g. Reid 2013: 288) and the commencement of tabernacle building from ch. 35 confirms that the resumption of 'priest' language in Exod. 35 is significant and that any silence until the middle of ch. 38 is not contemptuous.

to his protestations of innocence (32:22–24), the narrator repeatedly indicts him (24:14; 32:2–5, 25) and proffers Aaron's lame rationalization in order to elicit mocking. We have not yet heard the position description summarized in Leviticus 10:10–11, but readers with foreknowledge can hardly miss Aaron's distinct failure at differentiating and teaching appropriate behaviour in the vicinity of God's mountaintop presence. God's grand mediator-elect hits the skids and Exodus splashes it across the front pages of the tabloids.

Such prominence is significant; perhaps Moses and his (auto)-biographer expected better of Aaron. Although the text does not join the dots directly, the wider cultic context may be hinting at further expectations of the high priest. Aaron's failure is juxtaposed with the recent declarations of his singular responsibility for the people before God (e.g. Exod. 28:29–30, 36–38).

Another juxtaposition ensues (cf. Childs 1974: 570): Aaron has failed to keep God and his people in harmonious communion. God plagues them (32:35) and, worse, distances himself from his recently covenanted people (32:33 – 33:6). The narrative is repeatedly interspersed with some of Moses' most passionate intercession, earning a measure of forgiveness and, better, a fresh commitment of God's presence among his people for their benefit (32:7–14, 30–32; 33:7 – 34:35). Although Aaron fails, the text is at pains to assure readers that successful mediation remains possible.[3]

We might reiterate another obvious lesson. Set in the cultic context of Exodus 25 – 40 and the wider Sinai narrative, chapters 32 – 34 confirm that the activity of mediation is not merely about communication. Certainly Moses conveys both God's pleasure and displeasure (e.g. 32:27–29; 34:32); regardless of the recording process of Exodus, much of the book itself publicizes the expectations God had issued behind closed doors. At stake is whether the holy God can dwell and travel safely among his stiff-necked people (e.g. 33:4–6; cf. 33:20). Though Aaron may not yet know about his pending promotion to the office of high priest, his first public actions are inauspicious as he fails to direct the people to safe behaviour and to ensure the retention of God's presence. Yet Moses demonstrates that reconciliation can be forged and God's presence sustained.

---

[3] Enns (2000: 568) thus summarizes Exod. 32 – 34 as a rounded drama of 'rebellion, mediation, and restoration'. Moses' later recounting of the incident amplifies the danger to Israel and to Aaron, along with the rigour and success of Moses' intercession (Deut. 9:7–21).

In arbitrating between God and humanity, Moses operates a little in the domain of each party. (The same notion, of having a foot in both camps, accords with ANE kings being ascribed divine attributes and priestly roles.) The biblical text certainly broadcasts the unprecedented intimacy Moses enjoys (Exod. 33:7–11; 34:33–35; cf. Num. 12:6–8; Deut. 34:10). We catch a glimpse of the privilege of this mediating task.

Finally, the golden calf incident also showcases something of the Levites and their zeal. Contrasted with Aaron's permissive anarchy, the Levites fulfil a representative role as they wreak God's judgment on their idolatrous kin (32:25–28). The text describes this as an 'ordination to Yahweh' (32:29, though precision here is elusive). Again, this first glimpse of their commissioning occurs in the context of protecting the boundaries of God's presence.

Korah's rebellion

Much the same scenario happens in the Korahite rebellion once the tabernacle is completed and the people have departed from Sinai into the wilderness (Num. 16 – 17). The same negative and positive points are made, even if the roles of protagonists and antagonists are assigned differently.

We observed earlier (ch. 2) that the Levites militate against Moses and Aaron, claiming that the whole community is equally holy (16:3). The unfolding confrontation concerns degrees of access: who is (more) holy (16:4–11)? Again the sense of graded holiness is at work; Moses acknowledges that the Levites have been 'differentiated' (*bdl*) from the rest of the Israelite community (16:9; cf. 8:14), but the point of the confrontation is that they are not as holy as God's priestly leaders.

On this occasion, Aaron joins Moses in receiving God's recognition and then in interceding that God might mitigate his judicial wrath (16:21). If anything, Aaron and his high-priestly dynasty here eclipse Moses as God's long-term leader (16:11, 16–17, 40; 17:1–10). When the wider community complains at the demise of Korah and his several hundred associates, and as God's anger starts to rekindle, it is Aaron alone who 'makes atonement' and halts the incipient plague (16:46–50). Aaron's peacemaking and prophylactic role is graphically depicted: 'he stood between the dead and the living, and the plague was halted' (16:48). Timothy Ashley (1993) is thus helpful in titling these chapters the 'Legitimation of Aaron's Priesthood' (295) and resolving that each incident recounted focuses on 'a need for intercession between the people and Yahweh that only the Aaronic priesthood could provide' (297).

Indeed, while the ensuing chapters revert from animated narrative to cultic instruction, it is hardly irrelevant that Numbers 18 and 19 further delineate tabernacle responsibilities and provisions for the priests and Levites in their ministries of keeping God's people clean in his presence. Numbers 20 returns to narrative – and Moses and Aaron forfeit their leadership when they themselves fail to promote God's holiness adequately (esp. 20:12–13).

Business as usual

Israel's final travels to the borders of Canaan in Numbers, and Moses' farewell sermon(s) in Deuteronomy, largely reiterate what we have already seen.

With Aaron having forfeited his leadership and his life, the high-priestly role and robes are handed on to his son, Eleazar (Num. 20). In turn, when Israel first encounters the Baal cult at Peor, Eleazar's son Phinehas acquits himself well. He kills the offending Israelite and, like his grandfather Aaron, halts God's wrath-fuelled plague (Num. 25). 'Phinehas is established in this, his first active appearance, as the faithful priest who can be counted on to defend the proper worship of Yhwh' (Organ 2001: 209). Both priestly heroes 'made atonement for' the nation (16:47; 25:13) and the results of their intercessions are phrased identically: 'and the plague was halted' (16:48; 25:8). This heralds an intentional comparison between Aaron and Phinehas, especially when such language occurs only twice more in the Old Testament. Psalm 106:30 recounts the present event in the same language (and the psalm earlier adds a word related to prayerful inter-cession [Milgrom 1990: 215]). Quite significantly, the other occurrence comes when King David builds an altar, sacrifices and prays (2 Sam. 24:18–25); the very last words of 2 Samuel recount that the king accomplishes the same as these two leading priests: 'and the plague upon Israel was halted'.

For this zeal, God commends Phinehas to Moses, granting Phinehas and his descendants 'my covenant of peace . . . a covenant of perpetual priesthood' (Num. 25:10–13). We have overlooked such a promise to Aaron and his descendants (Exod. 40:15; cf. 29:9). Given our expect-ation that the Aaronic priesthood fails and indeed may eventually be replaced altogether, what is this 'perpetual priesthood'? Given its intersection with several later passages, I shall defer scrutiny until later in this chapter.

In the meantime, Eleazar remains the high priest. Just as God led previously through Moses and Aaron, now we find Moses and Eleazar operating together and separately (e.g. Num. 26:1–4). In due course, Moses dies and the team becomes Joshua and Eleazar (e.g. Num. 34:17; Josh. 17:4; 19:51; 20:1). After all the preparation for the priesthood and the tabernacle (Exod. 25 – 40), the cultic instructions (esp. Lev. 1 – Num. 8) and Korah's failed challenge (Num. 16 – 17), the text largely keeps the spotlight on other matters. The priests and Levites remain active but are glimpsed only as background characters. As high priest, Eleazar contributes to decision-making and to investing Joshua as the new leader (e.g. Num. 27). The Levites are assigned special cities in the pending conquest of Canaan (Num. 35). Moses' recapitulation in Deuteronomy makes regular passing reference to priests and Levites, but adds little of note. Their typical tasks remain to the fore; Moses' farewell blessing on Levi's tribe commends their guarding and teaching of God's covenant and law, along with their sacrificial tasks (Deut. 33:9–10).[4]

The historical books

As we transition into another division of the Old Testament, much the same can be said for the historical books. Scripture's reduced focus in this corpus is not to diminish the role of God's representatives during this part of Israel's history (rightly McConville 1999).

While the priests are heavily involved with leading the sanctified people into Canaan (Josh. 3 – 6), the focus is squarely on the ark – and the presence of God that it represents – and not on its specialized handlers. Alert readers will observe that the priests, although serving in the background, have had something of a promotion. Pentateuchal instructions assign the carrying of the ark to Levites, and formally to the Kohathite clan (Num. 4:1–20) – a lesson that David and Uzzah will later be slow to learn (1 Chr. 13, 15). But this does not prohibit the priests participating who, after all, are *more* authorized to wrap

---

[4] To be sure, the *reduced* focus on cultic personnel is one source-critical factor in exploring the origins of Deuteronomy, as is the novel phrase 'the Levitical priests' (Deut. 17:9, 18; 18:1; 24:8; 27:9; cf. 21:5; 31:9). Such observations are relevant to their domains but need not detain us here. The novel phrase may also be symptomatic of alleged transformations of the roles of the Levites in the Deuteronomic writings (recently e.g. Achenbach 1999; Leuchter 2007; and the helpful summary of Boda 2016: 256–257); such arguments are intertwined with issues of composition and are more concerned with Levites than with the priests.

and direct such sacred items. Marten Woudstra (1981: 81) draws attention to similar passages where 'the priests', apparently distinguished from 'the Levites', handle the ark (1 Kgs 8:3–6; cf. Deut. 31:9) and it may simply be that the priests take the lead on major occasions, as when the ark is installed in the temple (Klingbeil 2005: 812). Of course, if God's human assistants on such occasions are drawn from the elite descendants of Aaron's family rather than from the broader tribe of Levi, it gives even greater dignity to God and his conquest leadership. The priests' participation is further apposite when we acknowledge the semantic and textual links to the theophany of Exodus 19 (Dozeman 2015: 284–287).[5]

Through the rest of Joshua, we simply find the Levites being allocated their cities (though no territory) and Eleazar assisting Joshua with the leadership of the people. Not unlike with an apprenticeship, Eleazar had risen to textual prominence (Num. 19) just prior to Aaron's death (Num. 20). Likewise here Eleazar's son Phinehas is shown entrusted with important arbitration (Josh. 22) just prior to the transition of power at the end of the book (Josh. 24:33).

We ought not, however, to overlook this leadership role. As Moses was anticipating arrival in the land, we start to find priests involved in everyday decision-making. Not only does the high priest discern divine decisions (e.g. Num. 27:21), but Moses foretells a time when the priests will work alongside judges in determinations (e.g. Deut. 17:8–12; 19:16–21; 21:5; cf. 2 Chr. 19:8–11). This is consonant with Exodus 18, where Moses' priestly father-in-law aids him in maintaining civic order, and consistent with God's declaration that a high priest's death marks the end of an epoch in certain criminal verdicts (Num. 35:25, 28, 32 ≈ Josh. 20:6). Apart from priests' familiarity with God's expectations, there may be a representational element. Deuteronomy 19:17 likely offers an appositional construction, whereby defendants stand before Yahweh *by* standing before Yahweh's priests and judges (NET, NAB, NLT; McConville 2002: 307).

The decline of priesthood

Every facet of Israel's life is painted in darker hues in the book of Judges. The nation wanders from Yahweh's leadership, such that even human kingship seems a desirable remedy.

---

[5] As with 'the Levitical priests' in Deuteronomy (previous note), absolute certainty is difficult. Commentators note how the notion of *priests* carrying the ark grieved the LXX translator, who here clarified 'our priests *and* Levites' (Josh. 3:3). Indeed, the LXX could be read as restricting the carrying entirely to the Levites.

The place of human priesthood is difficult to ascertain. There is certainly no hint that cultic behaviour has ceased; Daniel Block (1999: 37–39) catalogues many of the normal characteristics of the Israelites' worship, such as their sacrifices, prayers and oaths (e.g. Judg. 2:5; 5:2–9; 6:22–24; 16:28; 21:1–9); the book clearly presupposes the religious ideals of the past (esp. 2:20–22). The Israelites' requests for guidance (e.g. 1:1–2) are likely answered by priestly intercession or the high priest's Urim and Thummim: later instances expressly name the cultic site at Bethel, and particularly the presence there of the ark and the ministry of Phinehas (20:18, 23, 26–28).[6]

There is otherwise very limited mention of any cultic personnel. For all their zeal, the judges themselves have no revelatory role. Messages from God are conveyed neither by judges nor priests but via messengers, through prophets or directly from God himself (Block 1999: 40). The sparse mentions include the following:

- The first of the closing, anarchic stories (Judg. 17 – 18) describes several attempts at creating a potentially independent human priesthood. An Ephraimite named Micah crafts a shrine, ephod and idols and ordains his own son as a priest (17:5). Micah soon recruits and ordains a passing Levite for the role (17:7–12). For all his flagrant waywardness, Micah still voices an understanding of the superiority of appointing a Levite (17:13). For his part, the Levite fails to uphold Yahweh's boundaries of holiness; he readily accepts the title of 'priest' and speaks on God's behalf (18:1–6). He fickly switches allegiances when threatened by the migrating Danites, who themselves see the prestige of obtaining a Levite (18:18–20), and he becomes the inaugural priest at their new cultic centre in the north. Only now at the end of the drama is it disclosed that this itinerant Levite – cast as loyal only to his own best interests – is a descendant of Moses (18:30)!
- The second story of depravity (Judg. 19 – 21) likewise revolves around an unnamed Levite. This nomenclature, used sparingly (19:1; 20:4), links the second story with the first. It may also have broader religious connotations (see below), though there is nothing expressly cultic about his behaviour here.

---

[6] Such a conclusion is generally accepted (e.g. Block 1999: 86–87; Webb 2012: 94–95), though Webb wisely warns against presuming entirely orthodox cultic functions at this time.

• Only the noted mention of 'Phinehas son of Eleazar son of Aaron' (20:28) makes an overt link with prior cultic expectations, although his role here is largely left to inference.

Other fleeting mentions of cultic issues, such as the ephod constructed by Gideon (8:23–27) and 'the house of God at Shiloh' (18:31; possibly also 19:18), are inconclusive for our investigation. What, then, can we make of the way Judges presents the notion and accoutrements of priesthood? The lack of foregrounded details suggests caution. But studying the adjoining biblical histories gives us some bookends or boundaries between which to navigate. Faithful loyalty to God in Joshua and a dysfunctional priesthood in Samuel invite us to pinpoint a substantial decline during the period of the judges.[7] There may be various allusions as the book unfolds. Given points of contact between the accounts of Abraham and Jephthah sacrificing their children (Gen. 22; Judg. 11), is Jephthah's pagan sacrifice contrasted with Abraham's priestlike uprightness (Schrock 2013: 175–176)? Perhaps the strongest evidence for the overall decline is the persuasive thesis of Don Hudson: if the identities in Judges 19 – 21 are intentionally anonymized, this Levite's behaviour is typical of *any* Levite's.[8] Another literary touch is found in 18:30, where we find three matters succinctly and sinisterly juxtaposed (cf. Mueller 2001: 73). As did Aaron at Sinai in the past (Exod. 32:1–6), and as will Jeroboam at this same site in Dan in a future known to readers (1 Kgs 12:26–33), an Israelite tribe sets up an unauthorized idol; readers are familiar with such a future because the narrator adroitly foreshadows 'the day of the exiling of the land' (which is elsewhere expressly blamed on idolatry, e.g. Lev. 26:27–33; Deut. 4:25–28; 2 Kgs 17:5–23); and, wedged between these two ominous and linked observations, the narrator names the Mosaic dynasty as responsible.[9]

---

[7] Commentators offer some general reconstructions, attempting to incorporate the limited Judges data; e.g. Block 1999: 41–44; Webb 2012: 13–15.

[8] The insights of Hudson 1994 are widely echoed; e.g. Block 1999: 517–518; McCann 2002: 118–119; Younger 2002: 348; Butler 2009: 417; Chisholm 2013: 497–498. Independent of Hudson, the same generalization is inferred in Moster 2015.

[9] Strictly, Mosaic descent does not condemn the Aaronic priesthood. I follow here the substantial consensus that the reading 'Moses' is only later corrupted to 'Manasseh' (retained by NASB). The character analysis of Moster 2014 offers rare dissent, that the lineage at 18:30 (probably) does not apply to the Levite and that the text (probably) names 'Manasseh' anyway.

Though we should handle carefully arguments from silence, we might also speculate whether the narrator tacitly (or even inadvertently) indicts the priesthood by what is not said. We have noted that a foundational mandate for priests is to teach the Israelites all God's commands (Lev. 10:11). What blame then attaches when Judges charges successive generations with ignorance (Judg. 2:10; 3:7; 8:34)? We should add the repeated testimony that 'Israel (again) did evil in the eyes of Yahweh' (2:11; 3:7, 12; 4:1; 6:1; 10:6; 13:1) and the theme of the closing chapters that 'everyone did what was right in their own eyes' (17:6; 21:25). Even while we catch glimpses of cultic personnel in the background, any effective teaching appears absent.

Pending termination

The limited but foreboding evidence of Judges is corroborated by the opening of Samuel.

Samuel the individual is a transitional figure. Within a single New Testament book, he is described as both the last of the judges and the first of the prophets (Acts 3:24; 13:20). The deliverers in Judges are said to 'judge' or 'lead' Israel, especially in the summary formula 'X judged Israel for Y years' (Judg. 10:2–3; 12:7, 8–9, 11, 13–14; 15:20; 16:31; cf. 3:10; 4:4). The verb carries on into successive books. Ruth is set in the same period (Ruth 1:1), and Eli's life and dynasty close with the same formula: 'he judged Israel for forty years' (1 Sam. 4:18). It is telling, then, that Samuel himself 'judges' the people (7:6) and that the chapters introducing his life conclude that he 'judged Israel all the days of his life' (7:15). His sons are appointed and operate as judges, apparently in their father's stead (8:1–2). Indeed, in his farewell speech Samuel lists his ministry alongside the deliverance wrought by Jerub-Baal (Gideon), Bedan (Barak?) and Jephthah (12:11).[10]

Samuel the book is likewise concerned to narrate the change of Israel's leadership. While scholars typically debate whether God willingly or begrudgingly introduces a human monarchy, the opening chapters are equally concerned with a transformation of the *priestly* dynasty: 'the books of Samuel begin not with a crisis over the absence

---

[10] Reading 'Samuel' here accepts the MT text. A few have baulked at Samuel's third-person self-reference (e.g. NRSV, NEB/REB; cautiously McCarter 1980: 208, 211), but I have demonstrated elsewhere (Malone 2009) the validity of such a phenomenon, not least in Samuel. The identification of Bedan/Barak (and, perhaps, thus of Jephthah) remains debated. Block (1999: 22–23) recounts those such as Noth who see the book of Judges extending as far as 1 Sam. 12.

of a king, but with the failure of the priesthood' (Deenick 2011: 327). This warrants some closer attention.

The story introduces Elkanah and his wives, along with their regular pilgrimages to the tabernacle at Shiloh (the location confirmed by Josh. 18:1; Judg. 18:31). But such piety commences with mention of 'the two sons of Eli: Hophni and Phinehas' (1 Sam. 1:3) and only a few verses later Eli plays a speaking role. Indeed, once Samuel is miraculously born and settled into ministry, the story's focus sharpens to the reassignment of priesthood from Eli's house to Samuel. Interspersed with praise for the youth who will, only eventually, be identified as the successor, Eli's dynasty is progressively denounced by the narrator, via a man of God, and through God's direct words to Samuel (respectively 2:12–26, 27–36; 3:1 – 4:1).

Each of these sections is quite detailed, often and unsurprisingly concerning priestly matters. Some of the core issues include:

- The initial condemnation of Eli's sons emphasizes their mistreatment of God's people and his sacrificial system. Especially indicted at the start and end, these 'sons of Belial did not know Yahweh' (2:12) and their extortionate intimidation is summarized as 'very great sin' concerning their ignorance or disregard for 'the offering of Yahweh' (2:17).[11]

- The sacrificial system is again the focus of the accusation brought by Yahweh through the man of God. He spells out how Eli's ancestor (probably Aaron; again just 'priest' rather than 'high priest') was *chosen* by God for such cultic ministry, a ministry now scorned by Eli's family (2:27–29). Yahweh admits he had promised Aaron and even Eli himself that their priestly dynasties would operate 'for ever', but he now pronounces their premature, graphic demise (2:30–34).

- That speech continues unbroken, but its climax requires special attention. Readers know that Samuel soon will express God's disappointment with Saul's kingship and his plan for a faithful successor, especially in 13:13–14:

---

[11] None of the possible senses of 'sons of Belial' is complementary (e.g. Tsumura 2007: 122–124)! And one wonders if 'the practice/duties [*mišpāṭ*] of the priests [towards?] the people' (2:13) directly indicts their leadership responsibilities (cf. 'judge/lead' [*šāpaṭ*] throughout Judges and pending in 1 Sam. 4:18; 7:15; etc.). Every aspect of the *mišpāṭ* phrase is variable: its placement here (connected with what precedes?), the breadth of *špṭ*, any prepositional import concerning the people, and the apparent echo of Deut. 18:3. Further, Organ (2001: 217) suggests that the sexually lax Phinehas here (2:22) is intentionally contrasted with Aaron's upright grandson.

You have not guarded the commandment of Yahweh your God which he commanded [*ṣāwâ*] you, for now Yahweh would have established your kingdom over Israel for ever ['*ad-'ôlām*]. But now your kingdom will not stand [*qûm*]: Yahweh has sought for himself [*lô*] a man according to [*kĕ-*] his heart [*lēbāb*] and Yahweh has commanded him as prince over his people, for you did not guard what Yahweh commanded.

A preview of such language occurs here in 2:29–35 as God's spokesman likewise promises Eli a replacement priesthood:

Why do you scorn . . . what I commanded [*ṣāwâ*]? . . . I certainly said that your house and your ancestor's house would walk before me for ever ['*ad-'ôlām*] . . . I will raise ['make stand', *qûm*] for myself [*lî*] a faithful priest who will act according to [*kĕ-*] what is in my heart [*lēbāb*] and in my mind. And I will build for him a faithful house and he will walk before my anointed one all the days.

Already we see that a 'perpetual' dynasty, whether regal or sacral, can be terminated. In 2:35 we observe that Aaron's dynasty, even though promised 'for ever' (Exod. 40:15; Num. 25:13; Deut. 18:5), can find its contract annulled.

- Still on that same verse, one key question concerns with what God will replace the Aaronic priesthood. It is commonly construed that the priesthood here passes from Eli's family to Zadok's, as formally implemented by Solomon (1 Kgs 2:27, 35). Karl Deenick raises the intriguing suggestion that the Hebrew reads not 'a faithful priest . . . before my anointed one' but 'a faithful priest . . . before me (who is) my anointed one'. Rather than a priest and a king, perhaps the solution to the failure of the priesthood is a role that combines both. Apart from tidily prefiguring the multi-talented ministry of Jesus, this could explain some of the priestly roles exercised by monarchs such as David and Solomon (see below). The solution further anticipates Hebrews 7: it 'is not simply an issue of replacing one Aaronic priestly line with another – the Elides with the Zadokites – but of replacing the Aaronic priesthood in general' (Deenick 2011: 328).[12]

[12] Independently of Deenick, Diffey (2013) proposes that 1 Sam. 2:35 points to a Davidic priesthood. And, though grounded upon certain critical reconstructions, Milstein (2016) hypothesizes that the opening chapters of 1 Samuel hint that King Saul (rather than Samuel) 'was remembered as a figure of priestly background who was tied

- Later texts certainly refract such priestly connections for Samuel. Psalm 99:6 pairs Moses and Aaron with Samuel on the basis of being Yahweh's priests. And the author of Chronicles, with a recognized emphasis on the temple and its operation, furnishes Samuel's biological or adoptive lineage as a Levite (1 Chr. 6:27–28, 33–34) along with other temple-related activities (e.g. 9:22; see further M. J. Evans 2005: 863).
- Samuel's success is overtly contrasted with the paucity of divine revelation. His call narrative starts and, especially, finishes on this note (1 Sam. 3:1, 19–21). Where mediating God's words is a core priestly task, Samuel succeeds where Eli's house has overtly lapsed (Schrock 2013: 157).

Such observations bring to light some significant transitions, which can be summarized simply and starkly. Eli and his sons are clearly cast in priestly roles. Plenty of hints likewise intimate such a priestly future for Samuel (2:11, 18; 3:1, 3, 15; 7:9, 17) and relevant studies have no qualms in describing Samuel's behaviour as that of a 'priest' (e.g. Armerding 1975: 80; Tsumura 2007: 418). However, the narrative gives more weight to Samuel's capacity as a 'prophet' (3:20) and then as a 'judge' (7:6, 15). Again, it is these latter labels by which the New Testament remembers his ministry (Acts 3:24; 13:20).

All of a sudden, and perhaps startlingly, we start to observe not only the demise of the Elide priesthood but the apparent demise – or at least demotion – of priests as prominent Israelite leaders altogether. We have seen religious functions performed by the patriarchs, and perhaps even intended of all antediluvian humans. Moses and Aaron and their respective successors retained cultic elements as an essential part of guiding God's people into Canaan. Under the judges, that priority appears to have dwindled; any mention of religious activity appears marginalized and compromised. The Elides oversee a corrupted priesthood whose termination is pronounced. And, as much as biblical categories permit differentiation, Eli's protégé is cast far more in secular terms than with religious overtones. If we fairly call Eli a 'priest-judge', Samuel is regularly a 'prophet-judge'.[13] Frank Spina (1994: 72)

to the House of Yahweh at Shiloh' (100). And, whether or not 2:35 expects unique fulfilment in Jesus, the language of Heb. 2:17 clarifies Samuel's foreshadowed 'priest' as a 'high priest' (deSilva 2006: 298).

[13] 'Priest-judge' is overtly used of Eli by Tsumura (2007: 197; cf. 188), who likewise collocates 'prophet' and 'judge' of Samuel (e.g. 234, 251, 273; cf. Bergen 1996: 34–35, 52–53).

proposes that we readers are witnessing a transition 'not simply from one man or family to another, but from one *kind* of leadership, namely priestly, to another *kind*, namely prophetic'. All these labels may betray our modern tendency to delineate too strictly between categories. Certainly we have already found Moses himself engaging in priestly behaviour, yet he also operates as a judge (Exod. 18:13–26; cf. Num. 25:5; 27:5) and as a prophet (Deut. 18:15–18; 34:10). And there are hints that Samuel's own multivalent ministry is modelled on Moses' (Ps. 99:6; Jer. 15:1; perhaps even 1 Sam. 1 – 3; see Leuchter 2013). So the various elements may differ in their emphases, but the existence of such combinations is not in itself remarkable. Spina's observation remains valid but, at least until the monarchy firmly takes root, we should be speaking of emphases rather than rigidly distinct job descriptions. Certainly a prophetic role in Israel's leadership is on the rise.

Serving in shadows

Spina's observation also rings true when we realize that the whole institution of priesthood now seems to take a back seat in the historical narratives. Granted, our narrators are concerned to foreground the newly arrived monarchy: its faltering start with Saul, its golden era under David and Solomon, and then its mixed report card until the respective fates of the divided kingdoms.

The biblical text itself reflects this. References to priests (and also to Levites) become sparse, certainly when contrasted with our study of the Pentateuch. Occasional mention of temple personnel can be found, including particular priests such as Ahijah, Ahimelech, Abiathar, Zadok, Jehoiada, Uriah and Hilkiah.[14] Most of their actions appear as standard background colour: priests going about their regular rituals (e.g. 2 Sam. 15:24; 1 Kgs 8:3–5, 11). More disturbing, their actions appear subordinated to the behest of kings (e.g. 1 Sam. 18:18–19; 21:1–9), even to the point that some monarchs override divine sensibilities or slaughter uncooperative priests (1 Sam. 22:6–23; 2 Kgs 16:10–18). The author of Kings continues to use the language of 'priests' even for impostors who enjoy no divine authorization. Obvious examples include the rival priests interposed by Jeroboam I and the private priesthoods of wayward kings such as Ahab (1 Kgs 12:31 – 13:3; 2 Kgs 10:11, 19; cf. 11:18; 23:5, 20). These political

---

[14] Representative chapters include 1 Sam. 14; 21 – 23; 30; 2 Sam. 8; 15; 1 Kgs 1 – 2; 2 Kgs 11 – 12; 16; 22 – 23. As in the Pentateuch, the language of 'priest' tends to suffice for the central or 'chief' priest.

manoeuvres and rival systems demand their own investigation, but for now they serve to illustrate the importance and power associated with cultic systems. Conversely, there are occasional glimpses of the priesthood contributing to good order. Their duties in the newly established temple run smoothly, just as Solomon's royal deference to God is cast positively (1 Kgs 8). And Gordon McConville (1999: 82–85) helpfully notes the prominence of priestly language and priestly action in guiding Joash's restoration of the temple (2 Kgs 11 – 12) and, to a lesser and perhaps even contrasting extent, during Josiah's reform (2 Kgs 22 – 23). We see priestly concern not just for God's sacred space but also for his anointed leaders; orthodox priests remain concerned for God's human representatives. Finally, the leading priests are prominent among those with whom the narrator chooses to end his graphic depiction of the fall of Jerusalem (25:18–21).

It seems safe to see something of the Aaronic priesthood at work, even though the priests are not prominent in the biblical narratives. Of course we need to be careful not to overinterpret such silences. Among conservative scholars, at one extreme Clive Thomson (1961) minimizes the place of legitimate priests, judging them all to have failed and that any locums nominated by David in the absence of the ark and of the tabernacle or temple were 'improper'. Israel is left without cultic mediators and God distances himself from his people. At the other extreme, Carl Armerding (1975) delights that 'it seems plain that David himself was the chief sacrificial and priestly intermediary between Yahweh and his people during his reign' (82), leading a viable priesthood. (More sceptical scholars simply assume that a number of families or guilds were vying for power, and/or that the victors had not yet written themselves back into prior narratives.) Neither extreme seems necessary, especially if we allow that a lack of narrative mention does not especially correlate with a lack of priestly activity.

Kings as priests?

Casually in passing, one difficult passage lists that 'Zadok son of Ahitub and Ahimelech son of Abiathar were priests . . . and the sons of David were priests' (2 Sam. 8:17–18). Especially when the same word (*kōhănîm*) is used each time, how have Judahite princes become confused with Levite priests? Does this smack of a growing priestly corruption, now transgressing tribal boundaries? Or is it some kind of recognition that, from the beginning, Aaron's family was sired through his Judahite wife (Elisheba, Exod. 6:23)? Knowing that the biblical story ends with a great high priest – and 'clearly it was from Judah that our Lord descended' (Heb. 7:14) – is God already foreshadowing the validity of a Judahite priest-king?! As the marginal notes of the NET translation summarize tidily, there are two leading options for David's sons. Perhaps Samuel intends some kind of role wider than that of a cultic 'priest'. The Greek Septuagint introduces a unique term, describing David's sons as 'courtyard leaders' (cf. NASB, CSB), though we do not know which courtyard is in view. The parallel in 1 Chronicles 18:17 likewise tones down the cultic connotations, describing David's sons as 'leading officials' (NET).[15]

The second option is that royal figures participated in priestly service. We have already seen examples of this, such as David recently sacrificing before the ark and before Yahweh, clad in an ephod and blessing the people (2 Sam. 6:12–19). It is commonly suggested that there were additional priestly roles that laymen could participate in: 'David's sons were priests, though not in the Levitical sense.'[16] Of great interest to our study is that this allows significant overlap between royal and priestly roles: kings such as David could readily participate in certain priestly activities. Whether or not such a prerogative is available also to others in the Israelite community, we certainly observe kings joining in sacral activities. In addition to David's ephod-wearing sacrifices, we have already seen how the very last verses of Samuel show David building an altar and offering sacrifices and prayers, which halt God's wrath-fuelled plague (24:18–25) – wording otherwise used only of similar success by the priests Aaron and Phinehas (Num. 16:48; 25:8; Ps. 106:30)! Although the narrator makes no explicit comment,

---

[15] Even a conservative scholar of the stature of Wenham is willing to entertain the possibility of textual emendation for Samuel (Wenham 1975, proposing *sōkĕnîm* [royal administrators] for *kōhănîm*). Note also the possibility raised by Chapman (2016: 55, n. 145) that it may be the word 'sons' that could be re-evaluated: Chapman wonders if it could connote 'appointees'. This possibility gains weight when, akin to Solomon's dedication of the temple (Dillard 1987: 228–229), Hezekiah summons 'the priests and Levites' and addresses them as 'my sons' (2 Chr. 29:11). The titles 'priest' and 'adviser' are collocated in 1 Kgs 4:5; my gratitude to Greg Goswell for this observation.

[16] Firth 2009: 399, noticing also Ira the Jairite at 20:26; cf. Cody 1969: 100–107. Armerding 1975 remains influential, with similar notions echoed by the likes of Gordon 1986: 234, 247; Baldwin 1988: 225–226; Davies 2004: 89–90; and Long 2009: 453. Some perhaps go too far when they move beyond seeing Melchizedek's dual role as an example of a separate order of priests, to validating a dynasty of Jerusalemite priest-kings (e.g. Merrill 1993; Bergen 1996: 331–332, 352). Armerding and Merrill, in particular, collate some of the examples raised in this paragraph.

readers only a few decades later would recognize Araunah's threshing floor as the site of the temple (2 Chr. 3:1). Royal psalms can introduce priestly language, most obviously Psalm 110; Willem VanGemeren (2008: 684) collates examples that demonstrate that 'Although not an Aaronic priest, the Davidic king has sacerdotal functions.' Back in the historical narratives, two of David's sons offer public sacrifices as part of seeking to succeed David's reign (2 Sam. 15:10–12; 1 Kgs 1:9 with 1:11–25). A third son, Solomon, earns praise for many things, including his participation in cultic sacrifices (1 Kgs 8:5, 62–64; 9:25; 10:5; cf. 3:3–5). Granted, it is unclear that these mark David's sons as priests rather than pious worshippers. But the narrators do continue to show kings participating in such ways, singling out the *corruption* of their practices rather than the *fact* of their participation (1 Kgs 12:32 – 13:1; 2 Kgs 16:12–13). There are, of course, limits on kings' participation, as Uzziah discovered (2 Chr. 26:16–20). Building on the hint of Deborah Rooke (2000: 19), we might even suggest that Israel's monarchy is somehow modelled on its priesthood.[17]

Both options are quite attractive. Even if we should distrust that Israelite kings could encroach on priestly roles, either option reminds us that the term 'priest' can be used more broadly than we might narrowly assume.[18]

Equally tantalizing is the occasional suggestion that Israelites from tribes other than Levi could be adopted into Levitical roles (and perhaps thence into priestly service). God claimed all firstborn Israelite males (Exod. 13:1–2; 22:29). The first generation was redeemed by the 'offering' of the Levites in their place (Num. 8:15–19), and subsequent generations are to be redeemed with an animal (Exod. 13:11–13). The attractive suggestion is that, on occasion, a firstborn might *not* be redeemed but might be donated directly to God's service

---

[17] In addition to these options, Crocker (2013: 199–200) wonders if – as with boundary-transgressing kings like Uzziah – David in 2 Sam. 8 is committing 'a grievous error' by ordaining his sons. Also interesting is that Crocker wonders if David's priestly behaviour is derived not from Aaron but from Israel's corporate priesthood (see ch. 6). The intersection of priesthood and monarchy is strengthened by those who would see Exod. 19:6 as connoting 'a kingdom ruled by priests under the supreme direction of a king who is also [a] priest' (van der Kooij 2006: 178).

[18] The possibility that the term 'priests' applies outside the specific temple role is not challenged by the language used of Jeroboam I. That his idolatrous leadership includes appointing 'priests . . . who were not Levites' (1 Kgs 12:31; cf. 13:33) contributes little to the wider investigation of priests (rightly Provan 1995: 112). Chronicles clarifies that authentic priests and Levites were expelled by Jeroboam (2 Chr. 11:13–15). So 'priests' here means nothing more than when used of pagan clerics (e.g. Gen. 41:45; 1 Sam. 5:5; Jer. 48:7; 49:3).

(Levenson 1993: 46–48; cf. Haydock 2015: 34, n. 10, 48–49). This may explain Samuel's uncertain heritage and authenticate his tabernacle ministry even though he was an Ephraimite (1 Sam. 1:1). It might also set precedent for other non-Levitical service – though David and other contenders cannot claim status as firstborns or Nazirites.

Later Old Testament writings

Those who venture into the wilds of biblical theology can be uncertain how best to catalogue their findings. Does one work canonically through the biblical documents, even when these can be repetitive and can revisit times and places already observed? Or does one iron out the variations by imposing some other organizing structure – often a chronological timeline of salvation history and the fate of the northern and southern kingdoms? There are advantages and disadvantages to any such ways forward.

As we traverse the prophets and writings that make up the latter half of the Old Testament, we find an easy synergy on this occasion. I will, however, lean towards a thematic synthesis; I trust that this draws together the main highlights without harming the individual emphases and contributions of the biblical authors.

Prophetic condemnation

The contributions of the writing prophets integrate cleanly with what we have already discovered in the historical books. In the language of the Hebrew Bible and its divisions, the Latter Prophets are in harmony with the Former Prophets.

Once the monarchy has been established, past multivalent roles are increasingly superseded by narrower specializations. Prophets and priests and kings are noticeably more distinct from one another. Certainly the rank of 'priest' is mentioned by the writing prophets, and significant priests are named, such as Uriah, Pashhur, Zephaniah, Amaziah and Joshua. Their role in society is sometimes for the better or, more commonly, for the worse.[19]

---

[19] General titles and specific names occur in passages like Isa. 8:2; 28:7; 61:10; 66:21; Jer. 1:18; 2:8, 26; 4:9; 5:31; 6:13; 8:1, 10; 13:13; 14:18; 18:18; 19:1; 20:1; 21:1; 23:11, 33–34; 26:7–16; 27:16; 28:1, 5; 29:1, 24–29; 31:14; 32:32; 33:17–22; 34:19; 37:3 (Lam. 1:4, 19; 2:6, 20; 4:13–16); Ezek. 7:26; 22:26; 43:19; 44:23–24; 45:1–5, 19; 46:2, 19–20; 48:9–14, 21–22; Hos. 4:6–9; 5:1; 6:9; Joel 1:9, 13; 2:17; Amos 7:10; Mic. 3:11; Zeph. 3:4; Hag. 1:1, 12, 14; 2:2, 4, 10–13; Zech. 3:1, 8; 6:9–15; 7:3, 5; Mal. 1:6 – 2:9.

Failed priestly leadership

The priests are often listed alongside other ruling classes and their failed leadership is harangued collectively. This is especially prominent in the pre-exilic prophets. As much as Israel's kings and (false) prophets, God's priests have failed in their duties. A sampling of these paints a consistent picture – one that is consistently bleak:

- Isaiah 28:7 condemns the priests (along with prophets) for drunken impairment. The claim is probably a literal one and not merely metaphorical; the language here emulates the uncoordinated walking and incoherent speech it derides (Oswalt 1986: 510), and such incoherence is further mocked in the ensuing verses.
- In much the same era, Hosea 4:4–9 condemns the priesthood (and, in passing, accompanying prophets). The priests are censured for having rejected knowledge and for wilful inaction concerning God's torah.[20]
- Using similar language to censure Israel's marital waywardness a century later, Jeremiah 2:8 slams the failed leadership of priests, 'shepherds' and prophets. The priests are overtly condemned for not even asking, 'Where is Yahweh?'! We learn more of the expectations of priests if the second clause parallels the first (e.g. NET, CEV, GNB; Thompson 1980: 168), which would further indict the priests as 'those handling the law [who] did not know me'.[21] Similar examples can be found throughout Jeremiah. David Schrock (2013: 147) compiles those passages that berate false teaching, lamenting the priests' failure at their responsibilities to teach truth and to oppose falsehood.
- Lamentations 2:6 recounts Yahweh's spurning of kings and priests. The verdict itself is no surprise, though the close pairing of priests with kings may help us better grasp the connection between the two.[22] Lamentations 4:13–16 is equally insightful.

---

[20] The Hebrew is difficult, especially of 4:4. I follow here the common emendation (e.g. NRSV, ESV; G. V. Smith 2001: 85; Dearman 2010: 155). Although 'priest' is technically singular, it is usually seen to encompass all 'priests' (so CSB, NET). Dearman further notes (159–161) several wordplays in these verses based on priestly activities. Priests are condemned also in 5:1 and 10:5.

[21] Some scholars certainly concur that this second clause indicts the priests also (e.g. Dearman 2002: 59; Allen 2008: 41) and torah is a priestly prerogative in 18:18. The next most likely identity is another group responsible for torah interpretation, such as the Levites (so Craigie, Kelley and Drinkard 1991: 29), who cannot be distanced greatly from the priests.

[22] E.g. Salters 2010: 133: 'Hence, the linking of king and priest here is significant: they[!] represent the cultic personnel.'

Variously condemned with Israel's prophets and elders, her priests are banished from Israel and foreign nations alike – damned as defiled and unclean!

- Ezekiel 22:26 presents a powerful indictment, not least when Ezekiel himself is a priest (1:3). The wider passage complains that princes, priests, officials, prophets and indeed the whole people have failed in their respective responsibilities (22:23–29). So it is poignant to read the charges on which the priests are arraigned:

> Her priests have done violence to my torah and have profaned my holy things; between the holy and the profane/common they have not differentiated [*bdl*], and between the unclean and the clean they have not informed. They have closed their eyes to [the keeping of] my Sabbaths so that I am profaned among them. (22:26)

We cannot miss here the way that Ezekiel has woven in the very terms of the central priestly commission (Lev. 10:10–11). And, where the central tenets of Leviticus are the recognition of and response to and publicizing of Yahweh's holiness, this later generation of priests has made his name common. Being common is no good thing, as it is when a celebrity successfully becomes a household name. Rather, Yahweh's hallowed reputation has been supplanted from its holy prominence and devalued like any other everyday vernacular.[23]

- Ezekiel's language is expanded from Zephaniah 3:4 (Duguid 1994: 72–75; Block 1997: 725–726). There, alongside Israel's officials and judges and prophets, 'Her priests have profaned the holy [place]; they have done violence to torah.' Marvin Sweeney (2003: 156, 165) reads that they 'profane holiness' itself; 'this statement charges them with complete abandonment of their expected role'.[24]
- Some of the most overt descriptions of priestly profanement are detailed in the lengthy second catechetical dispute of Malachi

---

[23] Schrock 2013: 147–150 helpfully infers that God's abhorrence of Israel, especially in Ezek. 8 – 11, is almost certainly a failure of the priests to preserve pure worship. 'Because the priests abandoned their duties at the temple of the Lord, the Lord abandoned the temple' (150).

[24] We are not investigating here exactly how the priests have executed such treachery, but commentators can readily suggest scenarios (e.g. Roberts 1991: 213–214). These reflect the broad range of priestly responsibilities we have already identified, including both religious and civic guidance.

(1:6 – 2:9). Even after God's gracious restoration of his people from exile, God's priests are yet again bringing his name into disrepute (1:6) rather than making it great among the nations and honouring it (1:11, 14; 2:2). The priests are called to emulate the earliest Levites in fostering reverence, fear, accurate torah, peace and uprightness – especially through their speech (2:5–7). Indeed, Mark Boda (2012) sees Malachi's indictment as the crescendo of a growing disquiet concerning the failure of priests to inculcate holiness even after the exile (cf. Hag. 2:10–14; Zech. 3; 7).[25]

No doubt Israelite priests are also often targeted when generic leaders or teachers are condemned in many other prophetic tirades. Matters have not especially improved by Jesus' day, where temple leaders are condemned for various degrees of ignorance, misdirection or hubris.

It is also possible that the third clause of Jeremiah 2:8 continues the indictment against Israel's priests. The possibility is significant and is entertained by the punctuation of the NIV, CSB and NAB. The language is as strong as any other condemnation: 'The handlers of the law did not know me / the shepherds revolted against me.' If 'shepherd' is a description connected with priests, it adds insights into priestly responsibilities.[26] It is pertinent that God himself is described as the 'shepherd' of individual Israelites and of the whole community (e.g. Gen. 48:15; 49:24; Pss 23:1–4; 28:9; 78:52; 80:1; Isa. 40:11; Jer. 23:3; 31:10; Ezek. 34:11–22; Hos. 4:16; Mic. 7:14), further reinforcing the thesis that God's priests act in God's stead. Further, we know that a shepherding role is bequeathed to other human leaders, especially to kings, on God's behalf (Num. 27:15–17; 2 Sam. 5:2, 7:7 // 1 Chr. 11:2, 17:6; Pss 77:20; 78:70–72; Isa. 44:28; 63:11; Jer. 17:16; 22:22; 23:4; Ezek. 34:23; 37:24; Mic. 5:4–5; Zech. 11:4–17; likely 1 Kgs 22:17 // 2 Chr. 18:16; also Nah. 3:18). Elsewhere, poor 'shepherds' – possibly

---

[25] It is tempting to explore whether Malachi is addressing not only cultic priests but the priestly nation as a whole. This would certainly fuel our later exploration. But there are few textual grounds to distinguish the options, and little scholarly uptake of the possibility (cf. the dismissal by Verhoef 1987: 214).

[26] Certainly the next chapter has God promising any repentant people new 'shepherds' whose role concerns 'knowledge and understanding' (Jer. 3:15). But the translation there is difficult, with the final phrase usually taken as descriptive of the *means* by which 'shepherd-kings' would lead (e.g. Allen 2008: 57) rather than a reference to shepherd-priests (though NASB remains suggestive). If, alternatively, none of the roles of 2:8 overlap, then we find already a distinction between priests and teachers of the law (Holladay 1986: 88–89).

priests – are condemned (e.g. Isa. 56:11; Jer. 10:21; 23:1–2; 50:6; Ezek. 34:1–10; Zech. 10:2–3).[27] While the connection between priests and 'shepherds' seems quite limited, any connection would enhance our understanding of priesthood. It would also strengthen the overlap we have observed between priestly and royal roles.

Whether or not we can attribute to them the title 'shepherds', Israel's priests are among her leaders who are culpable for the poor spiritual state of the nation (e.g. Schrock 2013: 161–163).

Glimmers of an improved priestly future

Though Israel's priests are regularly denounced and their privileged status revoked, prophetic expectations for Israel's future retain priestly images. An ongoing role for priests is no less certain than an ongoing place for Davidic kings. Already we might note that the most overt promises of a pending new covenant between Yahweh and his people, in flagship passages within Jeremiah 30 – 33 and Ezekiel 34 – 38, were uttered by prophets who themselves enjoyed a priestly heritage (Jer. 1:1; Ezek. 1:3). The same is likely true of the prophet Zechariah (Zech. 1:1 with Neh. 12:4, 16).[28] 'It would be priestly prophets who would declare judgment on the pre-exilic temple and its services (Jeremiah, Ezekiel), and priestly prophets who would envision a renewal of the temple and its services (Ezekiel, Zechariah)' (Boda 2016: 67).

Certainly many oracles foresee a joint restoration of royal and of priestly houses. God envisages renewed lines of kings and of priests. Going further, Crispin Fletcher-Louis (2006: 158–169) is confident that it is a priestly future, more than royal hopes, that dominates Old Testament and Second Temple expectations. Along with others (see n. 29 below) Fletcher-Louis confirms that 'The prophets, by and large, see the future in priestly terms' (168).

Perhaps the most graphic and direct image occurs in the vision of Zechariah 3. Joshua, the high priest among the exiles returning from Babylon, is beleaguered by an adversarial accuser (almost invariably presented as 'Satan'). The unrecorded accusation is silenced as God and his defence team have Joshua's desecrated clothing replaced, including a clean turban, overtly linked with the forgiveness of Joshua's sins. Joshua is addressed as 'high priest' and commissioned

---

[27] Other human shepherds are nominated in texts like Zech. 11:3–17 and 13:7, though their identity is hotly debated (Boda 2016; e.g. 607–609). Of immediate relevance is that these human shepherds may be temple leaders (so Boda).

[28] For such evidence concerning Zechariah, see Boda 2016: 16–17, 66–68. Weyde 2015 marshals evidence for counting Malachi also among the priestly prophets.

to lead Yahweh's people. This is explained as a 'symbol' or 'sign' of God's pending agent, codenamed 'Branch' or 'Sprout', who himself is linked with the removal of sin throughout the land. Priestly ministry is restored after the exile and into the future, 'a new start for the priesthood and the people' (Boda 2004: 261).[29]

Many of the same ideas – and the same terms – can be found previously in the restoration previewed in Isaiah 4:2–6 (Boda 2016: 241–242). Similar restoration language is also found in Jeremiah 23:1–8 and 33:14–26, although here royal motifs are as prominent as priestly roles.[30] Like Zechariah 3, Jeremiah 33 closely aligns the prospect of future royal rule with the restoration of an effective priesthood:

> For thus says the LORD: 'David will never lack someone sitting on the throne of the house of Israel. And the Levitical priests will never lack someone in my presence offering burnt offerings and burning grain offerings and making sacrifices every day.' (Jer. 33:17–18)

Similar sentiments, though in different language, naturally accompany Ezekiel's extended presentation of a new temple. Following the pronouncement of a permanent sanctuary dwelling among his people (Ezek. 37:26–28), the role of God's priests recurs throughout the graded holiness of Ezekiel 40 – 48 and is especially concentrated in the Pentateuch-sounding instructions of 44:15–31. Here a contrast is drawn with the Levites, perhaps including demoted priests, whose temple service is now abbreviated because of past sins (44:9–14).

If Joel be granted a postexilic setting (Allen 1976: 19–25; Dillard 1992: 240–243), then priestly intercession before Yahweh is again

---

[29] Further priestly connections and connotations are catalogued by commentators, e.g. Boda 2016: 259–261. Indeed, elsewhere Boda (2001; e.g. §§1.7–1.9) compiles the trend among scholars to see postexilic priestly roles expanding at the expense of kings and prophets. Certainly Joshua is repeatedly titled 'the high/great priest' (Hag. 1:1, 12, 14; 2:2; Zech. 3:1, 8; 6:11). So we must interpret carefully Ezekiel's silence on the (future?) high priest (rightly Block 1998: 637). At one extreme Milgrom fervently insists that, due to past failures, 'in Ezekiel's system there is *no place for a high priest* . . . who in Ezekiel's system is wholly and permanently evicted from the visionary sanctuary' (Milgrom and Block 2012: 168, 169). At the other extreme, Jenson (2012: 772) speculates that high priest and Most Holy Place may be absent because Ezekiel envisages a time when the Day of Atonement is unneeded. Related, but different again, is Duguid's suggestion (1994: 136) that God's glory now dwells in greater fullness (cf. Exod. 40:35; 1 Kgs 8:11).

[30] Pertinent to our earlier discussion of Jer. 2:8, Baldwin (1964) discerns priestly connotations in the ṣemaḥ passages – and even within the umbrella title 'shepherds' (e.g. 23:4).

proving effective (Joel 2:15–17, 18). One postexilic narrator certainly highlights the priestly pedigree of Ezra (Ezra 7:1–6) and delights in calling him 'Ezra the priest' (Ezra 7:11–12, 21; 10:10, 16; Neh. 8:2, 9; 12:26). The later chapters of Isaiah similarly foresee a time of renewed priestly activity. The description of the suffering servant of Isaiah 52:13 – 53:12 includes priestly connections (Abernethy 2016: 148–155). The language of 56:6 probably describes 'foreigners who join themselves to Yahweh to serve him' in a cultic sense (G. V. Smith 2009: 535), and this is spelled out quite overtly in 66:19–21. Distant antagonists will be summoned, by Israelite missionaries through their ethical living, to return Israelite exiles to Jerusalem as an offering to Yahweh, '"and I will even take some of *them* for priests and for Levites", says Yahweh' (66:21)! Indeed, 56:1–8 and 66:18–24 are probably intentional (and chiastic) bookends to the closing division of the book (e.g. Oswalt 1998: 461–465; Lessing 2014: 31–35), highlighting the unexpected magnitude of the mission of restored Israel.

Debate rages over the eschatological horizon of such predictions. How much were they fulfilled in the decades following the return from exile in the sixth century? How much did they await future figures (or even one individual figure) best matching these expectations? While the Isaiah passages in particular will return later in our study, our primary concern at this point is merely to recognize *that* a restoration was expected. The demise of the priesthood graphically announced by the pre-exilic and exilic prophets was not to be permanent.

Such a reading sits consistently within a conservative understanding of the Pentateuch's promises of '(a covenant of) perpetual priesthood' (Num. 25:13; cf. Exod. 29:9; 40:15; Deut. 18:5). Eli's family had their franchise terminated. Other priestly families at the fall of Jerusalem and the destruction of Solomon's Temple were cut short brutally (2 Kgs 25:18–21). But the priesthood as an institution had not yet run its course. This admittedly emphasizes a continuity of the office and not necessarily of the genetic longevity of particular dynasties. Narrower promises may need to be investigated further, beginning with the observation that 'for ever' in Hebrew may not be as permanent as it sounds in English.[31]

---

[31] Plenty of scholars remain concerned to trace specific priestly dynasties, particularly the putative handballing of the high priesthood between different descendants of Aaron. Such presuppositions surface briefly in passing (e.g. Milgrom 1990: 479, expanded in Milgrom and Block 2012: 141–148) and in longer works (e.g. Rooke 2000).

And one intriguing option that runs through many such passages is whether various promises of renewed priesthood will have priests serve alongside Israelite kings or even intersect with them. It is difficult for Christian readers to approach the Old Testament without familiarity with the conflation of the two roles in the person and work of Jesus Christ (to which we turn soon enough). It is certainly not uncommon to find quite scholarly analyses of Old Testament passages that acknowledge, at the least, some ambiguity. Thus Deenick (2011: 330–331) thinks that the book of Samuel and the rise of kingship hints at such conflation: 'In short, 1 Sam 2:35 is the beginning of the search for a priest not from the house of Aaron.' Exploring Zechariah at the other end of the Old Testament canon, others are equally confident that 'Nowhere else in the Old Testament is it made so plain that the coming Davidic king will also be a priest' (Baldwin 1972: 137; cf. Klein 2008: 151). Such an expectation is not completely met in Old Testament times – though we have already observed that kings could appropriate certain priestly privileges.

All the same certainties and uncertainties plague the difficult Zechariah 6:9–15. Again the high priest Joshua is honoured; again there are connections with royal reign and the pending arrival of 'Branch'; again, the Israelites are encouraged that the temple cultus will be restored. But it is unclear whether restored Israel will be led by separate regal and cultic figures, as in their recent past, or whether Yahweh now announces a single individual in a unified role for some unspecified time in the immediate or distant future. The dilemma is certainly significant for understanding the postexilic period. Regardless of the old-covenant application of Zechariah, we see shortly that any new-covenant connections resolve towards a single figure. Certainly the detailed studies of Anthony Petterson (2009: 120–124; 2015: 186–187, 189–190) are comfortable that Zechariah contemplates an individual king who enjoys priestly prerogatives.

Future prospects narrated

Our survey of the prophets cannot ignore the important turning point that occurs in the midst of their collected messages. Some of them have pronounced the demise of the first temple, built by Solomon, while others have celebrated and encouraged – and critiqued – the second temple restored under Zerubbabel.

Some of the postexilic narratives recount this transition. The book of Kings builds up to the destruction of Jerusalem in 586 BC, and the narrator's graphic climax gives much of its space to the brick-by-brick demolition of the temple and its governing priests (2 Kgs 25:9, 13–17, 18–21). When Judah's Babylonian captors are themselves defeated by the Persians, Cyrus decrees a return for the exiles. In particular, the biblical narrators present this decree as focusing on the rebuilding of the Jerusalem temple (2 Chr. 36:23). Starting with the same decree, the book of Ezra thus focuses heavily on this rebuilding and on the return of temple personnel, especially 'the priests and the Levites' who, as the star players, are listed before other Israelites (Ezra 1:2–4, 5–11; 2:36–63, 68–70; 3:1–13; 4:1–3, 24; 5:1 – 6:18; 6:20, 22; 7:7, 11–24, 27; 8:15–20, 24–30, 33–36; 9:1, 7, 9; 10:5, 18–24). Echoes of this continue into the next generation (Neh. 7:73; 10:28, 32–39; 11:3, 10–24; 12:1–26, 27–43, 44–47; 13:4–14, 22, 29–31).[32] Indeed, in keeping with the flagship roles of the Aaronic priests, we find 'Ezra the priest' delighting in the study of God's laws and then teaching them to the returnees and blessing them (esp. Ezra 7:10; Neh. 8:1–12, 13, 18).

Further, even as Chronicles recounts the prior history leading up to the exile, one of its slants is to authenticate ongoing temple ministry for the postexilic generation. The Chronicler certainly provides more detail on the priests and Levites, in the opening genealogies for example, and may even be 'legitimizing the authority of Levitical priesthood as the rightful successors to the royal authority of Davidic kingship' (Hill 2003: 61; cf. 132).[33]

As temple duties resume, we also notice the wider sharing of (high) priestly responsibilities. Under Aaron, the language had focused strongly on '*the* priest' with occasional mention of his assistants. Now we find a more democratized system. We read of 'Hilkiah the high priest and the priests of the second order and the door-keepers' (2 Kgs 23:4); shortly thereafter are named 'Seraiah the chief priest and Zephaniah the second priest' (2 Kgs 25:18 // Jer. 52:24). More than a century earlier we hear of 'the senior priests' (2 Kgs 19:2 // Isa. 37:2)

---

[32] Among these are many mentions of Joshua son of Jehozadak (Ezra 2:2; 3:2, 8–9; 4:3; 5:2; 10:18; cf. Neh. 7:7; 12:1–7, 26). We learn elsewhere (Hag. 1:12, 14; 2:2, 4; Zech. 3:1, 8; 6:12) that this Joshua was high priest. But Ezra–Nehemiah foregrounds the role of neither Joshua nor his civic counterpart Zerubbabel, highlighting instead wider community involvement (Rose 2005: 1017, summarizing Japhet 1982: 80–86).

[33] The statistics tidily compiled by Klingbeil (2005: 811–812) show that mention of 'priests' and/or 'Levites' occurs in one of every ten verses in Chronicles, Ezra and Nehemiah – even before we count other synonyms and allusions. By way of contrast and completeness, we should note that such language is all but absent from the wisdom literature and Psalms (Job 12:19; Pss 78:64; 99:6; 110:4; 132:9, 16; cf. 135:19–20). Haydock 2015 includes a chapter (ch. 3) on the psalter and its missiological highlights (to which we could add many other studies, such as Mascarenhas 2005), though his suggested connections with Israel's priesthood are slender.

and a century later of 'the leading priests' (Neh. 12:7). Such democratization continues into the New Testament period. The gentle evolution of the priesthood, and apparently more so its administrative roles, need not drive us to panic or revise the history of the Pentateuch.

So it is clear that God is not finished with a 'vocational' priest and priesthood through which he will deal with his people. We have seen this optimistic outlook relayed by Jeremiah in the midst of the sixth-century exile (perhaps also by Ezekiel, in a different kind of way) and by Zechariah shortly afterwards upon the people's return to Jerusalem. But such optimism does not find itself flawlessly realized. Promises of a restored Jerusalem were not eagerly embraced; hence the urging ministries of Ezra and Nehemiah and Zechariah. Expectation of a new priesthood did not translate into immediate enthusiasm to rebuild the Jerusalem temple; hence the ministry of Haggai. Indeed, among the postexilic historians and prophets we find the human priesthood harangued as much as it had been prior to the Babylonian punishment – a punishment for failures to which earlier generations of priests had contributed. Ezra and Nehemiah confront temple priests and personnel with compromised marriages (Ezra 10:18–24; Neh. 13:4–14, 28–29) and end their accounts on a mixed note.[34] Zechariah 7:1–7 queries the genuineness of priests' fasting and feasting. And we have already noted the tirade in Malachi 1:6 – 2:9. To this we might add 3:1–5, where the 'Levites' of God's temple probably comprise the priests as well (Hill 2012: 337; cf. 1998: 276); they require further divine refining and purifying before their actions are as acceptable as those of former generations. Thus for the prophets Boda (2012) detects 'a discernible development' (33) in the canonical presentation of Haggai, Zechariah and Malachi as each book progressively protests the ongoing *decline* of the postexilic priesthood. Beth Glazier-McDonald (1987: 46) paints a similarly bleak picture at the end of the Old Testament:

> Because the maintenance of holiness and the keeping of the law were essential to the survival of the community, the priests were necessary to the people. But often they perceived themselves as a privileged class who, by virtue of their birth, were entitled to service

---

[34] The point stands, even though these books separated in the English canon belong together. Major 'memoir' sections of Ezra–Nehemiah conclude with the need to 'purify' the priests and Levites (e.g. Neh. 13:30).

from the people. They tended to accept the honors appertaining to their position while inwardly mocking the cultic practices it was their duty to perform. It is precisely this to which Malachi refers.

The optimism proclaimed over the prior centuries has not yet reached full resolution. The bleak picture appears to remain when we reach the New Testament in the next chapter.

Summary

There are of course many more nuances that could be explored. Ezra introduces and exemplifies a new class of 'scribes' (Ezra 7:6, 11; Neh. 8:1, 4, 9, 13; 12:26, 36); several of these passages collocate Ezra's titles, giving rise to a new combination of 'priest-scribe' (Marx 1995: 325). In particular, I have invested little in the way that Levites are given more time in the spotlight in Chronicles. Some historians are keen to explore how much the Chronicler's 'promotion' of them is realistic recording and how much may be rhetorical hyperbole. Either way, Chronicles adds little to our understanding of the priestly family within the wider tribe of assistants. There are certainly clarifying insights but not much that is strictly novel.[35]

Although with its own nuances, we might crudely suggest that the trajectory of Israel's priests is not dissimilar to those of their prophets and kings. God's select leaders can accomplish grand feats in facilitating contact and communication between God and people – but they can also fail dismally in their responsibilities. The Old Testament furnishes examples of both failure and success. As with prophets and kings, there is a sense that God is not finished with his priests and that he has further reinstatement and renewal in store for the role. The way that the Old Testament plateaus, if not declines, assures us that this will be part of post-postexilic restoration. Knowing more of the story, Christian readers recognize that this continues beyond the strictures of the old covenant. And so we turn to the new-covenant era.

---

[35] For example, Chronicles regularly has priests playing trumpets at events involving the ark or the temple (1 Chr. 15:24, 28; 16:6; 2 Chr. 5:12–13; 7:6; 29:26, 28; cf. Ezra 3:10; Neh. 12:35, 41) and in battle (2 Chr. 13:12, 14). Such clarity is new and welcome. Yet this extends what is otherwise already known: that priests were among signal trumpeters (Num. 10:8–10), including in war (Num. 10:9; 31:6; Josh. 6:1–21), and that trumpets were played at cultic ceremonies (e.g. Lev. 23:24; 25:9; Num. 29:1; cf. Exod. 19:16; 20:18), including the entry of the ark (2 Sam. 6:15). Milgrom (1990: 372–373) distinguishes between 'trumpet' (ḥăṣōṣĕrâ) and '[ram's] horn' (šôpār), and especially between their different users.

Chapter Five

New-covenant transformations

Studies of the historical development of the priesthood are certainly concerned with the intertestamental period (VanderKam 2004; Rooke 2000). Israel's successive subjugators and internal wrangling climaxed in the decades before Jesus' birth, as summarized by Gottlob Schrenk (1965: 268):

> Herod destroyed the Hasmoneans. The hereditary and permanent character of the office was disregarded by the political rulers, and arbitrary depositions and appointments followed. The rights of the Zadokites were ignored. Representatives of other priestly families were accepted.

Mention of the Hasmoneans reminds us that at least once, under John Hyrcanus, the high priest was also political leader of God's people (134–104 BC), a civic role already glimpsed in the Old Testament (Grabbe 2004). Indeed, the progressive complications and compromises gave rise in some quarters to the hope of God's intervening with a messianic high priest (Fletcher-Louis 2013: 701–702, providing contemporary and modern sources).

Apart from questions of official bloodline and the method(s) of appointment, especially for the high priest, there is general continuity between the Old and New Testaments. The descriptions and functions of priests in the Gospels and Acts are immediately recognizable alongside the Old Testament forms we have surveyed (see D. A. Hubbard 1996: 960–961). The biggest change, already glimpsed in the postexilic era and not detracting from priesthood, was that priestly teaching became increasingly facilitated by a class of scribes. Extensively renovated by Herod the Great, the temple in Jerusalem likewise stood and operated in recognizable continuity with the temples established under Solomon and Zerubbabel (although Wise [2000: 1171–1174] narrates how increasingly fragmented Jewish sects variously assessed its legitimacy).

Thus between the end of the Old Testament and the start of the New there is substantial continuity with limited discontinuity. By the end of Jesus' earthly ministry the future of the Jerusalem cultus is condemned, and by the end of the New Testament writings a whole new mechanism between God and humanity is in place. My present chapter surveys this radical transformation, particularly in the individual, vocational sense of priesthood.

More business as usual

At the birth of Jesus, the sociopolitical landscape of Israel has obviously changed. The Jews have enjoyed little autonomy for the previous six centuries. Conquest by Alexander the Great has Hellenized the known world, with Greek language and behaviour a significant normalizing influence. And the mighty Roman Empire now reigns, firmly in charge here as elsewhere.

It is thus perhaps surprising that priestly behaviour in the Jerusalem temple exhibits such continuity with centuries of Jewish tradition. A quick survey of the New Testament shows that familiarity with the Old Testament is an excellent primer for the temple personnel we now meet.

Priestly references and referents

As in the Old Testament, the New Testament populates the background scenery with a chorus of nondescript priests going about their duties.

So familiar are they that the New Testament narrators make surprisingly little mention of them, though we do not doubt their activity. Jesus acknowledges their work in past generations (Matt. 12:4 // Mark 2:26 // Luke 6:4), which still continues, even on the Sabbath day (Matt. 12:5). He can employ them as a stock character in parables (famously Luke 10:31). Priests are mentioned interacting with Jesus and his apostles (John 1:19; Acts 4:1), and the epistles may allude to the ongoing priestly work continuing in the Jerusalem temple over subsequent decades (1 Cor. 9:13; Heb. 8:3–5; 9:6–7, 25; 10:1–3, 8; 13:10–11). We are thus left thirsting for more information when Luke reports that in the early years of the church 'a great number of the priests were becoming obedient to the faith' (Acts 6:7).[1]

---

[1] Concerning Hebrews, commentators almost universally acknowledge that the present tense does not guarantee a date prior to AD 70 nor that the epistle especially

More common is reference to the 'scribes'. Some sixty-five mentions of them are summarized by Gregory Thellman, who concludes that 'They were closely aligned with and, in many cases, overlapped with the priesthood and temple establishment, as well as with parties like the Pharisees' (2013: 844). It is no surprise that, however the overlap worked, such scribes are associated with the teaching of Jewish law. Indeed, Luke introduces some synonyms such as 'law-teachers' (esp. Luke 5:17, 21); so clear is the parallel that some Bibles consistently translate the usual word for 'scribes' (*grammateis*) as 'teachers of the law' (NIV, GNB, NCV) or similar. In this we find a continuation of part of the responsibilities of the Old Testament priesthood, and inter-actions with these scribes are obviously admissible in our investigation. The New Testament likewise knows of 'Levites', mentioned thrice and mostly alongside priests (Luke 10:32; John 1:19; Acts 4:36).

Robert Kugler's brief survey helpfully observes that Second Temple writing 'often focuses not on the priesthood as a whole but on the high priesthood alone' (2010: 1096). The four Gospel authors squarely fit this description. High/chief priests are mentioned far more frequently than generic priests. The 105 narrative mentions arise almost exclu-sively as opponents of Jesus and his followers and especially in adjudicating their respective trials.[2] Annas and Caiaphas are named (Matt. 26:3, 57; Luke 3:2; John 11:49; 18:13–14, 24, 28; Acts 4:6), as are Sceva (Acts 19:14), Ananias (Acts 23:2; 24:1) and the historical figure of Abiathar (Mark 2:26).[3]

Intriguingly, the Gospels and Acts often nominate 'the chief priests' in the plural. After our study of the Old Testament and its singling out of an individual paterfamilias, such plurals fairly grate. Even casual readers of Mark 14:53 cannot help but notice the odd

refers to *temple* sacrifices. Potential allusions to the first-century cultic system are plausible and alluring but beyond certainty.

[2] For completeness, and without indicating parallels, references to high priests are found in Matt. 2:4; 16:21; 20:18; 21:15, 23, 45; 26:3, 14, 47, 51, 57–59, 62–63, 65; 27:1, 3, 6, 12, 20, 41, 62; 28:11; Mark 2:26; 8:31; 10:33; 11:18, 27; 14:1, 10, 43, 47, 53–55, 60–61, 63, 66; 15:1, 3, 10–11, 31; Luke 9:22; 19:47; 20:1, 19; 22:2, 4, 50, 52, 54, 66; 23:4, 10, 13; 24:20; John 7:32, 45; 11:47, 49, 51, 57; 12:10; 18:3, 10, 13, 15–16, 19, 22, 24, 26, 35; 19:6, 15, 21; Acts 4:6, 23; 5:17, 21, 24, 27; 7:1; 9:1, 14, 21; 19:14; 22:5, 30; 23:2, 4–5, 14; 24:1; 25:2, 15; 26:10, 12. The seventeen additional occurrences in Hebrews are explored later. We should also note the 'captain(s)' of the temple (Luke 22:4, 52; Acts 4:1; 5:24, 26), widely acknowledged as a high-ranking priestly role.

[3] Jesus' apparent error in Mark 2:26, naming Abiathar when David encountered Abiathar's father Ahimelech (1 Sam. 21:1–9), continues to disturb Christian readers (Wilson 2015). A formal investigation is offered in Perrin 2013. The father of John the Baptist, Zechariah, is the sole regular (i.e. non-high) priest named (Luke 1:5). The case of Melchizedek is considered later.

juxtaposition: 'They led Jesus to the high priest, and all the high priests and the elders and the scribes gathered together.' Similar dissonance occurs when Luke 3:2 names 'the [singular] high-priesthood of Annas and Caiaphas'. Commentators regularly distil Josephus' records to explain that Annas was deposed by the Romans and then succeeded by five sons and his son-in-law Caiaphas. Thus whether through personal loyalty to Annas or religious commitment to a lifelong high-priestly appointment, first-century Jews accorded Annas due deference. In their eyes there were at least two current high priests. Caiaphas in turn would be deposed and replaced. We can thus grasp why in Acts 4:6 Luke retains the title 'high priest' for Annas, lists Caiaphas and other authorities, and mentions also 'all who belonged to the high-priestly class' (Schnabel 2012: 236). Craig Evans (2001; e.g. 179–180) exemplifies those who see a broader collection of authorities in the New Testament use of the plural; he translates as 'ruling priests' and catalogues the various deputies and under-studies of whom the class was composed. We ourselves have noted the rise of second-tier priests in the latter centuries of Old Testament history. Surveying the prominence of plural words in Luke and in Josephus, Craig Keener (2012–15: 1142) resolves that this 'was simply the standard terminology of the era', and lighter commentaries are often content to leave the phrase unremarked. In short, while the New Testament retains a single high priest, his authority is cast as more shared than in the earliest accounts of Aaron's role in the Pentateuch.

Priestly activities

Regardless of how they are identified, it is important to acknowledge that the priestly caste held sway in any number of official pronounce-ments. Throughout the Gospels and Acts it is commonly the chief priests (joined by the likely-priestly scribes) who oppose the fledgling Christian movement. Their role in the ruling Sanhedrin and its judicial decisions is prominent (e.g. Marcus 2009: 1099–1104; Fletcher-Louis 2013: 700–701). Undoubtedly also shaped by matters of politics and power, the Second Temple priesthood proactively avoids the apparent apathy of their Old Testament forebears.

In this regard, the temple personnel remain caught up in judicial matters. Such judgments are rendered throughout the Old Testament, though we have focused (as does much of the OT) more on their ceremonial roles. Priests and Levites are depicted as pronoun-cing civil verdicts at various times (e.g. Deut. 17:8–13; 19:17; 21:5;

Ezek. 44:24; 1 Chr. 23:4; 26:29; 2 Chr. 19:8–11). Similar passages depict further civic duties for Levites and priests, including organizing labour and finances (1 Chr. 26:20–32; 2 Chr. 24:4–14; 34:12–13; Neh. 10:37) (R. L. Hubbard 2009: 462–464). Certainly the judicial matters that the New Testament narrators emphasize are those concerning God's holiness, particularly concerning which people and what actions are more appropriate or less suited to represent or interact with God.

It is this judicial opposition to Jesus and his followers that fuels Christian impressions of 'the generally negative assessment of priests in the Gospels' (Ellingworth 2000: 699). We must interpret such sentiments carefully; Ellingworth himself expresses his concerns in the context of the increasing politicization of the (high) priesthood and the priestly leaders' hostility towards Jesus.

Beyond this familiar antagonism, and despite Jesus' pronouncements of the demise of an earthly Jerusalem cultus (see below), we ought to note that Jesus' earthly ministry does not directly supplant the authority of the priests of his day. In particular, after healing lepers Jesus acknowledges the aegis of priests in declaring cleanness (Matt. 8:4 // Mark 1:44 // Luke 5:14; 17:14) (Basser 2000: 826). Crispin Fletcher-Louis (2013: 703) likewise acknowledges that 'the Gospels do not position Jesus against the priesthood per se' and proposes occasions where Jesus laments the decline of the cultus.

Similarly, any angst heard in Acts has to do with individual priests misusing such positions rather than with the current validity of the positions themselves. Mention of Barnabas's Levite heritage suggests that Luke is *impressed* by such standing, in the same way as a mass conversion of priests caps Luke's first major summary (Acts 4:36; 6:7) (Keener 2012–15: 1182, 1291–1292). Keener further reminds us that Luke begins his Gospel narrative with John the Baptist's parents: two 'righteous' descendants of Aaron (Luke 1:5–6). Both parents are used by the Holy Spirit in God's praise as are other temple worshippers (1:39–45, 67–79; 2:25–35, 36–38). Both John's parents and Jesus' parents are cast as being torah compliant (1:56; 2:21–24, 39, 41). Christian antagonism and scepticism towards the Jewish priesthood described in the New Testament narratives make it difficult to interpret the exchange between Paul and the high priest Ananias before the Sanhedrin (Acts 23:1–5). Is Paul's response one of humble contrition at his short-sighted outburst or of further sarcastic vitriol? Scholars are quite divided. Importantly, though, either way 'Paul expresses respect for the office of high priest, even if he is critical of the behaviour of the one who currently holds the position' (Peterson 2009: 615).[4]

We can thus conclude, at least for our more general purposes, that we find in New Testament narratives the same kinds of functions for Israel's temple personnel that we found in the Old Testament. The priests, including chief priests and collaborating scribes, continue to oversee temple sacrifices, to teach and interpret the law, and generally to oil the wheels of the cultic system. All this appears to remain concerned for the sake of God's reputation and for the welfare of his chosen people. Most notably *missing* is any mention of high-priestly access into God's presence (the Day of Atonement) and of priests providing blessings.[5]

That said, for all the New Testament's relative neutrality towards the Jewish priesthood, the priesthood does not seem to have made huge strides in the quality of its incumbents. Nicholas Perrin's introduction (2014) summarizes some negative *Jewish* evaluations:

Countless first- and second-century Jewish witnesses agree that all the wrong people were at the helm of the temple. According to these sources, the higher levels of the priesthood in Jesus' time were populated with greedy, self-aggrandizing, and sexually immoral men. Rather than serving God, they were in fact serving themselves and desecrating the temple along the way.

While we might detect hints at this dissatisfaction in the biblical accounts, it is all the more surprising how less inflammatory the narrators are. That may be in part because their focus is on the better fulfilment arriving in Jesus.

---

[4] The mass conversion of priests in Acts 6:7 might draw our attention to John 12:42, where 'even many of the leaders believed in him'. Yet it is unclear (1) whether the 'leaders' here include priests (the generic term is used of Pharisees [John 3:1; Luke 14:1] and chief priests [Acts 4:5, 8; 23:5], but occasionally distinguished from chief priests [Luke 23:13; 24:20]); (2) how we should construe 'many' here (Michaels 2010: 711); and (3) whether John's ensuing qualification shows that their fear of excommunication ultimately belies their belief as superficial.

[5] While we are familiar with mention of Pharisees at prayer, Pharisees were rarely a formal part of the priesthood. Even if we should consider them to be functioning similarly to cultic religious leaders, direct references to Pharisees at prayer are fewer than we might imagine (Luke 5:33; 18:10–12; perhaps Matt. 6:5 [cf. spurious 23:14]).

Jesus as priest in the Gospels?

Eugene Merrill (1993:51) laments that, while Jesus is readily revered as prophet and king, his priestly role is much less prominent. This is not least because the Gospels and Paul 'gave scant attention to Jesus as priest'. We see shortly that others have reached a similar evaluation.

Jesus as priest

There are two fairly polarized views of Jesus' priesthood in the Gospels. Many share Merrill's view that there is 'scant attention' paid – if any. For example, Richard Averbeck's helpful biblical-theological survey (1996) mines Hebrews alone. Others protest such minimization. They outline evidence that Jesus behaved as a priest during his earthly ministry and that he is presented as such by his biographers. Though some proposed parallels are enticing, they are difficult to confirm with any confidence and leave the minimalist position more convincing.[6]

Some of the priestly connections require careful argument and depend on the validity of contributing evidence. Fletcher-Louis makes much of Jesus' self-designation as 'Son of Man' and is thus heavily reliant on seeing the figure in Daniel 7:13–14 as 'the high priest who is described receiving glory in God's presence' (2013: 702). Such priestly connotations for that title are hardly assured.[7]

Many of the potential parallels are broad and their interpretations as priestly are tentative. Yes, priests probably participated in the declaration of the forgiveness of sins (Fletcher-Louis [2007: 73] proposes Exod. 28:38 and Lev. 10:17). When Jesus forgives sins (e.g. Mark 2:1–12), is he portrayed as a priest – or as the God on whose behalf priests would pronounce absolution? Similarly, Jesus is recognized as 'the Holy One of God' (Mark 1:24 // Luke 4:34; John 6:69; cf. Luke 1:35; Acts 3:14; 1 John 2:20). Yes, the title reflects *Aaron's* (Ps. 106:16;

---

[6] More maximalist studies include Feuillet 1975, Cheung 1986 and Fletcher-Louis (2006/2007, summarized in 2013), all followed by Schrock (2013, showcased in Piotrowski and Schrock 2016). Many others are catalogued by Winkle (2012: 4–7), to which we might add O'Collins and Jones 2010.

[7] Certainly the recent biblical theology of J. M. Hamilton (2014b, esp. 147–153) finds the Danielic figure to be described in *regal*, if not also *divine*, terms. Any priestly connotation comes only as an afterthought, derivative from this royal role (189–190). Priests are, of course, connected both with kings and with God, but priestly imagery is hardly foregrounded in Dan. 7. Likewise, while Bock's recent summary (2013) of the title 'Son of Man' acknowledges the same acts of authority as does Fletcher-Louis, Bock at no point interprets these as priestly prerogatives. Winkle's survey (2012: 271–273) concludes that 'such provocative, high priestly perspectives have not garnered support from more than a scholarly minority'.

cf. Exod. 28:36; 39:30; Lev. 21:6; Num. 16:7). But the title 'Holy One (of Israel)' is regularly ascribed to *God*, especially throughout Isaiah. Indeed, the precision with which such epithets are negotiated – between testaments and their respective languages – makes it difficult to endorse the link (and Fletcher-Louis is ultimately focused on the inclusion or exclusion of a definite article). How should we balance the competing assertion that *Samson* 'is the only other person in the Bible to be called "Holy One of God" (Judg 16:17)' (Edwards 2002: 58)? The title and its interpretation are hardly conclusive for a priestly Jesus, especially when a divine Jesus is equally plausible theologically and textually. And while it has sometimes been common to describe Jesus as 'cleansing' the temple (Mark 11:15–19; pars.), and although Jesus' actions may fulfil the divine 'purifying' foreseen in Malachi 3:1–4, his biographers do not seem to draw these connections or conclusions.[8]

Some suggestions border on questionable exegesis altogether. Many priestly promoters (listed in n. 6) add supernatural healing as a form of priestly mediation. Some rightly note that Jesus is willing to make contact with the sick and unclean, those who are ritually not holy. While contact relieves them from maladies that render them ritually unclean, the evidence that Jesus is behaving as a priest seems circumstantial. Yes, certain priestly garments and offerings appear to communicate holiness. But the 'contagion formula' regularly cited (esp. Exod. 29:37; 30:29; Lev. 6:18, 27; Ezek. 44:19) is heavily disputed. While it is often translated 'X *becomes* holy [by touching]', it is regularly argued that it should probably read 'X must *be* holy [in order to touch]' (cf. NKJV, NCV).[9] Perhaps any holiness received from Jesus can be attributed to grounds other than his priestliness. In fact, any sense of holiness and its contagion in these healings is only inferred; it is not something the Gospel writers themselves narrate. Proponents are also in danger of freighting too heavily and narrowly the verb 'to be cleansed'. To take such a verb in its sense of cultic cleanness is as dubious as insisting that other verbs in these accounts that can mean 'to be saved' and 'to be delivered' (both in Mark 5:25–34) must signal *spiritual* redemption. The outcome of these healings may be ritual cleanness, but our authors take no pains to highlight Jesus' superseding the ministry of the formal priesthood. Tellingly, we have already

---

[8] Blaylock (2016) offers an exploration of how Malachi might foreshadow a priestly Jesus.

[9] Proponents of this revision include Levine (1989: 37–38), Hartley (1992: 97), Stuart (2006: 629), V. P. Hamilton (2011: 503); against the likes of Milgrom (e.g. 1991: 445–446), Kiuchi (2007: 124–125).

seen that Jesus does not arrogate to himself the priestly responsibility of declaring his healed patients ritually clean. If Jesus should be seeking to parallel or supplant the cultic system, it is also odd that he commands his patients to 'offer what [gifts] Moses commanded concerning your cleansing' (Mark 1:44 // Matt. 8:4 // Luke 5:14). Caution suggests we cannot follow a chain of logic where several of the links are weak.[10]

The closest Jesus comes to this kind of overt priestly behaviour is in his conflict with the Pharisees and scribes over cleanliness rituals. Whether or not 'the tradition of the elders' accurately reflected God's intentions in the Torah, Jesus' statements about foods and ritual contamination lead Mark to deduce bluntly that Jesus was 'declaring all foods [ceremonially] clean' (Mark 7:19). Jesus replicates the central priestly duty of teaching God's people how to distinguish clean and unclean – though he also radically redefines the boundaries previously set under the old covenant. It is thus difficult to express fluently how Jesus both continues and discontinues the expectation of Old Testament priests. In the light of Mark's presentation of Jesus for a new-covenant readership, and one that is traditionally seen largely to comprise Gentiles, Jesus' behaviour might be considered akin to that of old-covenant priests although with new-covenant content.

Much the same might be said for John 17, popularly described in some circles since the Reformation as Jesus' 'high-priestly prayer'. Jesus is certainly undertaking an act of intercession, and part of the content concerns the 'consecration' of his disciples for their pending post-resurrection mission (17:17–19). Such language can lead moderns to find here further support for a priestly Jesus: 'The "Lamb of God" of John's prophecy (1:29, 36) has become both Shepherd and High Priest, offering himself to the Father so that his disciples "might be consecrated in truth" (v. 19)!' (Michaels 2010: 874). It is telling though that Michaels immediately concedes that 'It is unclear how far the priestly imagery should be pressed.' Such caution can be found in the warnings of others and sometimes in outright refusals to explore priestly connotations at all. The survey by Harold Attridge (2013) is judiciously even-handed, yet even he concludes that any priestly imagery here is

---

[10] Such weak links are evident in the short study of Wenkel (2014). He himself acknowledges that his strongest arguments for Luke's presentation of a priestly Jesus come from biblical texts outside that Gospel. We might also wonder if Fletcher-Louis (2007) largely undoes his thesis when he suggests that Jesus conceives of himself as a priest *but is hiding that fact* (64, 77) and concedes that Jesus' priesthood 'does not conform to much' of its supposed OT model (78).

but a cautious 'gesture' – and is probably seeking to *disarm* any over-zealous appropriation of Old Testament antecedents. That is, Attridge finds in John 17 more discontinuity than continuity.

None of this is to dispute some priestlike behaviour on Jesus' part in the Gospels. We simply do not have much prominent evidence of his being cast in such a role. Ultimately, when all such claims from a preceding generation of scholars have been scrutinized, the verdicts have been equally restrained. John Baigent (1981: 34) highlights the difficulty of classifying the kinds of actions and titles at stake:

> Methodologically, the basic problem is to determine what is to count as evidence of a concept of priesthood. The problem is particularly acute when it is claimed that the idea is implicit rather than explicit. What sort of pointers are needed to be able safely to conclude that a writer had in mind a view of Jesus as priest?

Hence one reviewer of André Feuillet (1975) complains that 'Consistently he proceeds from what might be implied in the text to the affirmation that it must be implied' (Kilmartin 1975: 516). Helen Bond (2007) and Harold Attridge (2013; cf. 2016) advocate priestly comparisons and contrasts in John, and both consent how tacit these are. Baigent himself comfortably concludes that it is Hebrews alone that foregrounds Jesus as a priest, although we might revise Baigent's assessment of Revelation 1 and include its contribution as well.

Jesus and/as the temple

We should note in passing that one basis for (mis)construing Jesus as a priest has to do with the pending demise of the familiar Jerusalem-focused, bricks-and-mortar form of the cultic system. Jesus sometimes appropriates cultic imagery, often concerned with the *transformation* of the system. So we must discern whether such appropriations are more continuous or more discontinuous.

The study of Jesus and the temple is an industry in itself (e.g. Beale 2004; Perrin 2010). Complications abound. Jesus' earthly life and ministry, all but from start to finish (Luke 2:22–38; 23:45), intersect with the Jerusalem temple. He announces its destruction in parabolic action and overt declaration (Mark 11:15–19; 13:1–2; pars.), even intimating that he himself will be its replacement (John 2:19–22). As we anticipate our inspection of Hebrews and its prominent teaching of Jesus as the great high priest, we find that we are attempting to juggle variables on several axes. How much does a cultic allusion concerning Jesus have to do with the Jerusalem temple and its Aaronic priesthood, and how much with the new temple and its personnel? Are such allusions shaped by the language and function of the temple or of the priesthood, when Jesus is associated with both elements? The same problem applies when we eventually turn to look at the church: it likewise is described from both perspectives (and Perrin [55] speaks adroitly of 'the believing community as temple-*cum*-priesthood').

Moreover, what additional complications arise while the old-covenant and new-covenant systems are running side by side for the few decades between Jesus' death and the earthly temple's destruction (i.e. AD 30–70)?

The simplest of examples can sufficiently illustrate the complexity. Both Jesus and Hebrews describe Jesus as the 'way' to God (John 14:6; Heb. 10:20). To what extent is this a spatial metaphor that we could link with God's presence, and how much (as other sophists of the time used it) does it connote a manner of living? Are other mentions of a 'way' or a 'road' (e.g. Matt. 7:13–14) intentional allusions to Jesus or are they simple metaphors? When Jesus is in view, is he the road itself or a participant or leader on the journey (cf. Marcus 1992)? When the title is transferred to Christianity ('the Way', Acts 9:2 et al.), are any facets of its application to Jesus also transferred? How can we tell if other mentions, such as 'the way of truth' or 'the way of righteousness' (2 Pet. 2:2, 21), are allusions to Jesus or to Christian living or to thoroughfares? What about the compound form 'way out', from which comes our soteriologically rich term 'exodus'? When are similar images, such as 'the access (to the Father)' (Eph. 2:18; 3:12; Rom. 5:2), making similar points? The grammar of Hebrews 10:19 and 2 Peter 1:11 could be pressed to insist that Jesus himself is also our 'way in' or 'entry' into God's kingdom. Where could/would/should we stop such speculation?

I do not propose to explore these complications further here. But we are alerted to the potential depths that might be plumbed and to the certain overlapping of categories such as those of temple and priesthood. At a minimum, we are reminded that God's long-term mission to facilitate access to himself undergoes its most dramatic upheaval during the first century; we must remain alert to the various transformations taking place. This upheaval effectively flags the end of the working usefulness of the old-covenant elements, which gives us various grounds on which to gauge their partial, anticipatory purpose within God's long-game strategy. Their purpose and transformation is presented no more clearly than in Hebrews.

Jesus as (high) priest in Hebrews!

The heading well deserves an exclamation mark. It is the proverbial child's play to find quotations and whole studies lionizing the crucial contribution of this unique epistle. The following accolades are representative of varied publications:

- 'While the Epistle has in common with the other New Testament writings the representation of Christ as Revealer, it stands practically alone in explicitly naming Him a Priest.' (Vos 1907: 423)
- 'Focusing on the mention of Melchizedek in Ps. 110:4, the author of Hebrews brilliantly crafts a high-priestly Christology unique to the NT.' (Guthrie 2007: 967)
- 'Hebrews' development of Christ's high priesthood, however, is a unique contribution to NT theology.' (Cockerill 2012: 24)
- 'This portrayal of Jesus' death, whereby he entered the heavenly sanctuary and was designated a high priest according to the order of Melchizedek, is the most innovative and remarkable aspect of the author's theology. No other New Testament writer explicitly portrays Jesus as a priest, let alone as a high priest.' (Matera 2007: 335)
- 'The christology of the NT would certainly be impoverished should it have been deprived of Hebrews' deep and rich understanding of who Jesus was.' (Parsons 1988: 215)

Here in Hebrews, extensively and unmissably, the (high) priestly ministry of the ascended Jesus is extolled.

Already we might note the potential confusion between the language of 'priest' and 'high priest' in Hebrews. Such a distinction is unproblematic for our survey. Hebrews employs the two terms interchangeably, favouring 'high priest' unless (and sometimes even when) discussing the 'priest' language sourced from Psalm 110:4 (e.g. Ellingworth 1993: 183–184). My own study has repeatedly observed that the Old Testament, and the Pentateuch in particular, is likewise focused on the central priest rather than on any assistants.

Priesthood and the shape of Hebrews

The nuances of the structure of Hebrews are frequently debated (hence the survey of Joslin 2007), but it is relatively straightforward to observe how central is the notion of Jesus as our great high priest.

We shall soon delight at how prominent this point is to the message and purpose of the homily. First we can observe how significant the theme is to the very shape and flow of the book. The opening verses praise the Son through whom God has definitively spoken (Heb. 1:1–4). His accolades include having accomplished 'purification of sins'. The writing pastor showcases Jesus' deity and humanity in the opening chapters before reaching 2:17–18. Gareth Cockerill (2012: 86) speaks for many when he summarizes as follows: 'These first two chapters climax in 2:17–18 with a word of encouragement that announces the main theme of Hebrews – the eternal Son is the all-sufficient High Priest.'

It can be tempting to overlook 3:1 – 4:13 as not intersecting much with the notion of Jesus' priesthood. The comparison of Moses and Jesus as each being faithful with respect to God's 'house' might bring us to think of notions of tabernacle or temple; we might then hastily retreat when we resolve that this is barely the nuance of 'house' on this occasion. And yet our initial instinct drives us in that direction and any subsequent retreat ought not to be unconditional. After all, the section does begin with a passionate reminder to focus on 'the apostle *and high priest* of our confession, Jesus' (3:1) and our preacher feels ready to resume strong priestly language as he moves from these chapters into his next topic (4:14–16). His line of argument concerns the wilderness generation led by Moses. We have already observed how this generation witnessed the advent of the Aaronic priesthood and God's presence among them in his portable dwelling place, although admittedly Hebrews does not capitalize yet on those particular elements.

Any vagaries are dispelled at 4:14. Still without having explained his claim in full detail, the pastor confidently moves to his next exhortations on the basis that 'we have a great high priest . . . Jesus the Son of God'. Thus 4:14 – 5:10 overflows with mentions of high priests and sacrifices and their pastoral benefit for weak and flagging sinners. While vexing to many readers, 5:11 – 6:20 is a pastoral aside as the preacher directly urges his congregants to lift their game and keep up with his complex teaching. His initial desire to talk about Melchizedek at 5:10 is repeated at 6:20, from which he launches into his detailed comparison in Hebrews 7.

These central chapters continue the cultic imagery throughout 8:1 – 10:18. Although the merits of the new covenant and Jesus' sacrifice are invoked, their purpose is to magnify the superiority of Christ's priesthood (e.g. 8:1, 6; 9:11, 15; 10:14). From this demonstration of Jesus' superiority, our pastor erupts into another overt series of exhortations. Just as 4:14–16 initiates the long central teaching about Jesus' priesthood, so 10:19–25 exults in the pastoral consequences of that priesthood. Believers are to continue their Christian journey because of the unprecedented access to God secured by the 'great priest over the household of God' (10:21).

Having persisted with the priestly and cultic imagery through this extended central argument, the closing chapters revert to a different kind of encouragement. These exhortations feel more dominated by athletic imagery (esp. 12:1–2, 12–13). Yet various cultic allusions recur (e.g. 12:14–29; 13:9–16, 20), several of which we shall inspect in due course.

While scholars are far from an exact consensus, the vast majority now more or less follow George Guthrie (1994). This structure acknowledges the turning points of 4:14–16 and 10:19–25, adding even more prominence to their own priest-based exhortations and the high-priestly arguments concentrated in the intervening chapters. As we turn to consider more intensely the message of Hebrews, already we can appreciate how central is the notion of priesthood from the shape of the book itself.

Hebrews and the language of priesthood

Commentators happily adopt superlative adjectives as they repeatedly describe the 'distinctive' prominence that Hebrews gives to Jesus' 'unique' high-priestly ministry (respectively, Ellingworth 1993; Lane 1991). To modern Christian readers, Jesus' sonship would seem the far more foundational notion. So the contribution of Hebrews is even more significant when its focus on priesthood is intertwined with such sonship and even explicates it (Lane, cxl–cxliii). Indeed, though it may make us uncomfortable, Gerald O'Collins and Michael Jones (2010: 239) bluntly assess the way that moderns tend to prize a selective canon and thus possess an underdeveloped Christology:

> over the centuries Hebrews has not drawn the kind of attention that Christians gave to the Gospels, Romans, and other books of the New Testament. One might speak of a 'marginalizing' of Hebrews, a marginalizing that was associated with, and even encouraged, a diminished interest in the priesthood of Christ.

Returning later to the same lament (291–292), they embarrassingly expose that

The [Niceno-Constantinopolitan] Creed of 381, accepted and used by all Christians, has privileged three other titles: 'Christ (Messiah)', 'Lord', and 'Son of God'. Down through the centuries 'Saviour' (used of Jesus sixteen times in the New Testament) and 'Redeemer' (curiously, never applied to him in the New Testament) have also proved enduringly valuable Christological titles. Jesus' title as 'priest', along with the theme of his priesthood, has been somewhat marginalized . . .

When Hebrews makes at least twenty overt references or clear allusions to Jesus as '(high) priest' and to his 'priesthood', even before we consider additional terms and implicatures, the basic statistics should alarm us. A survey of church music would only reinforce the bias away from priestly language.[11]

While everyday Christians may still be unfamiliar with priestly language in general and with Hebrews in particular, studies of such elements are accelerating. They still typically scrutinize one topic at a time, such as the way Hebrews treats Christ's priesthood.[12] As we seek to synthesize a range of biblical teaching on mediatorial priesthood, some of the key contributions of Hebrews include the following:

- The sermon is concerned to showcase Jesus' full humanity (esp. 2:10–18). This humanity demonstrates that he is 'perfect' for the priestly task of representing his human brothers and sisters before God (2:10; 4:15; 5:7–10).
- Yet, even before Jesus' humanity is established in Hebrews 2, the opening chapter works hard also to establish his divinity (esp. 1:1–4). Although Hebrews is almost exclusively concerned to focus on how Jesus brings his human brothers and sisters before God, we read occasional hints from the obverse perspective. Jesus is the one who encapsulates – most completely – God's message to humanity (1:2; 2:1–4). He is cast as God's 'Son' and 'heir' (1:2, 5–14; 3:6; 4:14; 5:5, 8; 6:6; 7:3, 28; 10:29) along with the unique descriptors as God's 'radiance' and 'representation' (1:3). He represents God to his people.

---

[11] The same lament is raised by Fletcher-Louis (2006: 156): 'In general, priesthood has been marginalized in modern biblical studies.' He judges that renewed interest has reached scholarship of the OT faster than that of the NT. Such an imbalance is one more rationale for my present canonical synthesis.

[12] Among myriad shorter essays on this particular topic, note Vos 1907, Philip Hughes 1973–4, Parsons 1988 and Hagner 2005. Book-length treatments include Scholer 1991, Mason 2008 and McKelvey 2013.

- Building on Old Testament precursors, Jesus is shown as facilitating the better, new covenant between the two parties (esp. 7:18–19; 8:6; 9:15; 12:24; cf. 10:9).
- He accomplishes this by the offering of a superior sacrifice – himself – a singular act that need never be repeated (9:11–14, 25–28; 10:10, 12, 14). This results in a 'purification of sins' and atonement for them (1:3; 2:17; 7:27; 9:26, 28) that cleanses more than skin deep (9:13–14; 10:22; cf. 10:1–4, 11). Its sufficiency is heralded by language such as 'once ever' (7:27; 9:12, 28; 10:2, 10); its completion is flagged by the image of Jesus 'sitting down', and at the honoured position at God's right hand (1:3, 13; 8:1; 10:12; 12:2).[13]
- With his initiatory ministry completed, Jesus is now 'alive always to intercede' for those who approach God through him (7:25).[14]
- His priesthood operates in the real sphere of God's presence (8:2; 9:11, 24). The earthly sanctuary in which Old Testament priests operated was only a 'model' or 'shadow' of this (8:5; 9:23–24; 10:1; cf. Exod. 25:9, 40).
- Jesus' priesthood is superior because, unlike any Old Testament antecedents, he was appointed by God's oath (5:5–6; 7:20–22, 28). Both the oath and Jesus' indestructible life are connected with the enigmatic Melchizedek (5:5–10; 6:20; 7:1–19). This adds royal overtones and a rationale for Jesus' non-Aaronide lineage.
- Moreover, this priesthood is permanent because, unlike mortal predecessors, Jesus lives eternally and need not be replaced upon dying (7:16, 23–25). Nor is his holiness compromised in any way: he is fully sinless (4:15; 7:26–27; 9:14) and his mediation is not impeded by his own weaknesses (7:26–28).

All these factors combine to exalt Jesus as the ultimate and incomparable high priest. That he qualifies as the mediator par excellence is no mere intellectual curiosity: it becomes the basis for the superbly pastoral purpose of the letter. In turn, this gives us insights into the

---

[13] Our study is not concerned further with the nature of Jesus' sacrifice, though those keen to explore its substitutionary nature will certainly find Hebrews accommodating (e.g. 2:9, 17; 9:15).

[14] Although the language accords nicely with studies of priesthood, the precise nature of this intercession is not spelled out. Assuming a causal participle, Jesus' ongoing intercession is whatever action facilitates the 'thorough saving' described at the start of the verse. It is thus potentially different in content to any intercessions offered by OT priests. Note also the matching verb in Rom. 8:34 and the corresponding sentiment in 1 John 2:1.

overarching purpose of the Old Testament cultic system that prepared God's people for Jesus' unsurpassable ministry. We turn now to these matters.

Hebrews and the message of priesthood

Hebrews is compulsory reading for a biblical theology of priesthood (and of tabernacle and sacrifice, etc.). But our first-century preacher was hardly discoursing on some scholastic peculiarity. His transparently pastoral concerns provide great insights into his understanding of priesthood. From there, we can further clarify some whole-Bible emphases on priests and their cultic system.

Hebrews operates with various metaphors that are primarily spatial. Believers are characterized as participants in a journey or a race (famously 12:1–3). Jesus has led the way, having passed through the heavens (and) 'entering' the true sanctuary (4:14; 6:19–20; 9:11–12, 24–25, mostly *eiserchomai*). Thus his followers are urged to 'enter' God's rest (esp. 4:1–11) and, more frequently, to 'approach' God – access not previously available under the old covenant (4:16; 7:19, 25; 10:1, 22; 11:6; 12:22, mostly *proserchomai*)! With the paving of such a 'way' (9:8; 10:19–20) we find Jesus commensurately described as its 'pioneer'. The term used is relatively unique (2:10; 12:2; cf. Acts 3:15; 5:31) and, although debated, the proactive and spatial sense of 'trailblazer' captures the image brilliantly (cf. Witherington 2007: 149–150; Bruce 1990: 80). The same sense probably applies also to the unique term 'forerunner' in 6:20.

Various other images intermingle with these spatial ones. Our Lord Jesus is 'the great shepherd of the sheep' (13:20). He is the 'guarantor' of the better covenant (7:22) and 'minister' of a superior ministry (8:2, 6; cf. 10:11). He is this covenant's 'mediator' – a key term I have picked out to explore priesthood (8:6; 9:15; 12:24; cf. 1 Tim. 2:5). And, of course, there is the array of (high) priestly language applied to him (overtly 2:17; 3:1; 4:14–15; 5:5–10; 6:20; 7:11–28; 8:1–6; 9:11; 10:21). Each term has merit in its chosen usage, but their collocation within the overall homily suggests a degree of overlap. Their overlap concentrates on the benefits brought to Jesus' human brothers and sisters, and these benefits are further hinted at by the prepositional phrase 'on our behalf'. Jesus experienced being fully human 'so that he might taste death *on behalf of everyone*' (2:9). He is a 'forerunner *on our behalf* . . . having become a high priest for ever according to the order of Melchizedek' (6:20). He has entered the true heavenly sanctuary 'now to appear before God *on our behalf*' (9:24). An extended summary in 7:24–25 collocates several such notions: 'But because he continues [in office] for ever, the priesthood he has is permanent. Thus he is thoroughly able to save those who approach God through him, for he is always living in order to intercede on their behalf.'[15]

Whenever and wherever in the first century Hebrews is addressed, its pastoral author urges his friends to avail themselves of this superior access into God's presence. While there is an immediate degree of access to God (esp. 4:14–16; 10:19–22), it is not yet complete (e.g. 9:27–28; 10:35–39). Shunning certain Old Testament exemplars and emulating others, the Christian readers are to persevere in their journey until they reach the land, city, inheritance, finish line, or rest that awaits. Again, in virtually all these images it is Jesus who leads the way. Again, his full humanity allows full identification with and empathy for his human charges. Again, the most dominant image is that of approaching God in his sanctuary, and it is Jesus as our great high priest who facilitates everything foreshadowed in the earthly cultic system. He offers the ideal sacrifice, accomplished once for all time, that entirely cleanses the objective status and subjective consciences of worshippers, to lead them to God.[16]

Hebrews thus brings the biblical storyline of an individual mediator between God and humanity to a stunning and permanent perfection. Moreover, to do this our author is entirely reliant upon the continuities and discontinuities foundational to biblical theology. His regular use of the rhetorical feature called *synkrisis* combines both (positive) comparisons and (negative) contrasts as he highlights both the merits and shortcomings of the human Aaronic priesthood. Yes, the high priest gained access to God's presence – but only for himself and but once a year. Jesus is thoroughly able to save those who approach God through him. Yes, Aaron and his descendants sometimes interposed themselves to curtail God's plagues. Jesus is always living in order to

[15] Other terms or constructions could be added, as in 10:20: 'he has opened a fresh and living way *for us*' (a dative of advantage). Hebrews describes Jesus as the means of access as well as the agent who effects it. Small (2014: 178–196) compiles a helpful list of Jesus' titles/roles in Hebrews, and more broadly his other characterizations.

[16] This last clause, from Heb. 2:10, reminds us that there are glimpses of 'access' language elsewhere in the NT. Paul thrice mentions access to God through Jesus (Rom. 5:2; Eph. 2:18; 3:12). The middle of these three occurs in a passage with temple imagery, though Jesus and other leaders are cast as part of the temple's architecture rather than its staff. The language of 1 Peter 3:18 is perhaps closest to Heb. 2:10, though the priestly sentiments in Peter's prior chapter have not carried forward (Michaels 1988: 203). Davids (1990: 136) recognizes Peter's resonance with Hebrews but overstates his case that 'Peter is creating a new metaphor, for no other NT writer has this active picture of Jesus leading the Christian to God.'

intercede. Such overt contrasts, already well observed in 7:24–25, can be supplemented by some comparisons that Hebrews makes less directly. A primary function of the Levitical priests was to differentiate between the holy and common, between the unclean and clean. Jesus (and the better sacrifice he administers as part of the better covenant) *makes* holy and cleanses (1:3; 2:11; 9:13–14; 10:10, 14, 29). Where the Levitical priest was to teach God's commandments, in these last days God has spoken definitively by the Son (1:2; 2:3). Where high standards of holiness were set for the high priest (and thence the priests and then the people), and though each still sinned (5:2–3; 7:27), our great high priest is 'holy, blameless, undefiled, separated from sinners and exalted above the heavens' (7:26; cf. 4:15; 9:14)! Nor is this some dry academic exercise. Even as he models biblical theology for us, our author utilizes biblical theology to care for his congregation pastorally. We misread Hebrews if we mistake it for some dry intellectual treatise or an indulgent piece of obscurantism!

Our author's pastoral *synkrisis* inherently relies upon the unfolding developments found in salvation history and progressive revelation. Hebrews even foregrounds this temporal axis. Akin to our initial tapestry illustration, Hebrews compiles and analyses the time-lapse elements concerning God's mediators, no more clearly than in Hebrews 7. The Levitical priesthood was instituted, but God had not finished speaking and he foreshadowed a 'change' (7:11–12). Our author finds this change announced centuries later in Psalm 110:4, which envisages a priestly figure later than Aaron and of an order other than Aaron's (7:15–22; 5:6). Still more centuries later, Jesus effects this change. This is no isolated snapshot of a single priest but a progressive movie revealing transformation over time. The comparisons and the contrasts, taken together and mapped across the unfolding story of the Bible, inform our understanding of the role of the individual, vocational priest throughout Scripture. That an individual human mediates between God and humanity is glimpsed in Adam and Eve, sampled in the patriarchs, exemplified by Moses and formalized in Aaron, variously managed or mangled by Aaron's successors, and revitalized and bettered by the past and present ministries of the incarnate Christ.

Although a number of application points await my concluding chapter, many of my own goals are met if a biblical theology of priesthood leads us to doxology: to unbounded praise of God for his work through Jesus. The more we study of the Old Testament's fledgling and imperfect and incomplete cultic system, the better equipped we are to grasp something more of the magnitude of the access to God that Jesus has secured. Of course, the two ends of the biblical-theological spectrum mutually inform each other: where the Christian diet is heavily saturated with the New Testament, it may be that elements of Jesus' ministry can be employed to develop a growing appreciation for the painstaking scale models that God implemented in the Old Testament. As these cultic threads are traced through the biblical-theological tapestry, may God's people be nurtured in the magnificence of God's long-term planning, attention to detail and meticulous execution.

Jesus as priest in the rest of the New Testament?

In the bright spotlight of Hebrews, any remaining New Testament allusions to Jesus as a priest are difficult to discern. As when one stares at the sun and then sees an afterimage for some time, there is certainly the danger of finding a priestly Jesus elsewhere because of the theme's prominence in Hebrews (rightly Baigent 1981: 39). Yet, even though we may not be confident in the exegesis of some of the more maximalist presentations, they rightly observe that a number of New Testament themes align closely with matters of priesthood.

Revelation

The most overt of these remains the image of the risen Lord Jesus in the opening chapter of Revelation. As John turns to see the voice he has heard, among the lampstands he sees 'one like a son of man' dressed in distinctive clothing and with startling personal characteristics (Rev. 1:12–16). We can readily acknowledge that a range of allusions is inferred here; a mixture of features from Daniel 7 and elsewhere gives this figure overtones that are divine, royal/messianic and judicial. So there are good reasons why some interpreters are distracted from any priestly connotations (though we have been increasingly alerted to the fact that a priest *does* represent God and kings and judges). Even while not joining them, Grant Osborne (2002: 89) admits that the majority of interpreters do find priestly imagery mingled within the Revelation montage. The priestly imagery is reinforced if the golden lampstands, which John sees first, are themselves cultic allusions tended by this priestly figure (Beale 1999: 208–209). We ought to recall that the opening doxology includes cultic imagery: sins are alleviated by 'blood', producing 'priests to God' (1:5–6). Other cultic images pervade Revelation, affirming that John is entirely conversant with the Old Testament cultus. Certainly the detailed study of Ross Winkle (2012) draws on all these observations to resolve confidently that John's opening vision, and especially the 'ankle-length robe', does indeed present the risen Jesus in high-priestly terms. We can thus follow Winkle in observing the helpful summary of Ian Boxall (2006: 42):

> We know from Hebrews that the understanding of Christ as High Priest in the heavenly sanctuary was able to emerge within New Testament Christianity; Revelation 1 suggests that Hebrews might not be as unique in its christology as is sometimes assumed.

1 Peter

Nonetheless, Revelation merely adds this high-priestly motif to its arsenal of allusions without any overt development or application (Matera 2007: 335, n. 2). And we are hard pressed to discern any other substantial allusions in the rest of the New Testament. There is certainly no shortage of cultic images, but at best these are connected only derivatively with Jesus' priesthood (see chapter 7). It can be too hasty to enforce our categories or terminology where priestly intention is indirect – or is absent altogether.

Thus we should note the dissonance when O'Collins and Jones (2010: 35–38) proffer a section entitled '1 Peter on Christ's Priesthood' with an opening paragraph that rightly confesses that '1 Peter uses priestly, sacrificial language for the Christian community but not for Jesus himself.' They correctly catalogue the relevant images: Christ as an unblemished lamb whose sacrifice ransoms and sprinkles God's elect, temple imagery that includes Christ, and the sacrifices thence offered by his priestly people (1 Pet. 1:2, 18–19; 2:4–10). But such cultic images do not particularly contribute to *Jesus'* priesthood, no matter how suggestive they may sound. By far the strongest repetition in Peter's letter portrays Jesus as the willing and uncomplaining sacrificial victim, who gives his suffering people a model to emulate (esp. 2:18–25; 3:13–18). I shall have much to say about the priestly service of God's *people* in our next chapters, but 1 Peter is hardly about 'Christ's Priesthood', a point O'Collins and Jones all but concede several times.

Ironically, they regularly mention 1 Peter 2:5, drawing out many of the important elements in the verse that we ourselves will tackle. They twice spell out an important phrase therein, and it is this phrase that perhaps offers the best, untapped potential for thinking about Christ's active priesthood in this letter. God's elect 'as a spiritual house are being built into a holy priesthood in order to offer spiritual sacrifices acceptable to God *through Jesus Christ*'. The italicized phrase provides a tantalizing glimpse that Jesus might somehow contribute to the offering of these spiritual sacrifices – but a fleeting glimpse only. Ramsey Michaels (1988: 102) notes identical uses of 'through' Jesus (1:21; 4:11) but they affirm only that Jesus *somehow* assists in facilitating faith and praise. Although it is entirely plausible, we cannot press a distinctly *priestly* agency, any more than we can clarify how governors are appointed 'through' the Lord (2:14) or how Peter wrote his letter 'through' Silvanus (5:12).[17]

For our purposes, one last enticing parallel presents itself. Reliant on a number of variables, I present it here as a possibility rather than as an accomplished fact. Exodus 28:38 makes an enigmatic statement about Aaron 'bear[ing] the guilt of the holy things'. It is sometimes also thought that at sacrifices it might be the (high) priest, rather than the sacred animal, who bears the weight of sin (e.g. Wenham 1995: 79, following Kiuchi 1987). Similar phrasing may be found in Leviticus 10:17 and Numbers 18:1. Is there then a hint of this priestly behaviour in 1 Peter 2:24 (and/or Isa. 53:12 on which Peter draws) when the suffering Christ 'bore our sins in his body'?[18]

Anything more?

As it stands, there seems little further data to draw from. The New Testament concentrates its descriptions of Jesus as a high priest almost exclusively in Hebrews, with some recognizable but passing allusions in Revelation. There is certainly a lively debate between minimalists and maximalists. Both sets of interpreters acknowledge the possibility of investigating more nuanced claims. But we have already seen above that this gives rise to unagreed boundaries and unagreed interpretation of such nuances. Indeed, the interpretation of what *is* described

---

[17] The latter example provokes the investigation of Richards (2000). He resolves the meaning of *dia* in 5:12 from wider context and comparable usage – precisely because of the preposition's imprecision on its own. Such imprecise options are not often mentioned for 2:5, though note Nelson 1993: 163, n. 5.

[18] There might be a symbolic enactment of this guilt-bearing in Ezek. 4:4–6, where the prophet, himself a priest, 'will bear [Israel's and Judah's] iniquity' for 390 and 40 days respectively. Block (1997: 179) identifies this as priestly behaviour, in keeping with Exod. 28:38, but Duguid (1999: 90–91) observes that Ezekiel's actions are for illustration purposes only and do not actually *deal* with the people's sins. Episcopal readers might leap to find further support for a priestly Jesus in Peter's next verse and its description of Jesus as a 'bishop' (NKJV, ASV)!

in texts remains open to polarized inferences. Winkle's sober dissertation concludes (2012: 371) with a surge of enthusiasm; having found high-priestly Christology beyond Hebrews in Revelation, Winkle hopes that the minimalist position might be crushed! Yet the converse position is equally demonstrable: studies focused on Hebrews commonly see the letter's sustained and detailed argument as evidence of how unfamiliar the notion of Christ's priesthood was to its first readers (e.g. Lane 1991: cxli–cxlii; Koester 2001: 22, 109; Tait 2010: 133–135).

My own reading and presentation of the evidence in this chapter is certainly more sympathetic to the minimalist hermeneutic. We have already noted earlier in the present chapter a few weaknesses. Maximalist studies of the Gospels (e.g. Fletcher-Louis 2007) largely maximize *silences* left unexplained by the Gospel authors. Such studies also present a logic that is difficult to untangle. They seem to argue that Second Temple Jews expected a *priestly* leader, that Jesus presented himself as an authoritative leader, and thus that his leadership should be interpreted as priestly. Moreover, they argue – rightly – that authentic high priests are the earthly representatives of God. It is this equation that gives rise to the imprecision of the maximalist argument. When Jesus starts behaving like God (e.g. in forgiving sins or redefining the Sabbath or the law), why should this favour interpreting the evidence more towards a human high priest than towards God incarnate? I think Fletcher-Louis (69) largely concedes this point when he allows that 'Jesus' contagious holiness, we might say, is not the product of the apparatus of *office*, but rather a manifestation of his *person*.'

Evidence from subsequent church writings, no matter how early, adds no further confidence that the doctrine of Christ's priesthood circulated in forms other than we can see in the Scriptures. Various scholars (e.g. Koester 2001: 21–23) demonstrate that 1 Clement, written around AD 96, is dependent on content in Hebrews; there is no need to posit a wider tradition of which we have but a glimpse. It seems to me that more maximalist attempts are in danger of cherry-picking parallels that are plausible but inconclusive and that are open to charges of interpretative fallacy. We have seen that teaching is an important responsibility of priests, but that does not automatically class all teachers and Jesus as priests. Aaronic priests oversaw the *evaluation* of skin diseases such as leprosy, but Jesus' *cleansing* of lepers does not in itself confirm a sacral role. Such parallels may be suggestive, and they may even invite further evidence and argument, but they are not often presented convincingly.

It is with such caution that any other New Testament proposals should be approached. David Schrock (2013: 355–356) is correct that cultic images can be used even where 'priesthood' is not named, as in Revelation 1. But, again, what constitutes a cultic image that is adequately priestly? We have seen that O'Collins and Jones (2010) have faltered with 1 Peter, talking about Christ's priesthood in a cultic context that emphasizes other elements (not least the readers' own priesthood). Schrock invites us to consider Ephesians 2:11–22. He is certainly right to identify cultic imagery here and even that Christ Jesus behaves generally in a mediatorial fashion. Any priestly role is hard to discern when the pericope is as much about horizontal reconciliation as vertical reconciliation (Hoehner 2002: 383), and general cultic notions such as circumcision and temple confirm nothing about Christ's priesthood. Reconciliation language admittedly sounds like our prominent mediation theme. Yet, while we might safely describe Old Testament priests as conducting a ministry that approximates reconciliation, the Old Testament itself hardly presents us with such language or imagery. We must be wary of conflating modern descriptions that, for all their broad similarities, may not forge a confirmed link in the biblical text. If anything, New Testament language concerning reconciliation is judicial, as when it is paired with justification (Rom. 5:9–11; 2 Cor. 5:18–21).[19]

Summary

There are many additional cultic images in the New Testament, as when Paul and other authors describe their ministries or the ministries of Christians in sacrificial terms. We might consider these to be derivative or democratized from the high-priestly ministry of Jesus, and it is to these that we turn in the next chapters.

The present chapter has sought to provide the basis for those derivative descriptions. Certainly the New Testament writings were crafted first for an era fully immersed in the cultic system of the old covenant. Jesus and his apostles lived and moved in the orbit of the Jerusalem

---

[19] One classic example of unwarranted conflation is narrated in Naselli and Gons 2011: the theological conviction that the Holy Spirit is personal does not entail that masculine pronouns in John's Gospel betray John's own insights into this truth. Another example comes from my own study of alleged OT christophanies (Malone 2015); we must be careful how plausible NT hypotheses intersect with the interpretation of OT texts. Yet another illustration comes from J. M. Hamilton (2006), who demonstrates that NT teaching on the indwelling of the Holy Spirit can be wrongly imposed upon OT passages.

temple, restored after Babylonian destruction and exile and now zealously guarded by the various Jewish stakeholders. Alongside contemporary glimpses and future hopes the letter to the Hebrews reflects on the lessons cast between the shadow of the wilderness tabernacle and the heavenly reality. It is Hebrews in particular (and almost exclusively) that helps consolidate God's purposes for introducing the Old Testament cultic system, for facilitating old-covenant worship, and for training God's people throughout the ages to appreciate the surpassing magnificence of Jesus' priestly ministry. Various such elements are regularly identified, and T. W. Manson (1958: 58) captures several in his own summary of Hebrews:

Here we have the essential characteristics of a perfect high-priesthood: on the one side an unbreakable link with God the Father in the unfailing obedience of the Son; on the other an unbreakable link with his brother men through an unfailing sympathy and understanding. This solidarity with God and man uniquely fits Christ to be the Mediator, to represent God to men and men to God, to make the Holy One of Israel real to his children and to fit those sinful children to enter into the divine presence.

Part II
God's corporate priesthoods

Chapter Six

Israel as a kingdom of priests

There are two significant benefits of a biblical theology of priesthood, especially as we move from the 'individual' role of vocational priests to the more 'corporate' identity that describes the status and purpose of God's covenant people. The first benefit is that this connection is drawn throughout the biblical canon – overtly and repeatedly. So we are tracing an important thread through the tapestry of Scripture. The second benefit is that the Bible uses this connection to identify and commission God's people for their own priestly ministries as part of God's world-saving mission.

The present chapter surveys how this connection is drawn under the old covenant. We see that Israel is commissioned to function as a national 'priest' between God and the wider peoples of the earth. This lays the foundation for chapter 7, where we investigate what this corporate priesthood looks like under the new covenant.

Starting with the Old Testament itself has two advantages. The first is that it continues to walk us through the Bible in order, tracking the theme as it unfolds. A second advantage concerns our finishing point. Most Christian readers are concerned to know what all this teaching about priests might look like today, whether for lay believers or for formal clergy. That is certainly where a number of studies end up (e.g. Feuillet 1975; O'Collins and Jones 2010). It seems to me, though, that the temptation might be to explore new-covenant priesthood as a derivation of Jesus' priestly ministry. Rather, the derivation might be better drawn differently. Two diagrams can aid our approach. Figure 6.1 shows the temptation to derive Christian ministry from Jesus. While there are obviously important links between Jesus and his people, I propose that there are better parallels if we consider

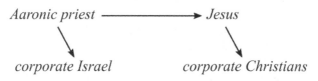

Figure 6.1

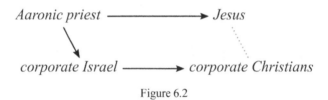

Figure 6.2

Christians' corporate ministry in the light of Israel's corporate commission, as shown in figure 6.2. It is with this approach in mind that we turn to consider what can be said of Israel's corporate priestly commission.

A kingdom of priests

The crucial passage has long been recognized as Exodus 19:6. Our interest is especially attracted to the invitation for Israel to become 'a kingdom of priests', a phrase unique in the Old Testament. The whole paragraph and chapter in which it occurs are central to Israel's national identity and, thence, for the identity of the new-covenant people of God. It is worth unpacking the phrase and its context in some detail.

A privileged status for Israel

We have already noted the substantial space given over to the design and construction of the tabernacle: Exodus 25 – 40 forms nearly half the book. That proportion jumps to 60% when we realize that Israel arrives at Mount Sinai sometime before Exodus 19 (see 18:5). So the making of the covenant and the giving of the covenant law is all a part of this Sinai narrative as well. Less than half the book is actually concerned with the 'exodus' out of Egypt.

The forging of the covenant commitment is the substance of Exodus 19 – 24, and it begins in earnest in the opening verses. Three months after leaving Egypt, the Israelites are encamped at Sinai. And the opening offer from God is astounding: he offers them an unparalleled position in his global rule. Having earlier identified them as his honoured 'firstborn son' (4:22–23), God reminds them of their dramatic rescue that has brought them to himself (19:4). Then comes the offer that they, indeed, cannot refuse.

If the Israelites accept the offer, God will exalt them among the wider nations. This privilege is seen clearly if we translate and structure carefully God's words in 19:5–6, perhaps a little woodenly:

126

Now if you heed thoroughly my voice and keep my covenant,

you will be to me a treasured possession
   from all the peoples;
   for to me is all the earth
but you, you will be to me a kingdom of priests
   and a holy nation.

This way of presenting the offer gives rise to several significant observations.[1] First, Yahweh indeed proposes a privilege for Israel. Studies regularly and rightly focus on the opening promise: that Israel would become God's 'treasured possession' (*sĕgullâ*). This is to be something prized and something personal (Wright [2006: 255] translates it as 'a special personal possession'). Nations past and present regularly have a head of state whose private wealth is distinguished from the national coffers he or she controls. King David was one such leader, who committed towards the building of the temple not only state resources but also donations from his private 'treasury' (*sĕgullâ*; 1 Chr. 29:1–5).

Second, this prized and personal possession gives shape to the phrase 'kingdom of priests'. The parallel presentation above suggests that, just as Israel 'will be to me' a private treasure, so too they 'will be to me' a kingdom of priests and a holy nation. Although scholars quibble about exactly how these three phrases interact, all agree that they mutually inform each other and that the latter two provide more detail about the first.

Third, Israel's promised identity is one that is defined with reference to the rest of the populated world. The two indented lines show that Israel is a treasured possession in contrast to God's general ownership of all peoples. The precise function of the second of those indented lines is frequently debated. The word translated here as 'for' could bring a number of nuances, as we shall shortly see. However we infer that nuance, the offer 'makes clear that the text is not only concerned to establish the nature of Yhwh's relation to Israel, but also Israel's relation to others' (Wells 2000: 44).

---

[1] The chiastic presentation here has proven to be persuasive among scholars. Championed by Mosis (1978), it is adopted by the focused studies of Exod. 19 in Wells 2000 and Davies 2004, in turn applied respectively in Wright 2006 and Williamson 2008. Each scholar emphasizes some of the following points made here, and Wells and Davies in particular explore in more depth.

These observations all influence how we understand Israel's commission to be a kingdom of priests in the final line. Israel is granted a position that is both connected with and distinct from the wider nations. The emphasis here is certainly on the distinction, with Israel marked out as a personal treasure and as a 'holy' nation. It is offered a status not enjoyed by the other nations. Of particular interest to us is the simple fact that 'holy' (*qādôš*) is that standard term applied to priests and their special standing before God. As with individual vocational priests, 'holy' marks out Israel as something more special and more suited to Yahweh. As with individual priests, we can consider this in spatial terms. 'Israel lives in his presence; Israel is particularly close to him' (Wells 2000: 55).

A privileged function for the nations

How then does this unique invitation to Israel envisage those wider nations? Are they merely a foil for Israel's privilege: those passed over for special treatment, eventually titled and derided as 'Gentiles' outside God's privileged covenant relationship? Such a corollary is certainly possible. But three lines of argument – three expanding levels of context – suggest a more optimistic fate for the nations. Israel's special status entails a special role within God's wider world for the nations' benefit.

Evidence from Exodus 19

The internal evidence of Exodus 19:5–6 is tantalizing but indeterminate on its own. My working definitions of priesthood might already entice us to resolve that Israel's commission as a collective priesthood means a mutual, two-way benefit between God and the nations. Tim Chester (2016: 142) articulates at a popular level such a conclusion:

> Israel were to be a kingdom which, as a whole, had a priestly function similar to the priests in [the] tabernacle . . . The presence and activity of priests therefore creates the possibility of a relationship between God and his people. In the same way, Israel as a priestly kingdom created the possibility of a relationship. As a priestly kingdom, Israel was to represent God to the world through mission, and represent the world to God through prayer. The world could not see God, but the world could see Israel and should have seen his glory in them.

This is indeed the conclusion towards which I want to argue. But the word 'priests' and the unique phrase 'kingdom of priests' require further support. Our study of priesthood ought not merely to assert the outcome we seek to confirm.

The other internal evidence available is the second of the two indented lines. The last line of verse 5 connects Israel's priesthood with the fact that 'all the earth is mine'. We have already heard that the word translated 'for' is quite contentious. At least four nuances can be divined (detailed by Davies [2004: 55–63] and tidily summarized by Williamson [2008: 100–102]). Is Israel chosen 'because' all the earth is God's and presumably Israel's election thus benefits the nations (cf. ESV, NASB, NKJV, NLT)? Is Israel chosen 'although' God might have claimed any of the other nations (NIV, CSB, NAB, NCV)? Could it be a more affirming claim that 'indeed' the whole earth is God's (NRSV, NJPS)? Or, as punctuated above, is it an explanation of what follows? It can be hard to distinguish any significant difference between some of these nuances. The immediate relevance for us might be considered as follows. All the options, along with the wider wording of God's offer, support the basic idea that Israel is chosen *from* among the nations. The question is whether we might go further and add the first nuance outlined above: that Israel is chosen not only *from* the nations but also *for* their benefit. Although this addition enjoys some scholarly and translational support, there are enough uncertainties raised to warrant caution. We should not thoughtlessly place too much weight on either the words 'priests' or 'for' – though they may ultimately be able to bear such weight.[2]

Further evidence from Exodus
We can garner further support for these individual words by looking a little further afield within Exodus. In particular, there are a number of parallels between the ceremonial consecrations of Israel in Exodus 24 and of the Aaronic priests in Exodus 29 (Averbeck 1997d: 1002–1003). Both the history of Israel and the text of Exodus seem concerned to show a parallel between Israel's corporate priesthood and Aaron's individualistic ministry.

The link is recognized even when interpreters differ over the direction of the influence. It is certainly reasonable to think that describing Israel with the language of 'priests' is derived from their experience of priests

---

[2] Indeed, Williamson admits to moving from the more missiological position (2003: 150; 2007: 97) to more staid caution (2008: 101–102). The two options outlined here ('from' versus 'from and for') are intertwined with the syntactic question: Do the latter lines *extend* the first promise of privileged status or *repeat* it? Wells (2000) argues that the descriptions of Israel are cumulative and include a missiological purpose.

within their own cultic system and of the priests of surrounding nations. After all, we have noted priestly language and priestly behaviour long before the formal election of Aaron and his descendants in the latter half of Exodus. In this view, the nation's priesthood is derived from individual priests. This is certainly the impression given in various useful explanations (e.g. Goheen 2011: 38–39).

More exciting for contemplating the wider ministry of the people of God, others take the corporate dimension as primary. John Davies (2004: 15; cf. 165–169) sees the Aaronic priesthood as a scale model of the more important reality: 'the Aaronic priests are intended by the writer of Exodus to present a concretization of the image of Israel's royal priesthood, a visual lesson on the ideal prospect set before the nation as a whole'. This is consistent with another central theme in Exodus: the tangible tabernacle is a localized scale model of the heavenly reality that it represents (see discussion in chapter 2, a point identified also by Davies [139]).[3]

We may not be able to resolve the direction of influence and it probably does not matter. No one doubts a connection, and the two senses of priesthood are mutually reinforcing. Our understanding of Israel's priesthood is clearly aided by the institution of the Aaronic priesthood.

Status versus function?

At this point we must acknowledge an important question that has commonly been overlooked. When a connection between Israel and Aaron is permitted, it is easy to assume that the connection is purely or primarily a functional one. We have already seen Chester's assumption of 'a priestly function' for Israel. The same idea is readily promulgated by those teasing out the missiological implications of Israel's priesthood. One often hears the maxim of Johannes Blauw (1962: 24): 'What priests are for a people, Israel as a people is for the world.' Variants are found in commentaries on the Pentateuch and its priesthood (e.g. Childs 1974: 367; Ross 2002: 57).

Such a missiological implication is attractive and one I seek to defend. But the missiological implication has been challenged somewhat in recent decades. Interpreters have had the forethought to ask *in what way* Israel is priestly.

---

[3] Although unconvincing in themselves, other variants also end up supporting this approach. One persistent proposal is that, because timid Israel failed to accept God's corporate commission, the Aaronic priesthood is a narrowed *substitute* for the nation (e.g. Clark 1935; Kaiser 1978: 109 = 2008: 76; Sheldon 2014).

In particular, it has been observed that being a priest is concerned with one's *status* in the worshipping community. We ourselves have seen the preponderance of 'holy' language concerning the Aaronic priesthood: the priest is 'holy to the LORD' and thus suited to being closer to God's presence. Likewise, as 'a holy nation', Israel is granted a special *relationship* with Yahweh and proximity to him. This emphasis of Davies (2004: 94–98) has influenced studies of priesthood and commentaries on Exodus (e.g. Schrock 2013: 254; Garrett 2014: 460). Similar notions can be traced earlier (e.g. Cheung 1986; *DBI* 663), though the impact is still being discovered in scholarly circles. Is a functional and missiological commission for Israel undone? Must we abandon Blauw and Chester and many, many others? Six immediate responses suggest that the function–status balance is an important one to seek and that the balance has not been completely and for ever tipped away from a functional role for the people of God.

First, Deborah Rooke (1998: 189) ponders if the Hebrew form of the noun 'priest' is cast as an active doing word ('thereby implying that the *kōhēn* is the one who carries out the action of the verbal root behind the participial noun'). Attractive though this would be, we ought not to place more weight on a hypothetical etymology than on a word's contextual usage.

Second, those who draw our attention to the 'status' side of the ledger are rarely pressing an all-or-nothing case. They acknowledge that, even though a special status might be the primary import of priesthood and the language of 'holy', this does not disqualify priestly activity. It is a matter of balance and of order. Thus Alex Cheung (1986: 267) acknowledges for Israel that 'The missionary/mediatorial consequences only resulted from her ontological worth.' Likewise, Davies (2004: 238) happily allows that 'it is not denied that there may be implications for human relationships of what it means to be the chosen and treasured people of God'. Such studies emphasize status over function, but they carefully use relative language such as 'primarily' as they seek to balance the two. They are not pressing exclusively for status and disregarding any subsequent function.

Third, much of the rest of the Pentateuch does not merely assume Israel's holy status but adjures Israel to function according to this status (e.g. Wells 2000: 56). Just as do the major apostolic writers to Christian believers in the New Testament (e.g. Eph. 4:1; 1 Pet. 1:13–16; 1 John 2:3–6), the Old Testament calls Israel to live in a way that reflects their status, to function in the family likeness and live

131

up to the family reputation. Even in the present context, Israel understands that God requires some kind of response. As soon as God conveys to the people the offer of 19:5–6, they respond that 'Whatever Yahweh has said we will *do*' (19:7–8; cf. 24:3, 7) (G. A. Cole 2009: 95).

Fourth, there may be additional categories that help clarify Israel's status and function. Michael Morales (2015: 232–236) suggestively explores how Adam serves as a priest-king over creation. Adam is described later as 'son of God' in juxtaposition with Jesus as God's 'Son' (Luke 3:22, 38), who proves to be the ultimate priest-king. Between times, Israel is cast as God's 'firstborn son' (Exod. 4:22–23) and commissioned to an active, ruling priesthood. There is even a hint of this in the priestly facets of the Davidic monarchs, themselves each singled out as God's 'son' (esp. 2 Sam. 7:14; Pss 2:7; 89:27). Morales thus traces a biblical theology of individual and corporate sons whose special status is to direct worship towards God.[4]

Fifth, consideration of the matter is muddied by the fact that different interpreters focus on different elements of cultic priesthood and of a more functional, missional ministry. Paul Williamson (2008: 103–105) fairly complains of enthusiastic evangelicals who cherry-pick the precise parallels – and even wishful similarities – that suit their cause. Such a temptation cuts both ways. Certainly those who emphasize priesthood as a status might overlook the functional entailments. Still, missional enthusiasts need to be cautious and recognize that, while Exodus 19 commissions Israel to some kind of worldwide ministry, the commission in itself is not as overt and active as some would wish.[5]

Sixth and relatedly, the nature of Israel's outward-focused mission is influenced by our understanding of two further factors. The first is the nature of priesthood. The second is that the status and function

---

[4] Morales further suggests that the combined role of *prophet* and priest and king was expected of each ideal son, with these roles splintered only during the time of old-covenant Israel. Nor do the implications end with Jesus: the NT regularly adapts 'sons/children of God' for his new-covenant people. It may also be that each son is involved with implementing a covenant, with Adam and Eve's priestly role further secured if we perceive God's making a covenant with/at creation. My gratitude to Matthew Emadi who suggested to me some of these lines of thought.

[5] Kaiser (2012) is a prominent example of one detecting an activist, centrifugal outreach by Israel. He thus emphasizes 'the missionary and ministry call issued in Exodus 19:4–6' (16). A more nuanced case in the same vein is made by Dickson (2003: 84), 'apparently premised on the notion of priestly presence (Exodus 19:5–6)'. *Pace* such enthusiasm, the recent consensus is hesitant to detect any organized Jewish mission (e.g. Schnabel 2004; Bird 2010).

of 'a kingdom of priests' is so flexible that we must be wary of introducing our own designs. So we turn to the second of these factors in a new subsection.

Evidence beyond Exodus

Exegetically, the question is how closely the three titles in 19:5–6 overlap. Are 'a kingdom of priests' and 'a holy nation' completely synonymous? If not, how do they differ? And how does their resultant compound duplicate or differ from Israel's primary description as 'a treasured possession'? We have observed that scholars are uncertain how best to answer these questions; it is easy to mould the answers to suit ourselves.

Many thus look beyond Exodus for their insights. Those who hold certain views of Scripture can be reluctant to allow this, especially when the authoring of the Pentateuch is subject to a range of reconstructions. Readers who are concerned with the final form of the text, however, are comfortable to let the narrative unfold as a related whole.

The most common intuitions for Exodus 19:5–6 are sourced from Genesis 12:1–3. There, in an equally structured commission (Wright 2006: 200–201), God charges Abram to leave his current context. God promises several outcomes. One outcome – which may be something of an outright command (Wright; asv) – is that Abram will 'be a blessing'. Certainly his obedience is linked to the prospect that all the families of the earth might experience blessing.[6] Thus interpreters can readily accommodate both elements in Israel's commission in Exodus 19:

> What that special position entails [in v. 5] is then explained in verse 6. They have a role that matches their status. The *status* is to be a special treasured possession. The *role* is to be a priestly and holy community in the midst of the nations . . . 'What the reader is given is not a description of Israel in isolation, but in relation to the whole of God's earth.' Or in other words, *the particularity of Israel here is intended to serve the universality of God's interest in the world. Israel's election serves God's mission.* (Wright 2006: 256, 257, citing Wells 2000: 49)

---

[6] The exact interpretation of the last clause of Gen. 12:3 is debated as Exod. 19:6. Is Abram to be active in bringing blessing upon the nations? Or will they be blessed by God or even bless themselves, leaving Abram and his family a more passive role?

Even here, it is important to note that the choice to distinguish status from function is as much a decision of the interpreter as it is an inescapable teaching of the text.[7]

The text's lack of clarity does not stop interpreters from proposing various missiological connections. Like many others, cited above and uncited, Douglas Stuart (2006: 423) sees a connection with the commission of Abram in Genesis 12. Stuart acknowledges that Exodus 19 offers little direct information, but he suggests a number of priestly activities for Israel, including to be a role model for the nations, to proclaim the truths of God and preserve his promises, and even to 'intercede for the rest of the world by offering acceptable offerings to God (both sacrifices and right behavior) and thus ameliorate the general distance between God and humankind'. Several of these will recur shortly. For now we might note (with Dickson 2003: 62–63) how Philo seems to have reached an interpretation similar to Stuart's final point about intercession. Philo wrote around the time of Jesus how the Supreme God had earlier chosen Moses' people 'out of all the other nations to be priests perpetually offering prayers on behalf of the race of humans' (*On the Life of Moses* 1.149).

I am not especially endorsing the latter suggestions that Israel is to pray for or sacrifice on behalf of the nations around it. But some of the other proposals are certainly borne out by further clarifications with the Pentateuch. Our investigation is increasingly intersecting with a biblical theology of mission, a topic admirably addressed by others (see within my bibliography various works of Beale, Goheen and Wright). We may thus get a taste for Israel's priestly mission even with a sampling that is representative rather than exhaustive.

A missiological intention

Certainly the commission prominently inaugurated in Exodus 19 is referenced as Israel's history unfolds. Several of these reminders include both the relevance of Israel's unparalleled status and confirmatory hints at the missiological consequences of this status.[8]

---

[7] Wright later returns to Exod. 19 (2006: 329–333), where he provides more circumspect investigation and balance, though he still does not make an exegetical demonstration that status ('a treasured possession') and function ('a kingdom of priests') must be treated more as disjoint than as identical.

[8] The sense of 'unparalleled' is endorsed by V. P. Hamilton (2011: 303), who sees the comparative of Exod. 19:5 akin to that of Gen. 3:1. God does not promise that Israel will be treasured *more than* the other nations, but that Israel will be treasured *rather than* the other nations. Similarly Goldingay 2003: 373 and Davies 2004: 54–55.

As Moses primes the next generation of Israelites to conquer Canaan, the rare language of 'a treasured possession' resurfaces in Deuteronomy (*sĕgullâ*; Deut. 7:6; 14:2; 26:18–19). Each occurrence also adds other language and sentiments from Exodus 19: Yahweh has chosen Israel 'from all the peoples' or 'above all the nations', and it is 'a people holy to Yahweh your God'. Israel is thus to live distinctively and not according to the behaviours and gods of the nations it is about to dispossess (cf. Millar 1998). The first occurrence (7:6) is juxtaposed with a famous reminder that the Israelites' privilege is purely because of Yahweh's covenant love and not because of any numerical or reputational superiority of Israel's own (7:7–11). A corresponding passage a few chapters later ominously recalls that the Israelites already have poor form when it comes to their 'righteousness' before Yahweh (9:4–6) – one of many hints that Israel's prospects are cast pessimistically (Barker 2004).

Deuteronomy certainly contains other passages of missiological value, perhaps none clearer than 4:5–8. Israel's behaviour in the sight of the nations is to elicit the nations' intrigue in the values and expectations and nearness of Israel's deity. Similarly, nestled among the blessings and curses for covenant obedience, 28:9–10 hopes that the other nations might see and respond to Yahweh's 'holy people' who are called by Yahweh's name. The same has already been hinted at earlier in the Pentateuch, where God explains to his people why they are to obey his distinctive covenant rules and their kosher food laws:

> I am Yahweh your God, who has differentiated you from the peoples. So you must differentiate between the clean animal and the unclean, and between the unclean bird and the clean, and you must not make yourselves cultically abhorrent by animal or by bird or by anything that crawls on the ground, which I have differentiated for you as unclean. You must be holy to me because I, Yahweh, am holy and I have differentiated you from the peoples to be mine. (Lev. 20:24–26)

Repeating the key idea of priestly 'differentiation' (*bdl*) as in Leviticus 10:10–11, God explains that Israel as a nation stands out from the other nations. The language here remains focused on Israel's status, but this 'holy' status and the ensuing kosher laws serve a proclamatory

---

The point is reinforced if Exod. 19:5–6 contrasts 'all the earth . . . *but* you . . .' (Wells 2000: 44–45; though see also 49–50).

purpose. From this, coupled with the passages from Deuteronomy, it is clear that Israel's distinctiveness is to be apparent to these other peoples and is not merely for Israel's own internal observance. A concern for Yahweh's reputation is also previewed in Moses' own mediation. In the shameful incident with the golden calf, Moses defends not the Israelites' actions but Yahweh's public standing (Exod. 32:11–12; note also 32:25). Later, when the advance scouting party leads the Israelites to distrust that God would conquer Canaan, Moses' intercession again stresses what the nations will think of him (Num. 14:13–16; Deut. 9:28).

We could keep multiplying the terms on which we focus and tracing the same combination of status *and* function for God's people. As well as being God's 'treasured possession', Israel is identified as his 'inheritance' (*naḥālâ*) and the like.[9] The language is found when God makes optimistic plans under the old covenant (e.g. Exod. 6:6–8; Lev. 26:9–13) – and even when prospects under the old covenant are pessimistic (Deut. 32:9 in the light of 31:19–22). The special relationship underpins a range of intercessions (Deut. 9:25–29; 1 Kgs 8:50–51; Joel 2:17). And Yahweh can claim all nations as his 'inheritance' (Ps. 82:8), a point poetically and powerfully brought home in the midst of Israel's eighth-century geopolitical upheaval with the promise that archenemies Assyria and Egypt will join Judah as God's people, his handiwork, his inheritance (Isa. 19:25). Such relational language is thus revived in hope for the new covenant and God's new-covenant people (esp. various references in Jeremiah and Zechariah).

All of this clarification follows Exodus 19:6 canonically but, as we noted in chapter 3, Exodus is authored or compiled alongside the rest of the Pentateuch. All these textual connections are admissible in understanding the key verse. We can retain confidence that God has missiological intentions for Israel even as he pronounces their privileged status. Priestly language appears to capture both senses, even if we allow that Israel's holy status may be to the fore. We can thus appreciate why the comments of John Durham (1987: 263) are frequently quoted, capturing well God's intent for his people in this seminal commission:

---

[9] Covering a range of points in Israel's history, see Exod. 34:9; Deut. 4:20; 9:26, 29; 1 Kgs 8:52–53; Pss 28:9; 33:12; 74:2; 94:5, 14; 106:40; Isa. 63:17; Jer. 10:16 // 51:19; Joel 2:17; 3:2; Mic. 7:18. Additional constructions include Israel as Yahweh's 'portion' (Deut. 32:9) and, quite simply and powerfully, as 'my people' (e.g. Exod. 6:7; Lev. 26:12; Jer. 7:23; 11:14; 24:7; 30:22; 31:33; Ezek. 11:20; Zech. 2:11; 8:8; 13:9). Some of the points here are derived from Wright 1997.

Israel as a 'holy people' . . . are to be a people set apart, different from all other people by what they are and are becoming – a display-people, a showcase to the world of how being in covenant with Yahweh changes a people.

Israel's priestly performance

As we come to assess Israel's priestly performance among the nations, we can use Williamson's summary (2008: 105) of Exodus 19:5–6 as something of a benchmark:

> Israel was a nation like no other; Israel was to be a holy nation, a nation set apart for God, living *among* the nations yet distinct *from* the nations – if you like, a nation *in* the world, but not *of* the world. Israel was to be a nation reflecting God's value system, modelling God's standards of justice by living according to God's code of ethics, a nation demonstrating God's paradigm for life and society.

Of course there are many ways to evaluate Israel's performance, and again the ensuing survey is selective and representative.

Some promising glimpses

After Moses recommissions the next generation and they advance into Canaan, we find several promising examples where Yahweh's reputation accompanies his people. Although Israel is never God's ideal son who perfectly broadcasts God's fame, there are glimpses that it can get things right.

Even as the nation breaches the Promised Land, Rahab in Jericho volunteers news of Yahweh's fame to Joshua's two spies (Josh. 2:9–11). She admits that 'terror has fallen on us', that 'all dwelling in the land have melted away before you' (notions already anticipated in Exod. 15:14–16; 23:27). Yahweh's work through his people is so prominent that Rahab can confess that 'Yahweh your God is God in heaven above and on earth below.'

Once the land is conquered and the monarchy eventually established, fame continues to be attributed to Israel's deity. When Israel is operating at peak religious and political efficiency, neighbouring monarchs honour Yahweh by name (1 Kgs 5:7; 10:9). We might suspect that this is only polite diplomacy, yet an intervening prayer from Solomon suggests otherwise (8:41–43). He acknowledges that foreigners will flock to Jerusalem and its temple in response to the spread of Yahweh's reputation, and prays that God will answer their prayers 'so that all the peoples of the earth will know your name, to fear you as do your people Israel' (and to recognize Yahweh's connection with the Jerusalem temple being dedicated at this time). Several of the psalms are likewise concerned that Yahweh's reputation be known throughout the earth, most notably Psalms 67, 96 and 117 (Mascarenhas 2005). And, whether or not we see Jonah as evidence of an active outward mission (as does Kaiser 2012), Jonah's story clearly serves to remind its Jewish readers of God's international sympathies. Other prophets are not shy in reminding Israel of Yahweh's quest for worldwide fame (a very short sample includes Isa. 2:1–4 [= Mic. 4:1–3]; 24:14–16; 49:1–7; Zech. 8:20–23; Mal. 1:11).

Some negative outcomes

Jonah's story seems addressed to readers who have started to scorn God's international sympathies.[10] Even if Jonah is not a direct corrective, other writing prophets are frustrated when Israel fails to meet the priestly mandate for which God commissioned them in Exodus.

This commission remains important throughout Israel's chequered history. Stuart's commentaries (e.g. 1987; 1989; 1998) make a point of the prophets as 'covenant enforcement mediators' (as he calls them in Fee and Stuart 2014: 190–192). The prophets are not composing new morals and expectations, but calling Israel back to Yahweh's longstanding expectations by recalling the covenant's promised blessings and curses, reaffirming that compliance means Yahweh's name will be known and revered.

This is certainly the sentiment of Amos 3:1–2. As the prophet turns to a fresh complaint, he expounds Israel's failure to embody their privileged status:

> Hear this word that Yahweh has spoken against you, people of Israel, against the whole family I brought up out of the land of Egypt:
> > 'You only have I known
> > out of all the families of the earth;
> > therefore I will punish you
> > for all your sins.'

---

[10] Surveys like those of Alexander (1988: 81–91) and Bruckner (2004: 17–25) warn us against oversimplifying the book's purpose. It is not solely or even primarily concerned with Israel's reactions to *all* Gentile nations or a call to evangelize them.

In the preceding chapters, God has condemned the surrounding nations (and Judah and Israel) for various overt misdemeanours. Here in Amos 3 condemnation is incurred by the Israelites for failing to live up to their unique covenant calling. Israel has been 'known' or chosen in a unique sense, and thus their accountability is equally magnified. The condemnation here is even more powerful if it introduces the remainder of the book and the prophet's indictments (D. A. Hubbard 1989: 147). Israel's failure to be a priestly nation to the surrounding nations is further highlighted when Amos invites such nations to witness the violence and destruction that *Israel* harbours (3:9–10). Familiar enemies, the Philistines and Egyptians, are summoned to confirm – and perhaps even to be repulsed by – the depths of Israel's depravity.

A similar pattern can be found in the longer and more complex message of Ezekiel. To pick out but one significant passage, Ezekiel 36:20–23 lambasts the Israelites for the influence their behaviour has had on Yahweh's reputation. Four times in four verses he is concerned that 'my holy name' has been 'profaned among the nations'. We must recognize that this is the cultic language of the tabernacle and its priests; 'to make/pronounce profane' (*ḥll*) is the opposite of 'to make/ pronounce holy' (*qdš*). Just as Ezekiel the priest has singled out vocational priests for not adhering to the expectations of Leviticus (Lev. 10:10–11 ← Ezek. 22:26), so his complaint here in 36:20–23 echoes the instructions of Leviticus concerning corporate priesthood. The Israelites had been instructed to avoid conduct that profanes Yahweh's name (Lev. 18:21; 19:12; 20:3), as had Israel's priests (Lev. 22:2, 32, the bookends of a chapter concerned with 'holy/sacred' offerings 'consecrated' to Yahweh and his 'holy' name, so that he will be acknowledged as 'holy'). It is from such concerns that Leviticus 17 – 27 is regularly titled 'the Holiness Code'. Similar concerns for the profaning of Yahweh and his name can be found elsewhere in Ezekiel and the prophets (Isa. 48:11; Jer. 34:16; Ezek. 13:19; 20:9, 14, 22, 39; 39:7; Amos 2:7).[11]

It is the people's behaviour (Ezek. 36:16–19) that has led to their present exile, and the present exile gives the Gentile nations opportunity to mock the Israelites and their God. Many of Yahweh's actions have the goal that 'they will know that I am Yahweh', whether Yahweh's actions engender punishment or restoration, whether the

---

[11] Rooker (2000: 140) helpfully observes that other pagan religions would not call their priests to alter their ethical behaviour.

object of those actions is Israel or the nations, and whether the bene-ficiaries – those who will know Yahweh better – are Israelites or Gentiles. All God's actions are driven by concern for his own reputation.[12] Other hints might be found throughout the prophets. Although Hosea 4:6 gives the impression of condemning the class of individual priests, it is certainly possible to read the verse as a rejection of Israel *as a nation* and a suspension of their *corporate* priestly status (so McComiskey 1992: 60–61). We might also wonder if Hosea 5 continues the tirade against the privileged nation as a whole when the dispute opens with a threefold call for the attention of 'you priests . . . you Israelites . . . royal house' (NIV, NJPS, CSB).[13]

Some future hopes

After the northern kingdom is all but wiped out and the southern kingdom carted off to exile, the latter chapters of Isaiah envisage something of the restoration that God has planned for his people. Some of these plans hint at a restoration of their priestly ministry – and the incorporation of others into that ministry.

There may be muted hints of a restored corporate priesthood in Isaiah 40 – 55. It is sometimes noted that *sĕgullâ* language is paired, at least in other ancient Semitic languages, with terms concerned with 'servants' and 'serving' (e.g. Davies 2004: 53–54; V. P. Hamilton 2011: 303). In turn, such studies and many others (e.g. Schultz 1997) observe the vast range of meanings of the 'serve' word group (Hebr. *'bd*): from an abject slave through to an honoured dignitary. So it is significant that the Bible itself can link *sĕgullâ* and *'ebed* in Ecclesiastes 2:7–8 and Malachi 3:17; the *'ebed* here holds an honoured position. When Israel is cast as Yahweh's 'servant' (*'ebed*) in Isaiah, and as God coaxes his treasured people out of exile and towards restoration, we might speculate that this is a tacit result of his ongoing commitment to them

---

[12] The eight resulting combinations of actions–objects–beneficiaries (of which only five occur) are explored in Williams 1998 and summarized in Wright 2001: 268–272. Williams highlights the less obvious combination: that Israel's delivery can be for the benefit of the onlooking nations (Ezek. 36:23; 39:7, verses full of 'profane' and 'holy' language). We might also note that Yahweh himself can 'profane' – deconsecrate, 'unholify' – his own sanctuary (Ezek. 7:22; 24:21) or his holy people (Isa. 43:28; 47:6; Lam. 2:2; Ps. 89:39) (see O'Kennedy 1997: 147–149).
[13] While I am yet to find this parallelism defended, it would resolve the kinds of tensions summarized in Kwakkel 2011. Certainly one notices similar parallelism in Ps. 115:12–13 ('us' / 'house of Israel' / 'house of Aaron' / 'those who fear Yahweh') and in Ps. 135:19–20 ('house of Israel' / 'house of Aaron' / 'house of Levi' / 'you who fear him [Yahweh]').

and a recognition of their persistent status in his eyes. This accords well with the significant priestly responsibilities that God seeks to restore in the final division of the book.

Isaiah 56:1–8 suggests that membership within Israel will be even more inclusive than in the past. Foreigners committed to Yahweh will not be 'differentiated' (*bdl*) from his people and will also be able to minister to him. Eunuchs have previously been banned from temple service if not also from the worshipping community (Lev. 21:20; Deut. 23:1). Yet Isaiah foreshadows a time when such eunuchs will be hugely honoured within the temple. Such outcasts are depicted as bringing acceptable offerings and sacrifices to God's altar. Looking at the cultic terminology here, Terence Fretheim (1997: 256) overtly wonders if 'something approaching the "priesthood of all believers" may be entailed in this vision of the future'. And it should not be lost on us that Jesus cites this passage at the moment he pronounces defunct the (second) Jerusalem temple and brings its operation to a grinding halt (Mark 11:15–18; pars.).[14]

Isaiah 61 likewise delights at God's future restoration of cultic worship, again with the participation of outsiders. The surrounding verses flow together, with 61:1–3 familiar in Christian circles and 61:5–6 of most immediate relevance to us:

> Strangers will stand and shepherd your flock;
>> foreigners will be your farmers and your vinedressers.
> But you will be called priests of Yahweh,
>> said to be ministers of our God;
> you will consume the wealth of the nations
>> and in their glory you will boast.

Here, at the high point of Isaiah 56 – 66 (see below), we find the repeated message that any advantage enjoyed by the nations will come from their recognition and servitude of Israel. Where 56:1–8 shocks its readers by presenting these foreigners on a par with God's people, 61:5 presents the foreigners as mere assistants. It is true that the nations benefit from Israel's overflow and not independently apart from Israel (Abernethy 2016: 193–196). And this may be the rhetorical point of the present chapter, addressed to Israelites. 'Priests'

---

[14] G. V. Smith (2009: 525–526) further explores how Isa. 56 is connected with what precedes: 'In many ways chap. 56 is an expansion of the offer of salvation introduced in chap. 55, specifying how two groups of people (and by implication all other non-Israelites) will be integrated into normal worship practices in the future.'

here may be an honorific, as we considered above for 2 Samuel 8:18. Nonetheless, the opening pericope of Isaiah's division has already confirmed – twice – that these foreigners are those 'joined to Yahweh' (56:3, 6) (Childs 2001: 457, 459). So the grand claims of 61:6 must be read in that light. Israel will once again be identified as God's 'priests' and 'ministers' in close association with their role in joining members of the Gentile nations to Yahweh. These titles may even be acclaimed of Israel *by* the converted Gentiles in praise of 'our' God (Oswalt 1998: 571–572).[15]

The closing paragraphs of Isaiah retain the inclusive tone. In 66:18–21 we read of God's remaining concerned to proclaim his glory worldwide and to gather together people from all nations and languages. The ensuing influx of nations is described in cultic terms; Zion is cast as the cultic centre of God's universal mission. The ethnic identity of the centrifugal missionaries in 66:19 is unclear. It may well include survivors of the nations (Begg 1999: 52–54)! Even if this is too eager, our exploration of Israel as God's international mediators is only enhanced if it proves to be Israel's survivors filling the proclamatory role (Oswalt 1998: 688–689). From the freshly consecrated Gentiles who flock to Zion, Yahweh 'will take some of them as priests, as Levites' as the prophet envisages a universal (though not universalistic) worship of Yahweh (66:23). Interpreters are jubilant at both the means and the outcome of this mission. 'This is the only unequivocally centrifugal articulation of mission in the Old Testament' (Wright 2006: 488). There are then two significant corollaries for our focus on Israel's priesthood. We see again that 'the election of Israel is not for Israel but for the world' (Oswalt 2003: 697). And Israel's priestly mission is self-replicating; certainly in 66:21 and probably also in 66:19, converts from the pagan nations will be invited to join this sacred ministry.

These three highlights from Isaiah 56 – 66 could be probed ever deeper, but three matters are most pertinent for us. First, we find concrete examples of Israel described as behaving as a nation of priests on behalf of other nations. As throughout Isaiah, the impression is that Israel is successful in broadcasting the fame of Yahweh such that other nations flock to Zion (e.g. 2:1–4). These nations bring their praises and their sacrifices (60:6–7), and the implication of Israel

---

[15] G. V. Smith (2009: 638) takes the difficult last clause of 61:6 as a further description of Israel's priestly behaviour. We might then translate it 'and you will get changed into their glorious (vestments)', linking the vestments with the Gentiles.

being called 'priests of Yahweh' and 'ministers of our God' (61:6) is that the nations recognize Israel's mediatorial role. Perhaps Israel is even portrayed in the priestly role of facilitating those sacrifices on the nations' behalf (Begg 1999: 50–51).

The second matter of significance is that the three passages highlighted in this closing division of Isaiah are not unrelated. Although precise boundaries and emphases remain debated, there is general acceptance of an intentional chiastic structure that pairs 56:1–8 and 66:18–24 as bookends, with some or all of chapters 60 – 62 highlighted in the centre (Oswalt 1998: 464–465; Lessing 2014: 31–35). Even if a chiasm is unsupported, it is clear that the themes are strongly repetitive and strategically placed. Israel is to bring the nations to Yahweh and the nations will enthusiastically join in ministering to him. John Oswalt (1998: 571–572) writes passionately and extensively about the implications for Israel's priesthood and its prominence in Isaiah, *part* of which reads:

> Israel's exalted position is to be one not of privilege but of responsibility. As a *priest* is to be a mediator between humans and God, assisting humans in their worship of God, and teaching humans the ways of God, Israel is to be a priest to the nations. This understanding of Israel's calling and function has been explicit in the book [of Isaiah] since ch. 2, and is fundamental to a correct understanding of its structure and function.

Third and less prominently to this point in biblical revelation, we catch a glimpse that the nations themselves will be adopted into God's corporate priestly ministry.

Even where priestly responsibilities are not overtly mentioned, we might speculate confidently about Israel's restoration to this kind of ministry among the wider nations and the Gentiles' subsequent incorporation into that ministry. Amos 9:11–15 assures Israel that God will restore David's fallen 'booth', and the promise refers as much to the entire nation as to their Davidic leadership (G. V. Smith 1998: 378–379; Goswell 2011). One goal of this restoration is 'so that they may possess . . . all the nations who are called by my name'. The early church certainly interprets here God's favour towards the Gentiles, as recorded at the Jerusalem Council in Acts 15:14–17. And we have already noted the international flocking to Zion expected in oracles such as Zechariah 8:20–23. Similar oracles punctuate that prophet's work. Like other prophets, Zechariah envisages a time when repentant

Gentiles must (on pain of further punishment) join Israel to 'worship the King, the LORD of hosts' (Zech. 14:16–19). The following verses, which close his book, take a number of (high) priestly images – especially the inscription 'Holy to Yahweh' (cf. Exod. 28:36) – and now apply them and their holiness to this multi-ethnic congregation (Zech. 14:20–21) (Stuart 2006: 616)! A consistent message runs through the prophets from among the earliest of their number to among their latest.

Indeed, at this point we might observe that God's priestly people have probably *always* possessed something of a multicultural nature. When we read of 'the motley collection of refugees from Egypt' (France 1998: 36) we might think it a claim about their journey-weary socioeconomic condition. But Stuart (2006: 303–304) in particular reminds us of Exodus 12:38: the wilderness generation with whom God covenants at Sinai includes 'an ethnically diverse crowd' (HCSB). Already, from the formation of Israel, other nationalities are being blessed by their association with God's chosen people, and there is no indication that they were excluded from God's commissioning of his corporate kingdom of priests.

Thus a biblical theology of Israel's priesthood is not dissimilar to many other studies of Israel's obedience to God's expectations. We can sense God's superlative intentions for his people, catch the occasional promising glimpse of early steps towards success, observe far more frequently Israel's inability under the old covenant to match God's intentions, and yet hear God continue to echo these intentions with the assurance that one day they will be met. From our perspective firmly in the midst of God's new-covenant era, we can certainly see this eschatological trajectory playing out more successfully in the New Testament. We return shortly in chapter 7 to continue the trajectory.

The intersection of individual and corporate priesthoods

In all this, we should acknowledge that our treatment of Israel as a corporate priesthood intersects with our survey of individual vocational priests. Yes, I have been distinguishing between the two, using different adjectives and providing distinct chapters. Yet we have already noted the positive parallels between the priestly commissions of Israel and of Aaron. Neither is it hard to see that the failure of Israel's individual Aaronic priests is a major factor in Israel's national failure to live as a priestly people.

It is certainly customary to berate the Levitical priesthood for skimping on their vocational responsibilities. In chapter 4 we have already surveyed various priestly failures, and the links with Israel's corporate shortcomings are not difficult to find. Among the earliest writing prophets, Hosea 4 is perhaps clearest in forging those links, railing against missed 'knowledge' (*da'at*). The Israelites are condemned because 'there is no faithfulness, no covenant loyalty, no knowledge of God in the land' (4:1) and hence, famously, 'my people are destroyed for lack of knowledge' (4:6). The prophet immediately turns on the priests:

> Because you have rejected knowledge,
>   I also reject you as my priests;
> because you have ignored the law [*tôrâ*] of your God . . .
>
> (4:6 NIV)

Andrew Dearman (2010: 158) joins the dots transparently: 'The failure of the priesthood is linked directly to that of the people . . . The priesthood failed in their task as mediators of divine instruction, and the ripple effect permeates the community.' God's positive expectations are reiterated at the end of the Old Testament, where, in correcting wayward priests, Malachi 2:7 insists that 'the lips of a priest should guard knowledge [*da'at*] and people should seek instruction [*tôrâ*] from his mouth, for he is the messenger of the LORD of hosts'.

We might even ponder if the old-covenant priesthood was *expected* to fall short. We might develop the kinds of parallels that permeate biblical theology:

- God seems intent to train his people through a series of stages, just as children progress from tricycles to training wheels to bicycles (and even to unicycles). In New Testament terms, the Old Testament sketches out a shadow of the greater realities to come (Col. 2:17; Heb. 10:1).
- The tabernacle for God's dwelling was a visible, small-scale model of God's dwelling (Heb. 8:5). It was a temporary instantiation, to be replaced by God indwelling his gathered new-covenant people (with an even more perfect dwelling envisaged for the future) (Beale 2004).
- The old (Sinai) covenant and its law served as a formative guardian until God's people attained maturity (e.g. Gal. 3:23 – 4:7). On its

own it could never facilitate observance and a new covenant would succeed it (esp. Jer. 31:31–34; Ezek. 36:24–27).[16]

- The old-covenant sacrifices effected a degree of ritual cleanness that permitted God's old-covenant dwelling among his people. While unprecedented among the nations and greatly celebrated, these would be replaced by one better sacrifice (Heb. 9:11 – 10:18).

- In similar vein, Hebrews celebrates the value of a human priesthood, but recognizes that such priests (and thus their dependent worshippers) are impeded by their own sinfulness and mortal lifespans – shortcomings from which Jesus is exempt (Heb. 7:23–28).

We are told that the tabernacle and the law were temporary devices by which God trained his people for their future counterparts. The sacrificial emphasis pervading the New Testament (e.g. John 1:29; 19:31–37; 1 Cor. 5:7; Hebrews; 1 Pet. 1:19; Rev. 5:6) strongly suggests that the sacrificial system was another intentionally prospective part of this training regime (cf. G. A. Cole 2009: 94–98). So it is safe to consider that the vocational priesthood of Aaron and his descendants was likewise preparatory for the high priesthood of Jesus. We ought not to expect that the Old Testament priesthood, as a shadow of a greater coming reality, would be any more permanent or perfect than the other temporary models.

If the vocational ministry of individual priests was never perfect under the old covenant and contributed to the failure of Israel's corporate priesthood, what does the superior priestly ministry of Jesus Christ contribute to the status and function of his new-covenant people? It is to corporate Christians that we now turn.

---

[16] We have already noted the pessimism of Barker (2004), who also champions Yahweh's faithfulness to the covenant. On the vexed issue of the NT's mixed view of the old covenant, especially in the writings of the Pharisee-turned-apostle Paul, see Rosner 2013.

Chapter Seven

The church's priestly commission

While we need to be nuanced in our phrasing and in any ensuing application, it would seem that the old covenant was expected, even designed, to fall short. So it is little surprise that the vocational priesthood *within* Israel faltered and that, in turn, the corporate priesthood *of* Israel stumbled. Such shortcomings do not mean that these institutions were intrinsically bad; they simply were not as complete as their successors under the new covenant.

What then of the corporate priesthood? Certainly Israel was not immediately and universally a blessing to the nations. Despite some notable successes, we have observed too many instances where Yahweh's name was *profaned* among the nations because of his people. As we turn to the New Testament, we find exactly the same kinds of continuity and discontinuity concerning the corporate priesthood of God's people as we do concerning matters of tabernacle, covenant and sacrifice. We should be encouraged that 'the notion of Israel as a corporate royal-priestly entity is not a passing metaphor, but represents a richer and more sustained ideology which has left its mark at a number of places within the Hebrew Bible and beyond' (Davies 2004: 16).

Proclamatory priesthood in 1 Peter

There are several relevant passages in the New Testament. A number of these trace the church as the replacement for the old-covenant tabernacle or temple; at least in geospatial terms, God's presence still dwells amidst the people of God but now without a physical building (e.g. Rom. 8:9–11; 1 Cor. 3:9–17; 6:19; 2 Cor. 6:16–18; Eph. 2:19–22).[1]

---

[1] Further references name 'the house(hold) of God' (e.g. 1 Tim. 3:15; Heb. 3:6; 1 Pet. 4:17), but this may be pursuing a different OT angle (e.g. Exod. 16:31; Num. 12:7; 2 Kgs 17:21; Jer. 12:7; 31:31; Amos 5:25; 9:11). Of course, NT authors can reach similar theological conclusions without using overt architectural language. Heil (1997: 76, 99) demonstrates 'that the Christian community replaces the temple in Mark', obediently becoming 'the "building" of God's communal household of prayer and authentic worship inclusive of all peoples'.

The same architectural imagery is raised in 1 Peter 2. Throughout the letter, Jesus is a model to be emulated (2:18–25; 3:8–18; 4:1–6; cf. 1:15–16) (Smalley 1961). The phrases of 2:21 are both rich and rare, where the outcome of Christ's suffering is described twice using two specialized terms for the example he left (Davids 1990: 110; Forbes 2014: 90). Believers are to bear up under unjust suffering because

Christ suffered for you,
leaving you a *template/stencil*
so that you might follow in his *footsteps*.

Peter then furnishes some specific elements of Jesus' placid suffering.

Peter's cultic language

Jesus leads not only in the path of suffering but also in the purpose of ministry. Earlier in the same chapter, Peter praises him as 'a living stone – by people rejected but, to God, selected and significant' (2:4). Peter soon reinforces his stone imagery by thrice citing the Old Testament, with Isaiah 28:16 confirming that this stone is 'a selected and significant cornerstone' laid by the Lord Yahweh (even if it is rejected by others and offensive to them). It is amidst these 'stone' verses that the centre of Peter's declaration in 2:4–8 is enshrined: his readers too are like living stones and are being built into a spiritual house.[2]

Of course there is much to explore in the house imagery itself. Does Peter choose 'house' language, rather than Paul's 'temple' terminology, because 'house' can refer not only to the building but also to God's 'family' (as at 4:17 NIRV, NCV) (Jobes 2005: 150)? Certainly 1 Peter 2 is central to a biblical theology of where God dwells among his people (e.g. Beale 2004). The more literal buildings in the Old Testament that were seen to house God's localized presence are now replaced by a spiritual house(hold).

More pressing is the observation that Peter himself overlays the static, building metaphor with a more dynamic, functional image. To the language of stones and houses he adds the language of priesthood and sacrifices. We can even argue, from narrower grammar and broader

---

[2] Although important, our current exploration need not determine whether Peter's participles (2:4–5) – the primary verbs here – are better interpreted as more indicative (so the vast majority of versions and commentators) or with an imperatival bent (RSV/ NRSV, NEB/REB, NAB, GNB, NCV). Regardless of the grammar, Gupta (2009) demonstrates how 2:1–10 and other metaphorical passages are designed to influence Peter's readers.

context, that the dramatic architectural language is itself surpassed by Peter's focus on the house's personnel and their activities.

At the grammatical level, the spiritual house is but a precursor to the spiritual priesthood. The point is illustrated well by Thomas Schreiner (2003: 105–106; cf. Forbes 2014: 62). The traditional presentation of 2:5 reads this way:

> You also, as living stones,
> are being built up
> *[into]* a spiritual house,
> *to be* a holy priesthood . . .

Paying attention to the italicized prepositions, we can reword (and reorder) the verse to make its point even clearer:

> You also, as living stones,
> *[already]* a spiritual house,
> are being built up
> *into* a holy priesthood . . .

The difference is subtle and it is not crucial to defend one reading over the other. Both recognize that it is Christians' priesthood, not their architecture, that is the climax of Peter's verbal portrait.

This interim climax is supported by Peter's wider message. Verse 5 adds further purpose to God's craftsmanship: 'You also . . . are being built up into a holy priesthood, *in order* to offer spiritual sacrifices.' These sacrifices are further described as being 'acceptable to God through Jesus Christ'. After consolidating his claims about Jesus in 2:6–8, Peter once again promotes his readers' priesthood. The overall flow of his presentation is hampered in many English Bibles, especially where a paragraph break introduces 2:9. The break was commonly omitted in the AV/KJV and once again is omitted in very recent versions such as the NET and LEB; this omission better preserves the flow of Peter's argument:

2:4	you come to *Jesus* (a living stone)
	rejected by people
	selected and significant to God
2:5	and *you* (like living stones, a spiritual house)
	are being built up into a holy priesthood
	to offer acceptable spiritual sacrifices

2:6-8   Scripture confirms *Jesus*
           as a selected and significant cornerstone
           who was also rejected
2:9-10   but *you* are a royal priesthood
           to declare his praises
           (illustrated by Scripture)

Peter oscillates Jesus–readers–Jesus–readers. Jesus is repeatedly a stone that earns a polarized reception. Peter's readers are repeatedly a special priesthood in God's service. We can see that 2:5 and 2:9 inform each other and that 2:9–10 forms the climax of 2:4–10 (cf. France 1998).

The importance of 2:9–10 is all the more dramatic when the language is drawn substantially from Exodus 19:5–6. We can summarize the detail available elsewhere (e.g. Carson 2007). Peter first describes his readers as 'a chosen race', in wording probably derived from Isaiah 43:20. The second and third descriptions come directly from Exodus LXX: 'a royal priesthood, a holy nation'. The fourth phrase, 'a people for possessing', unmistakeably evokes the 'treasured possession' that heads the Sinai invitation.[3] Peter is constructing a rich identity of the people of God. He has drawn from the foundational commission of Exodus 19:5–6, where God forms a people for himself after the exodus from Egyptian slavery. Peter has also integrated sentiments from Isaiah 43:20–21, where Yahweh cajoles his chosen people towards a new exodus out of Babylonian exile. (Peter perhaps also draws from yet another anticipatory promise in Mal. 3:17–18.) The Greek form of Isaiah speaks of 'my chosen race, my people, whom I possessed/acquired to detail my praiseworthy acts'. And Peter appends much of that same purpose for God's new-covenant people: 'so that you might declare [his] praiseworthy acts'. According to the parallel structure above, this purpose in 2:9 fleshes out what it means 'to offer acceptable sacrifices' in 2:5. Peter then details God's praiseworthy acts ('who called you out of darkness into his marvellous light') and, *still* not satisfied with the superlative identity and work to which God has called his new-covenant believers, Peter further portrays them in terms of the restoration foreshadowed by Hosea. That prophet had illustrated

---

[3] Throughout the LXX, several different Gk words translate Hebr. *sĕgullâ*, the controlling term in Exod. 19:5–6. Peter's exact phrase (*[eis] peripoiēsin*) is found in Mal. 3:17, another – and anticipatory – use of *sĕgullâ*. The corresponding Gk verb (in the form *peripoiēsamen*) occurs in Isa. 43:21 LXX, from which Peter has already drawn and will draw again immediately.

Israel's adultery through his own disastrous marriage. Hosea and Gomer's second and third children were named at birth Lo-Ruhamah, 'not shown mercy', and Lo-Ammi, 'not my people' (Hos. 1:6–9). But a time would come when the wayward family would be restored and these children would be renamed 'my people' and 'shown mercy' and be beyond counting (1:10 – 2:1). Hosea 2 narrates how God would woo his bride again, climaxing with the same reversals (2:23). Peter draws from the (Greek) language of these reversals as he further extols God's saving acts.

Peter's cultic application

I have laboured the details of 1 Peter 2:4–10 because they craft a dramatic contribution to the identity and activity of God's priestly people. This identity and its consequences should be unpacked carefully.

First, we might rehearse God's careful and persistent plan to choose a people for himself. Again we notice the importance of the temporal axis as biblical history and revelation unfold. After the creation of a (priestly) humanity and their breach of relationship, God planned to reclaim his universal fame. He started small, choosing one man (Abram) and his family, though already we glimpse God's intention to bless all the families of the earth (Gen. 12:1–3). God viewed his people as his firstborn son, whom he rescued from slavery (Exod. 4:22–23). These redeemed people were invited into a formal covenant, whereby they would be Yahweh's treasured possession – a kingdom of priests and a holy nation (Exod. 19:3–6). Even though their covenant faithfulness and priestly ministry were far from exemplary and they ended up in remedial exile, Yahweh offered them a second exodus (esp. Isa. 40 – 55), a fresh marriage (esp. Hos. 1 – 3), a new covenant (esp. Jer. 31:31–34) and a renewed priestly mandate (Isa. 56 – 66). This restoration did not appear to be completed with Israel's return from exile in the Old Testament, and research continues apace into how new-exodus motifs are continued in the New Testament.[4]

Second, the New Testament restoration accelerated God's blessing of all nations through Israel. Much to the surprise of the early church, Gentiles were accorded the status and blessings of God's chosen people. Peter celebrates this extension of God's election, ascribing to

---

[4] Major monographs such as Watts 1997 (on Mark), Brunson 2003 (John), Pao 2000 (Acts) and R. J. Morales 2010 (Galatians) are among the many studies surveyed in D. L. Smith 2016.

his Gentile readers the same status and mandate as God's first covenant people. In the short compass of 2:4–10, Peter encapsulates themes that range throughout the New Testament. We might note how Paul likewise cites Hosea 1:10 and 2:23 in Romans 9:23–28, to demonstrate that God's pre-prepared objects of mercy are called 'not only from the Jews but also from the Gentiles'.

Third, Peter uses this priestly identity in much the same way that we have seen it used of individual vocational priests and of corporate Israel. In a structure widely accepted, Peter builds up the identity of God's people (1:1 – 2:10) before spending much of his letter in direct instruction (2:11 – 4:11). Rhetorically, '2:11 marks a shift from the identity of God's people to their consequent responsibility in a hostile world' (Michaels 1988: xxxv) and 2:11–12 forms the executive summary of all the ensuing directives. What Christopher Wright (2006: 256) said of the Israelites in Exodus 19 can be applied verbatim to Christian believers in 1 Peter: 'They have a role that matches their status. The *status* is to be a special treasured possession. The *role* is to be a priestly and holy community in the midst of the nations.'

Fourth, in terms of his own detail, Peter does not spell out an obviously cultic series of behaviours for his priestly readers. He is certainly concerned with his readers' special status, repeatedly invoking their 'election' and 'holiness' before God (1:1–2, 15–16; 2:5, 9; 3:5, 15) and drawing from the Holiness Code in Leviticus 17 – 27 and its central command in Leviticus 19:2. He does not catalogue a list of verbally mediating roles, such as inviting his readers to intercede for their persecutors (though that can be found elsewhere in the NT). We have seen the important call in the priestly verses 'to offer spiritual sacrifices to God' (2:5), which is elaborated as 'declaring his praiseworthy acts' (2:9). The connection is readily recognized by many, such as Paul Achtemeier (1996: 157–158), who adds a string of confirming parallels from Psalms and the prophets. We should also observe that Peter's ensuing directives are focused on submissive, non-retaliatory and often non-verbal *behavioural* responses to persecution; Karen Jobes (2005: 167) gives the controlling commands in 2:11–12 the title 'Lifestyle Evangelism'. Nonetheless, such behavioural evangelism is intended to elicit the nations' own praises of God (2:12; 3:1–2; 4:11), and ensuing speaking opportunities should also be capitalized upon (3:15; 4:11).[5]

---

[5] Beale (2004: 249, 331) detects traces of Ps. 92:12–15 in 1 Pet. 2:9–10 (and in 1 Cor. 3). The psalm champions the praising of Yahweh and his covenant loyalty, and the closing paragraph on which Beale focuses speaks of 'the righteous' who are 'planted in the house of Yahweh' in order 'to disclose that Yahweh is upright'. Gupta (2009: 75)

More than any other passage, 1 Peter 2:4–10 furnishes contemporary Christian believers with an overt sense of what it means to be a corporate priesthood serving God. It continues the biblical-theological trajectory begun in the Old Testament, and my concluding reflections in chapter 8 on application rely substantially on Peter's key contribution.

Regal priesthood in Revelation

The next most overt New Testament passages concerning corporate Christian priesthood are found in Revelation. Three passages spread across the book name Christian believers as priests:

> To him who loves us and has freed us from our sins by his blood – indeed, he has made us to be a kingdom, priests for his God and Father – to him be the glory . . . (Rev. 1:5–6)[6]

> 'You are worthy . . .
> because you were slain and you bought, for God,
> by your blood
> people from every tribe and language
> and people and nation
> and you have made them, for our God,
> a kingdom and priests
> and they will reign upon the earth.'
> (Rev. 5:9–10)

> Blessed and holy is the one who has a share in the first resurrection. Over these the second death has no authority, but they will be priests of God and of Christ and will reign with him for a thousand years. (Rev. 20:6)

A range of other passages might hint at priestly connections (such as those compiled by Elgvin [2009]), but many are more circumstantial or corroborating rather than independently convincing. Especially

---

likewise concludes that Peter's rhetoric is intended to spur on his readers to 'mediation and witness'.

[6] The interjecting nature of the 'kingdom, priests' clause (cf. NASB) is supported by the change of verb mood and a resumptive pronoun afterwards. Aune (1997: 42) confirms 'an independent clause . . . in order to place great emphasis on this statement' (despite complaining about its 'impossible' Greek).

the three overt mentions of believers as priests can be approached using basic questions: who, what, when and where?

Who constitutes God's new priesthood?

The 'new song' of 5:9–10 is extremely explicit, identifying an international cohort. This is entirely consistent with the expectations developed throughout the Old Testament: God's chosen people will incorporate outsiders, to the point where Isaiah foresees a time when outcasts and Gentiles are overtly counted as not only living *among* God's priests but *as* God's priests.[7]

Of course, this adds further praise for the work of Jesus, whose definitive purchase of people from all races brings to fulfilment the expectations outlined in passages such as Exodus 19:6 and Isaiah 61:6. As throughout 1 Peter, God's promises to and expectations of his old-covenant people are extended to Christian believers of all backgrounds. These two observations are simple to write and to read – but profound in their implications for Christian identity and for biblical theology!

Revelation constitutes many Christians' vision of the eternal future, if not also partly of the present. So such international imagery and its profound implications influence how the book is read. Gregory Stevenson (2001: 240) reminds us of the prominent placement of the first mention of believer-priests and the significance of this theme for the whole book: 'Revelation thereby establishes from the outset (1:6) that the Christians are now the people of God and heirs of the covenant promises . . . who, as priests, have access to God.' Although not identical to 1 Peter, already we find important synergies.

What does this priesthood accomplish?

Apart from the general sense of access to God, what it means to be such a priest is not especially clear within Revelation. Each of the three overt passages above (Rev. 1:5–6; 5:9–10; 20:6) ties together 'priests' and ruling language ('kingdom' [*basileia*] and 'reign' [*basileuō*] both derive from the same Greek word group). The language of

---

[7] Studies have commonly sourced the 'every tribe' phrase in Rev. 5:9 from Daniel (e.g. Aune 1997: 361; Beale 1999: 359–360). The connection with Exod. 19:5–6 is even more profound if this is an adaptation of the phrase *there* (Bauckham 1993: 327; Osborne 2002: 260–261), and especially if, as we noted earlier, the Exodus phrase originally bore a sense of Israel's exclusive election *instead of* the wider nations.

kingship echoes throughout the book, commonly understood to be set in and against the increasingly oppressive Roman Empire. John's climactic title when introducing Jesus is 'the ruler of the kings of the earth' (1:5), a title later expressed as the superlative 'King of kings and Lord of lords' (17:14; 19:16). Such earthly kings are repeatedly portrayed as subject to God's power and judgment (esp. 6:15–17; 19:17–21). As an apocalypse is wont to do, John draws back the curtain to reveal that the concrete showdown between Jesus and human kings replicates the authority and conflict played out in the divine realm. God's reign is celebrated (4:9–11; 11:15–18; 15:3; 19:6), crushing those who defy him (16:10–16; 17:1–18). Ultimately – as envisaged by various Old Testament sages such as Isaiah – these earthly kings and their nations will bring tribute to acknowledge God's supremacy (21:24–26).

Being a priest is not especially distinguished from such regal language. We ought not be surprised at this, remembering that political leadership and religious leadership were closely associated in the ancient world. So a climactic image of heaven comes in 22:1–5, arguably *the* climactic paragraph before the vision closes and the book concludes. The heavenly city has just been described as a grandly decorated cube (21:9–21), undoubtedly evoking the Old Testament cultic system, its buildings and the cubic Most Holy Place where God dwells. Readers are then assured that there is no separate temple for God's distant presence: the glory of God and of the Lamb now fill the inhabitable universe (21:22–27). So the further description of the city in 22:1–5 is instructive. We find the throne shared by God and the Lamb (and associated trees and river), 'and his servants will [cult-ically] serve him'. It is in this context that, once again, we are assured in the very last words of the vision that God's human worshippers 'will reign for ever and ever'.

We can narrow down the issue of this priesthood's role by looking more closely at our three overt passages.

Each passage mentions not just generic priests but priests 'for God' (and, once, also 'of/for Christ'). God is the overt beneficiary of his priests' ministrations.

In the first two passages the NIV interpolates 'priests *to serve* God' (1:6; 5:10). This accords neatly with the recent, less overt passage where God's servants 'will serve him' (22:3). And the third overt passage (20:6) comes just after a fuller definition of the first resur-rection, where those who come to life and reign with Christ for a thousand years are those who have refused to worship the beast or its image (20:4–5). Again, our informal fourth passage conjoins the two activities: 'they will reign' and 'his servants will [cultically] serve him' (22:3–5). Even where Old Testament readers are more familiar with the *distinction* between kings and priests, Revelation seems to reduce that differentiation towards synonymy.

We might then ask whether the NIV's interpolation of 'priests to *serve* God' is of most help. Closer scrutiny of the first two overt passages brings the issue into sharper focus. The doxology of 1:5–6 praises Jesus because 'he appointed us as a kingdom, priests for his God and Father'. The song of 5:9–10 seems to distinguish the two privileges: Jesus appointed the myriad ransomed believers 'as a kingdom *and* priests for our God'.[8] On the surface it might be argued that 1:6 sees the two words as describing one outcome, while 5:10 sees the two words as denoting two separable roles. But this gains little mileage. Some interpreters see both verses describing *one* outcome: a hendiadys meaning 'a royal house of priests' (Harrington 1993; e.g. 45–46, 83–86). Other interpreters take both verses as offering *two* distinct roles (Aune 1997; Koester 2014). Such approaches follow the general assumption that the two verses intend to communicate the same thing; encapsulating her 1972 dissertation, Elisabeth Schüssler Fiorenza (1998: 68–81) believes that 1:5–6 is a formalized doxology that John then clarifies in his wording of 5:9–10. If the two roles are seen to be distinct, then in what way is 'a *kingdom*' appointed 'for our God'? We might appreciate the interpolation of 'to serve' as a further description of being priests, but the Greek of 5:10 makes clear that 'for our God' qualifies both terms.

The complexities of Greek grammar here are difficult. This is compounded by John's apparently irregular applications of it in Revelation (see now Moṭ 2015). Are the paired terms in 1:6 intended as a hendiadys or even as epexegetical? Is this coloured by our determination of John's source (which here most closely matches the LXX renditions of Theodotion and Symmachus)? Does the 'and' (*kai*) in 5:10 conjoin two distinct terms, or does it make the latter

---

[8] My language of 'appointing' in both verses removes any sense of Jesus' mechanically constructing an army of priests from scratch. This is the helpful translation of the NET and the way that all versions portray the same verb (*poieō*) in Mark 3:14 when Jesus 'makes/appoints' the Twelve. While English translations uniformly render the same verb as 'made' in Acts 2:36, it can likewise be understood there in the sense of 'appoint' (Schüssler Fiorenza 1998: 72; Keener 2012–15: 964). Schüssler Fiorenza helpfully observes the same phenomenon in the LXX, where the direct object can be 'he appointed *priests*' (e.g. 1 Sam. 12:6; 1 Kgs 12:31–32; 13:33; 2 Kgs 17:32; 2 Chr. 13:9).

epexegetically qualify the former?[9] Although frankly tentative, my own temptation is to lean towards the notion that the two terms are more closely linked than distinguished. It is certainly grammatically plausible in both 1:6 and 5:10. It acknowledges the close association between political and religious leadership. It recognizes that most occurrences move quickly to add phrases about 'reigning' (5:10; 20:4–6). And, despite the occasional mention of 'worship' and 'serving' and many *general* cultic allusions, Revelation does not seem to provide any great insights into what these believer-priests are to accomplish. Craig Koester's preference (2014: 228, 390) that Christians honour and worship God by bearing witness to him certainly touches on one of the book's themes, but its precision seems more reliant on 1 Peter 2:9 than on any overt explanation in Revelation. Schüssler Fiorenza (1998: 74) more rightly resolves that 'The author, however, appears to be more interested in the *basileia* [kingdom] motif than in the priest motif', though she may be incorrect in seeing the two motifs as too distinct.

If priesthood is not as prominent or as distinct as we might at first think, we should counsel caution. Perhaps we ought not, as many do, to race to overly emphasize a role for believers in the offering of incense-like prayers (5:8; 8:3–4) (e.g. Stevenson 2001: 290). While the Greek of 8:3–4 is itself difficult, and it is unclear whether the quantities of incense *are* the prayers or *accompany* them, it is still the angel rather than the saints who operates in God's presence.[10] Of course the value of prayer for new-covenant believers is important and is found elsewhere in the Bible (see below). And we can still explore the cultic imagery in Revelation, including the role of the saints *in* and *as* the temple of God's presence (e.g. Beale 2004: 313–333). Yet even Beale (331) resorts to 1 Peter 2:9 and Psalm 92:15 to discern the actual activity and purpose of 'the church as a temple and priest'. Beale draws little from Revelation, merely inferring from 6:9–11 and 11:1–6 that believer-priests are witnesses – perhaps even only relatively passive

---

[9] Aune (1997: cxcv) acknowledges the epexegetical use of *kai* elsewhere in Revelation. Compare the translation of Elgvin (2009: 260: 'a kingdom, priests') or the related ascensive presentation of Bandstra (1992: 15: 'a kingship, even priests').

[10] Some additional examples of 'angelic priestly ministry' in Revelation are adduced by Elgvin (2009: 263); he ponders if they are modelled on Levitical assistants. Beale (1999: 455–457) struggles with the tension. He acknowledges 'the angel's mediatorial role' here, the wider representative function of angels in the book, and 'the mediatorial role of angels in prayer' in particular. Yet he wants also to preserve for believers 'their direct access as priests to the divine throne', even though any access is more implicit than explicit.

witnesses – to the wider world through their 'sacrificial calling' (318–319) and later deriving a sense of witness from the symbolism of '"lampstands" shining God's revelation to the world (Rev. 1:13, 20; 2:2; 11:1, 4)' (389). Such evidence is sparse and only mildly indicative.

But, where hopes might suddenly be dashed when some of the New Testament's most prominent teaching on corporate priesthood appears to be inconclusive, we ought also to note the promising lines of argument that flow from the presentation of a *regal* priesthood. Several of these can be sketched here.

At the very foundational level, we are further assured that the imagery of Revelation – as also in 1 Peter 2 – is applying to Christian believers the identity and task assigned to God's people in Exodus 19. The language of 'a kingdom of priests' (Exod. 19:6) might still be unclear, and the connotation of 'kingdom' remains debated, but we ought to recognize that something regal is being associated with Israel's priesthood. We can also recall that the controlling term of God's corporate commission here is that Israel will be his 'treasured possession' (*sĕgullâ*). John Davies (2004: 55) notes that the term itself has royal conntations, both in its biblical uses and in its various extra-biblical instances. He concludes that 'Israel, the recipient of the title *sĕgullâ* is the "cherished possession" of the divine king, enjoying the status of a favoured royal retainer, if not royal status themselves, and doing so uniquely among the nations.' The admixture of royal and priestly language gives us confidence that God's intentions for his old-covenant people are extended to new-covenant believers. Yet the New Testament does not merely echo the Old Testament but extends God's priestly privileges to members of all nations; biblical theology tutors us in both continuities and discontinuities.

In turn, and perhaps most excitingly, the regal connotations produce a *better* correlation with our biblical theology of priesthood. We realize once again that a simplistic division between kings and priests might be unfortunate. It was not a division regularly found in ANE cultures. Nor is it one that fills more than a single millennium of biblical history. We might even argue that a rigorous distinction applies for less than five centuries, starting with the rise of the Israelite monarchy around 1050 BC and formally defunct with the fall of Jerusalem in 586 BC. However, it is these five centuries or so that form the focus of the Old Testament historical books and in which are set the majority of the writing prophets and many of the Writings. If we crudely read all of Samuel through to Zephaniah as set in this era, then around 70% of the Old Testament operates during this era and we can easily earn the impression that the division between kings and priests applies more broadly and more permanently. Yet either side of the monarchical era we find the more culturally normal experience of overlap between the two vocations. For one, Beale regularly populates the various tabernacles of God's presence with priest-*kings*, a term that he applies to Adam and all humanity, to Noah and the patriarchs, to the Israelites before and after exile, to Israel's expected Messiah, and to 'Christ as the ultimate Adam and priest-king' (2004: 70, 81, 87, 93, 115, 299, 301). Beale is comfortable to identify *all* of God's followers as 'his evangelical priest-king image bearers (e.g., cf. Exod. 19:6)' (326). Any tendency to overly separate priests and kings is too simplistic, and the phrases of Revelation offer a corrective antidote. From the Revelation use of 'kingdom (and) priests' Beale thus confirms 'the dual kingly-priestly role of the corporate church' (323).[11]

Pairing priests with kings has both explanatory power and theological consequences. It certainly helps explain why the narrators of Old Testament history have no qualms in ascribing priestly prerogatives to kings such as David and Solomon (e.g. 2 Sam. 6; 1 Kgs 8; and the even more cultically elaborate records of 1 Chr. 15 – 16; 23; 2 Chr. 6 – 7).[12] We should be less surprised to find, prior to the monarchy, a description of Melchizedek as both king and priest (Gen. 14:18) and, after the institution of the monarchy, the expectation of Yahweh's delegated ruler who is both lord and priest (Ps. 110). The same mingling of civic and religious leadership is encouraged by the post-exilic prophets Haggai and Zechariah, especially the difficult passage in Zechariah 6:9–15. Regardless of how many individuals and crowns and thrones are involved, once again there is a close association between (high) priest and pending ruler. It is twice affirmed that this approaching king 'will [re]build the temple of Yahweh', all the more

---

[11] Even for the OT, Rooke (1998: 187) confidently affirms that 'The idea of the Israelite monarchy as an example of sacral kingship has become an accepted piece of received scholarly wisdom' and later (193) speaks of the king having 'what might be called an *ex officio* priestly status'. Gupta (2009: 73) draws attention to several passages in Philo; during the Second Temple period it is still affirmed that 'the law invests the priests with the dignity and honour that belongs to kings' (*On the Special Laws* 1.142).

[12] It is instructive to note that it is Solomon's 'burnt offerings which he offered at the house of the LORD' that climax the list of sights that impress the Queen of Sheba (1 Kgs 10:5 // 2 Chr. 9:4, though the text might refer to a different element of temple worship; so NASB, AV/KJV). Dillard (1987: 1–7) confirms that 'the Chronicler has written his accounts of David and Solomon largely in terms of their involvement with the temple' (7).

significant if he is not to be identified *as* the priest.[13] Such connections draw attention to other passages that intertwine God's promises of a perpetual Davidic dynasty and a perpetual Levitical priesthood (esp. Jer. 33:17–18). We can understand why intertestamental Jews held various views of the anticipated Messiah(s), whether this be an individual priest-king or separate royal and priestly messiahs (sources in Bird 2009: 31–62). We can accommodate the mixed illustrations that the New Testament uses. These are not only for Jesus as an individual but also for his corporate followers; believers are not only portrayed as inaugurated priests (as in 1 Peter 2:4–10) but also as forthcoming rulers (e.g. Matt. 19:28 ≈ Luke 22:29–30; Eph. 2:6; Rev. 2:26–27; 3:21). Revelation itself is full of such mixed imagery. The barely describable one who sits on the throne is both 'holy, holy, holy' and 'Master Almighty' (Rev. 4:8). John's vision of heaven intermingles temple and throne-room imagery (esp. 21:22 – 22:5). Here, as elsewhere in the New Testament, God's priest-kings are not infrequently described as his 'holy ones/saints' (5:8; 8:4; 11:18; 13:7, 10; 14:12; 16:6; 17:6; 18:20, 24; 19:8; 20:9; 22:11).

There are commensurate theological consequences. We should *expect* the behaviour of Old Testament monarchs to advance or imperil true cultic worship of Yahweh, as evaluated both by the Former Prophets (in the historical books) and by the Latter Prophets (the writing prophets addressed as much to Judah's and Israel's *royal* leaders). Christians familiar with a pacifist, enemy-loving Jesus will need to acknowledge that priests in both Old and New Testaments are sometimes cast in military postures.[14] The eschatological tensions between present and future priestly service for God's believer-priests match the eschatological tensions for God's believer-kings (e.g. 1 Cor. 4:8). This leads directly to further questions.

[13] It is not uncommon to find conservative interpreters ascribing the priestly and kingly imagery here to a single and future figure, 'Branch/Sprout', distinct from sixth-century Joshua and Zerubbabel (e.g. Baldwin 1964; 1972; Petterson 2015). This recognizes, perhaps with NT hindsight, a pending priest-king Messiah. Others argue that only Joshua and Zerubbabel (identified as 'Sprout') are in view (e.g. Boda 2001; 2004; 2016; Merrill 1994). Schniedewind (1994) explores briefly how king and priest are also presented by Chronicles as equal authorities in its postexilic retelling of Israelite history, as when focusing on Solomon and his high priest being simultaneously anointed/installed/reconfirmed (1 Chr. 29:22, differing from 1 Kgs 1:39).

[14] We have already noted (chapters 2, 4) the role of OT priests in battle, especially as signallers. Elgvin (2009: 275) reminds us of Levi's own military vigilance in chapters such as Gen. 34 and Exod. 32. Phinehas establishes his priestly dynasty through similar vigilance in Num. 25. Elgvin then judges the corollary for believer-priests: 'As the enthroned Messiah shall rule by an iron rod, so shall his church.'

When and where is this priesthood exercised?

The temporal question is fraught with the same difficulties as is any other question concerning the timeframe of Revelation. How much depicted is already in play? How much is reserved for some future implementation? When should we expect to see God's believer-priests serving him (and these same believer-kings reigning)?

Interpretation of the three statements concerning corporate priest-kings in Revelation will be influenced by one's eschatological views. The third statement (20:6) casts priesthood in future terms, and this statement and the second (5:10) speak of reigning also as if future. However, the first two statements (1:6; 5:10) confidently extol that believers are appointed priests at the moment they are released from sin and purchased for God, events clearly seen as completed.[15]

Without venturing far into a recognized minefield, we should have every confidence to proclaim an inaugurated priesthood. Those investigating corporate priesthood from an amillennial perspective see the priestly reign of believers to have already begun (e.g. Bandstra 1992: 17–18; Beale 2004: 397–398). Already believer-priest-kings can declare God's praiseworthy acts to the nations and perhaps intercede for the nations. It integrates nicely with what we have seen in 1 Peter as well as with the new-covenant cultic responsibilities expected of readers of Mark's Gospel (esp. Heil 1997). Few Christians would object that such ministries are already expected of them, even if they have yet to grasp fully the priestly vocation that much of Scripture uses to frame such ministries. Nor does this inauguration of believer-priests' service rule out an extended or different form of that service (or of believer-kings' reign), as may be anticipated by premillennial interpreters.[16]

Of course, *where* this priestly service is executed is interrelated to questions of what is accomplished and when it occurs. The inaugurated stance outlined here accommodates both an initial earthly service as well as ongoing activity in the new heavens and new earth. In turn,

[15] Temporal matters are muddied when the text and tense of 'reign' in 5:10, and the ensuing sense of that tense, are heavily debated. Jesus' inauguration of believers' priesthood, however, is not in doubt. In defence of the present impact of Revelation's inaugurated eschatology, see Bandstra 1992.

[16] Indeed, Bandstra (1992: 22) explores the possibility that Rev. 20:6, for one, may even teach that Christian 'priests' are able to extend their priestly reign *after* their deaths – a feat that Hebrews denies was possible for old-covenant priests in the order of Aaron.

the different timeframes and locations remind us that believer-priests' ministries will by necessity be transformed. While declaring God's praiseworthy acts appears to be an eternal delight, their future rule will afford them more proximate access to God's presence even as there becomes no further opportunity to engage with or intercede for unbelievers. God's people will continue to join in devotion to God *alongside* whoever of 'the nations' and 'the kings of the earth' repent and flock to God's city-temple – but no longer *on behalf of* those who have failed to repent (21:22–27). Some interpreters focus on the futuristic elements of Revelation. Schüssler Fiorenza (here 1998: 123–124) emphasizes the futuristic expressions and an overly literalistic application of the cultic imagery when she resolves that

> Nowhere in Rev[elation] does the author speak of a Christian liturgy or priestly liturgical service on earth . . . As long as eschatological salvation, which is represented in Rev[elation] by the symbol of the throne of God, is not yet present on earth, Christians are not in the immediate presence of God and the Lamb and therefore cannot directly take part in the heavenly liturgy.

It is easy to concur that we do not see believer-priests operating cultically in such a literalistic fashion. But her claims border on suggesting that the Lord God Almighty has not yet *started* to exert his reign. Along with Andrew Bandstra (1992: 24) and the *Introduction to Biblical Theology* of Desmond Alexander (2008: 96–97), I find better clarity in G. B. Caird's presentation (1984: 297) of inaugurated priest-kings already at work:

> [T]he past fact of salvation must also be made contemporary in the experience of the church and the world . . . But more depends on the conduct of Christians than their own individual destiny. The church has been appointed by Christ to be 'a royal house of priests' (i. 6; v. 10), to mediate his royal and priestly authority to the whole world. Through the church he is to exercise his sovereignty over the nations, smashing their resistance to his rule and releasing their subjects for a new and better loyalty (i. 5; ii. 26 f.; xi. 15 ff.; xii. 5; xv. 3–4; xvii. 14; xix. 11 ff.). Through the church he is to mediate God's forgiveness and lead the world to repentance (iii. 7–9; xi. 13; xiv. 6–7; xx. 1–6).

A summary of Revelation

While we might not follow Schüssler Fiorenza in her eschatology, she is surely right to observe a number of textual and theological connections between Revelation's 'priest' passages and God's slaying of many Passover lambs in Exodus: 'As Israel was freed from the slavery of Egypt and constituted as a kingdom of priests and a special nation through the covenant with Yahweh, so also are those who are purchased for God by the Lamb made a kingdom and priests' (1998: 76). The last book of the Bible reaches back to the second (if not also to the first) to bookend the identity of God's people convincingly in priestly terms.

Just as Hebrews is full of cultic terminology focused on the tabernacle, so Revelation is full of cultic terminology focused on the temple.[17] Yet, for all the cultic context, there is surprisingly little cultic detail. We are left comprehending corporate Christian priesthood as *somehow* connected with an inaugurated reign alongside God and his victorious Lamb, but perhaps left to infer priestly behaviours from other biblical sources. There is no doubt that there is a priestly element to the present and future of God's people, but we cannot distil it in any way independent of those other images and other texts.

Nonetheless – and not discounting the importance of the *regal* imagery that is especially prominent in Revelation – the Bible's closing book reinforces what we have found in other corporate passages such as Exodus 19 and 1 Peter 2. Schüssler Fiorenza (1998: 123) rehearses the Old Testament's focus on the high priest as *the* priest when she describes redeemed Christians as 'the eschatological "high priests" of the New Jerusalem'. Such an inference is made fairly from the persistent description of God's priestly worshippers bearing his name upon their foreheads as did Aaron (Exod. 28:36–38 → Rev. 22:3–4; cf. 7:3; 14:1) (cf. Koester 2014: 228).

Priestly access in Hebrews?

Revelation is almost universally dated as being written after the demise of Jerusalem and its temple and priests. Conservative interpreters are comfortable that 1 Peter was written by the apostle; with his

---

[17] The temple is certainly the basis of many of Beale's studies, not least his 2004 work. Elgvin (2009: 268) builds on other studies to pronounce superlatively that 'Revelation is more permeated by temple symbolism than any other first century Jewish writing.'

death traditionally located around AD 64, the Jerusalem temple is still standing when he applies Israel's cultic terminology to Gentile Christians. So the books' overlapping message of Christians as believer-priests gains additional momentum. The dating of Hebrews is less certain than either of these and is the New Testament document that is next most mined for hints of Christians as a corporate priesthood. The arguments of Hebrews work regardless of whether the homily was composed before or after the fall of Jerusalem in AD 70. As various scholars note, the letter draws on the Mosaic tabernacle rather than the monarchical temple, so we cannot demand that the Jerusalem temple is still standing. Thus while some seek to pin down a narrow window (Lane [1991: lxvi] favours AD 64–68), others acknowledge only broader boundaries (Koester [2001: 50–54] correctly identifies roughly AD 50–90 as the plausible extremes).

Equally debatable is whether Hebrews – for all it has to contribute to Jesus' individual priesthood – contributes anything to a study of corporate priesthood. We can approach the issue in several ways.

Believers' status and access

Certainly Hebrews is confident in the ephemeral and expendable nature of the Aaronic priesthood as it stands under the old covenant. With the rise of a great high priest in the order of Melchizedek, humanity no longer needs any vocational priest other than Jesus. Jesus' individual priesthood is described largely in terms of Aaron's. Where 1 Peter and Revelation describe corporate Christian priesthood with reliance upon Exodus 19:6, Hebrews makes no such obvious connections or claims.

The arguments proposed

Some scholars still discern priestly hints for God's people in Hebrews. Among them, Beale (2004: 306–309) speaks confidently of Christians' 'priestly duty', 'priestly service', 'priestly manner of living', 'priestly qualifications' and 'priestly activities'. Certainly Hebrews describes Christian believers as those who are 'holy/sanctified' (e.g. 3:1; 6:10; 8:10; 12:10; 13:24) and a command to holiness is primary among the pastor's instructions. In 12:14, towards the end of his mixture of gentler exhortations and stronger imperatives, he insists that 'You must pursue peace with everyone and holiness, without which no one will see the Lord.'[18]

---

[18] The exact 'tense' of sanctification remains debated, especially when positional sanctification is entertained (esp. Peterson 1995). Some constructions hint at an ongoing transformation (2:11; 10:14), while others bear a more completed flavour (10:10, 29; 13:12).

This issue of access to God remains one of the author's primary concerns. It obtains here in 12:14, throughout the sermon, and especially at its rhetorical turning points (4:14–16; 10:19–25). Believers are urged to 'approach' God through Jesus (esp. 4:16; 7:19, 25; 10:22; 12:22) and to 'enter' into his presence and the rest/completion/maturity that it entails (esp. 4:1–3, 11; 6:19). The related verbs catalogued here (*proserchomai, eiserchomai*) are spatial and active, modelled primarily on approaching God by entering into the Most Holy Place, of which the earthly tabernacle is an illustration. The latter verb in particular is used also of Jesus' entry into the full presence of God (6:20; 9:12, 24–25).[19]

Because Jesus is a great high priest who enters into God's presence, some interpreters argue that the call for believers to enter likewise is an acknowledgment of corporate Christian priesthood. Once hinted at, any number of corroborations are allegedly discovered. A key call to enter God's presence includes mention of being 'sprinkled and washed' (10:19–22). This is almost certainly a reference to atonement and baptism. Is it a New Testament equivalent of the sacrifices and washings that marked the ordination of Old Testament priests? Such is the thesis of Peter Leithart (2000, developed in 2003) reflecting what he believes to be 'the majority view'. Not only does he argue that 'Hebrews 10.22 describes baptism with imagery borrowed from ordination'; he insists (2000: 53–55) that 'baptism fulfills and replaces ordination' such that 'All those baptized and sprinkled with the blood of Christ have privileges of access beyond those of Israel's High Priests.'

There is every reason to applaud the primary sentiment here. Leithart has captured well the elements of *access* with which Hebrews is doggedly concerned. This intersects well with Leithart's own concern (1999) that the notion of priesthood should be broadened beyond cultic connotations to embrace a more general sense of 'personal attendants to Yahweh in his house'. Certainly Leithart's definitions and foci are internally consistent and accord well with Hebrews's own passion to encourage Christian believers to celebrate their unprecedented access into God's presence. Any hesitance we might experience is grounded in (1) the way that Leithart has arranged a target sufficiently wide that he can barely miss it, and thus (2) the circumstantial connections he claims to forge.[20]

---

[19] Scholer (1991) offers a study of these two verbs (along with a third, *teleioō* = 'to perfect [access to God]').

[20] Leithart also suggests repeatedly (e.g. 2000: 59–60) that *this* is the ultimate fulfilment of 1 Sam. 2:35: Jesus is the 'faithful' (high) priest raised up for God's house *and* Christian believers are the members of his (Jesus') priestly house (Heb. 2:17 – 3:6). Of course

Similarly broad is the language of David deSilva. Looking at issues of persecution and application, he concludes (2000: 79) that the call in 13:16 to the 'sacrifices' of doing good and sharing are means 'to fulfill our priestly service' to one another. Certainly spurring on fellow pilgrims is a persistent instruction to these discouraged believers (esp. 3:12–14; 10:24–25). And, as we shall see shortly, the concrete points of application collated in Hebrews 13 are cast in terms of acceptable worship or service to God. But, like Leithart, deSilva may be overeager in inferring that those who offer these sacrifices should be construed as priests. It is equally likely that Hebrews casts these as the pleasing activities of those who *worship* God and who are still reliant on another, greater priest's mediation.

John Scholer's (1991) exploration of the readers' priesthood draws on elements such as Leithart's and deSilva's and focuses especially on the language of 'approaching' God and 'entering' his presence. Scholer acknowledges (e.g. 11) that the readers are not named as priests and that we cannot discern obvious corporate language such as that found in Exodus 19:6 or Isaiah 61:6. Yet Scholer (89–90) still deems the believers' kinship to their brother Jesus (prominent in 2:10–18) sufficient grounds for their own priesthood. Others have found Scholer persuasive (e.g. Small 2014: 310–311).[21]

The arguments critiqued
It is precisely here that questions of derivation and dependence become important. Scholars such as Scholer present an enticing parallel akin to the overall panorama of priesthood that I have been sketching. Aaron and each successive high priest was appointed to facilitate the Israelites' approach to God; his ministry was also a model for the Israelites' status and role among the wider nations. Jesus was appointed to facilitate believers' approach to God; his ministry is also a model for his brothers' and sisters' status and role among the wider families of the earth. Thus, goes the argument, just as Israel was identified as a kingdom of priests, Hebrews parallels 1 Peter and Revelation in heralding the priesthood of Christian believers. Hebrews

(note 20 *cont.*) I am sympathetic to the resulting corporate priesthood of believers, but I wonder if Leithart has cut some corners by blurring the various familial images of Hebrews and the possessive pronoun of '*his* house' (3:2, 6).

[21] One further hint, not regularly explored, concerns Heb. 5:14. When the pastor chides his friends for being too immature 'to distinguish between good and bad', might he intimate the kind of discernment expected of priests (esp. Lev. 10:10–11)? My gratitude to Neville Carr for drawing the possibility to my attention.

teaches this implicitly rather than predicating the word 'priest' directly of them or drawing on Exodus 19. It is here that the earlier parallelogram diagrams in chapter 6, pp. 125–126, are again important. I do not intend them as prescriptive but as an illustration to aid thinking. We have seen that 1 Peter and Revelation model Christians' corporate priesthood directly on *Israel's* corporate ministry (fig. 6.2). So we can be confident of the 'corporate Israel' → 'corporate Christians' link. That derivation is not ignored by scholars.

The claims for Hebrews trace a different route, supposing that the idea of believer-priests is derived from *Jesus'* individual priesthood (fig. 6.1). Alex Cheung's study (1986: 273) acknowledges this route: 'As the Israelites were all in principle priests through their identification with the Aaronic priests, so also Christian believers, by virtue of their being in union with Christ, obtain a priesthood that is derived from Christ's.' Cheung's ongoing paragraph rightly observes that there are discontinuities between old-covenant worship and new-covenant privileges, especially where Hebrews 13:10 celebrates that 'We have an altar from which those who worship/serve in the tabernacle have no authority to eat.' But this is one of few connections between corporate Christians and the corporate old-covenant priesthood. It provides little clarity and may not reference Israel's *priesthood* at all (see below). The remainder of Cheung's evidence, like the evidence presented by others, is drawn almost exclusively from links between Christ's and Christians' priesthoods. So it is telling and perhaps inconsistent that Cheung's same paragraph concludes (274) by drawing *another* interconnection in the parallelogram: 'In short, the OT priesthood was superseded by a priesthood that embraces all NT Christians.' The claim might sound similar to that which I have confidently made for 1 Peter and Revelation, but it differs in terms of its antecedent and, anyway, it finds minimal support in Hebrews.

Thus one ground for caution asks to what extent corporate Christian priesthood is modelled on Jesus' individual priestly ministry. Certainly for 1 Peter, Achtemeier (1996: 157) is adamant that 'The attempt to find here a link between the priesthood of the community and Christ as high priest, whereby the community is to participate in the priestly function of Christ, has no foothold in the letter itself.' When it comes to Hebrews, we might echo previous complaints raised of various passages. Of course the imagery of approaching God and offering sacrifices is associated with the priesthood, but is it associated uniquely enough for us to be confident that Hebrews is marking out Christians as *priests*? Although a detailed case could be mounted, we can summarize the weaknesses fairly briefly.

We need not deny that the verbs outlined by the likes of Scholer are associated with sacred approach to God. But a brief survey of the LXX usage of the verbs suggests that any conclusions drawn from them should be tentative:

- Such verbs are sometimes used of secular agents. The First Temple is 'entered' and (thus) defiled by foreign invaders (Jer. 51:51 [LXX 28:51]; Lam. 1:10; cf. 1 Macc. 1:21; 2 Macc. 5:15; cf. 3 Macc. 1:10–15).[22]
- Some of Israel's monarchs invite the wider population to join them in the temple. Jehoshaphat brings with him 'every man of Judah' (2 Chr. 20:27–28). Hezekiah *commands* 'all Judah and Israel' to 'give glory to the Lord God and enter into his sanctuary' (30:8). Before the Second Temple is completed and consecrated, Haggai 1:14 attests that – at the Lord's behest – Zerubbabel and Joshua and 'the remnant of all the people . . . entered and were doing works in the house of the Lord Almighty their God'.
- We find that general worshippers may 'enter' into God's house or God's presence. Hannah 'entered the house of the Lord at Shiloh' and, together with Elkanah, 'brought [Samuel] before the Lord' (1 Sam. 1:24–25). A range of psalmists, sometimes associated with David but sometimes not, celebrate their entry and call for others to enter (Pss 5:7; 43:4; 66:13; 73:17; 100:2, 4; 132:7). Psalm 100 is particularly inclusive, inviting 'all the earth' to worship the Lord, to 'enter before him', 'to enter into his gates . . . into his courts'.[23]
- On various occasions, unordained Israelites are commanded to 'approach' and 'stand' before God, to the point that they witness something of his glory (e.g. Exod. 16:6–10; Lev. 9:5, 23–24; Ps. 34:5; cf. Sir. 1.28 – 2.1).
- For his primary verb, 'approach', Scholer (1991) repeatedly allows its occasional use for regular, unordained worshippers (e.g. 91, 94, 100–102). He notes (101) one construction that 'characterizes the participants as worshipers' rather than as priests, and

---

[22] A range of Israelite kings also enter the temple (e.g. 2 Sam. 7:18; 12:20; 2 Kgs 11:13; 19:1; 2 Chr. 12:11; 20:27–28; 23:12; 26:16), but we have been developing a sense of the overlap between royal and priestly prerogatives.

[23] Psalms versification here is given in English, from which the LXX persistently differs by a verse or a chapter.

finds this key construction in the major injunctions of Hebrews, especially the key exhortations in the turning points of the homily (4:16; 10:22). His detailed studies of each passage (103–113, 125–131) fail to disarm his own claims, admitting – if not encouraging – the possibility that Hebrews addresses Christian believers as worshippers rather than as priests.

Consequently, Scholer's argument hits only half his target. We need not deny the importance of such verbs, and Hebrews applies them well to *Jesus'* priestly accomplishments. But the verbs apply also to the *beneficiaries* of such a priest without making them to be priests also. Scholer all but admits this (127–128) when he cites James Moffatt (1924: 144): 'He [the author of Hebrews] does not mean that Christians are priests . . . but, as to approach God was a priestly prerogative under the older order, he describes the Christian access to God in sacerdotal metaphors.' Christian access is *like* priests' access.[24]

Thus when such terms are found in the New Testament, as in Hebrews, it is not especially certain that they refer to approaching God in a priestly fashion. Perhaps they are sufficiently general that all God's worshippers might be considered to be priests – a point I am broadly keen to support. At the same time such words are so general and metaphorical that I am hesitant to place much weight upon them. Hebrews marvels at the access that all believers have to God through our great high priest; believers can begin to follow our forerunner into 'the inner sanctuary behind the curtain' (Heb. 6:19–20; cf. Lev. 16:2). It may be another way of associating believers with the privileges of God's holy priests, or it may merely be a cultic way of describing more generally the access won for worshippers by Christ's ministry. The same sense of access is illustrated in Mark 15:38, where the tearing of the temple 'curtain' may indicate the same point – without any mention or intimation of priests.[25]

---

[24] It is also difficult to accept Scholer's apparent presentation (204–205) of 'worship' as the exclusive domain of priests. Scholer's thesis is further diluted by his largely futurist eschatology. For Heb. 6:19–20 he acknowledges (177) that Jesus has 'entered' the true sanctuary but insists that it is only believers' hope that has so far followed him there. His barely inaugurated eschatology is cogently reflected in the adjective of his title: *Proleptic Priests*. These complaints are upheld precisely in the review of Scholer by Cockerill (1993) and moderately in that by Übelacker (1995). Nelson (1993: 150–153) provides a much more circumspect connection of Christ's and Christians' priesthood in Hebrews.

[25] For the popular sense that the torn curtain indicates access to God (even if the outer curtain rather than the inner), see e.g. Edwards 2002: 478–479. Of course, the event may indicate something different in the Gospels, such as further judgment upon the denounced temple (e.g. C. A. Evans 2001: 508–510; France 2002: 656–658).

We might also query whether other such parallels adduced are convincing. Hebrews certainly extols Jesus as the great high priest for his brothers and sisters. And we can infer that the brothers of an Old Testament high priest were priests themselves. But the Old Testament has little to say about any other kudos for the siblings of a *high* priest; it is focused more on the high priest's *children*. Contrary to some readings (e.g. Scholer 1991: 90; Lane 1991: 60), 'the children' of Hebrews 2:13 seem only to be other children of *God* and not somehow descendants and heirs of Jesus and his unique high-priestly privilege.

Believers' sacrifices and worship

The foregoing has touched on the fact that Hebrews ascribes the language of 'sacrifices' and 'worship' to Christian believers. Such terms are often invoked to teach the priesthood of all believers – but may be no more precise than some of the language of approaching God or entering his presence.

We have already noted the cultic imagery applied to the readers in 13:10–14. William Lane (1991: 530–537) acknowledges the dispute over the language here and that our interpretation of the cultic imagery is dependent on the command in 13:9 to avoid 'varied and strange teachings'. The nature of the Christians' altar and participation depends on the contrast being drawn, and our author's rhetorical point is precisely one of *disjunction* between old and new. That 'those who worship/serve in the tabernacle have no authority to eat' from the new altar makes no overt claim about this new altar. So we are largely left to infer what our author has in mind. The surrounding context highlights Jesus' death, which would mark believers as beneficiaries of the altar and sacrifice rather than as contributors to them. This is thoroughly in keeping with the tone and theology of the rest of the book and does not brand Christians as priests.

In turn, this helps us put into perspective the calls in 13:15–16 for Christian sacrifices. Believers are encouraged 'continually to offer a sacrifice of praise to God', confessing his name. Similarly, 'God is pleased with such sacrifices' as doing good and sharing (cf. Acts 10:4). These verses connect nicely with 12:28, a verse that largely controls the ethical examples of Hebrews 13 (esp. Koester 2001: 554–556).[26] Christian readers are exhorted, 'Let us have gratitude/grace, through

---

[26] Scholarly superlatives abound. Cockerill (2012: 675) names Heb. 12:28–29 as 'the pastor's richest description of the life of faith'. DeSilva (2000: 473) judges the exhortation to 'show gratitude' to be 'the basic summons of the whole letter', such that he incorporates it into his commentary title (*Perseverance in Gratitude*).

which let us serve/worship God acceptably with reverence and awe.' When we recall the near-identical sense of spiritual sacrifices that are 'acceptable/pleasing to God' in 1 Peter 2:5, it might sound like yet another call to corporate Christian priesthood. Again, however, we discover the blurred boundary that may not clearly distinguish cultic priests from the worshippers they assist. This identification between priest and worshipper is a helpful element of mediation, but here that overlap makes it difficult to assert that Hebrews is calling Christian believers into a specifically priestly service.

Nor should this surprise us. While we have focused on God's special commission of Israel in Exodus 19:5–6, a 'kingdom of priests' for the nations is not devoid of its own worship. Even as God commissions Moses to rescue his people from Egypt, the stated purpose is that they may *worship* God (Exod. 3:12; 4:23 and nearly a dozen echoes) (so Block 2014: 21, offering a whole biblical theology of worship). We can also observe that this is another indicator of an intended *function* for God's people and their special status. If anything, it again models Christian behaviour upon corporate Israel rather than upon individual Jesus.

In all this we must remember that metaphorical language relies on certain points of contact and excludes other potential points of contact. God 'is' a rock or a consuming fire in certain respects – and not in others. So deSilva (2000: 500–503) constructively rails against those who misinterpret the cultic imagery here in Hebrews 13 or who infer the wrong cultic metaphors. DeSilva argues that believers are not withdrawing from cultic proximity, as when an unclean Israelite moves away from the sacred space at the centre of the tabernacle and the Jewish camp. Rather, the language in 13:13 of 'departing' (*exerchomai*) joins 'approaching' and 'entering' (*proserchomai, eiserchomai*) as another description of moving *towards* God. If deSilva is right, parallels with the tabernacle are unhelpful, and instead we should envision Moses' tent of meeting outside the Israelite camp (Exod. 33:7) or the better homeland for which Abraham and the other patriarchs abandoned their established security (Heb. 11:8–16). If so, then seeking here evidence for Christians' priesthood is even less appropriate. At most it might produce some very indirect and derivative hints at some kind of access to God or of mediation in the wider world.

Of course we must also note that every element of the discussion in Hebrews of priestly access to God trends heavily towards the *discontinuities* with Old Testament precursors. Christian believers have greater access to God than did *any* of the Israelite people, the Aaronic priests or the high priest himself. Seeking *favourable* comparisons for corporate believer-priests is difficult.

In summary, Hebrews offers us some glorious insights into Christians' special access into God's sacred space through Jesus' priestly ministry. In turn, Christians are to respond to God's grace with 'sacrificial' praise and acts of service. While this access readily parallels many of the issues surrounding priestly access to God, it is unlikely to constitute direct teaching on Christian believers as priests to God.

The priestly mission of Paul

Every study of New Testament priesthood observes that Paul applies priestly language to describe his Gentile mission. Romans has a significant Gentile readership, and from first to last the letter emphasizes Paul's ministry among them (esp. Rom. 1:5–6, 14–15; 3:29–30; 4:16–17; 9:22–24; 11:13–14; 15:7–12, 17–19; 16:25–27). As he moves towards the close of the letter and the more pragmatic summary of past missions and future plans, he includes the following explanation (15:15–16):

> because of the grace given to me by God that I should be a minister of Christ Jesus unto the nations/Gentiles, functioning as a priest for the gospel of God so that the nations/Gentiles might be an offering acceptable [and] sanctified by the Holy Spirit.

Already we can detect a number of ideas relevant to our study. Paul's goal is that the Gentile nations should be an 'offering' or sacrifice, presumably to God. Paul strives to make this offering 'acceptable' or pleasing to God – the same adjective that describes the spiritual sacrifices that God's holy priesthood is to offer in 1 Peter 2:5 (and semantically similar to the term in the calls to sacrifice and worship in Romans 12:1 and Hebrews 12:28). This offering is also 'sanctified' or 'made holy' by God's Spirit.

Further, Paul describes his role in preparing this offering by applying priestly imagery to himself. He is a 'minister' or worshipper of Christ (inconclusive on its own) and behaves as a priest towards God's gospel. This latter verb leaves open many alluring connections. It might woodenly be translated '(that I should be) *priesting* the gospel of God'. Paul is not somehow ordaining the gospel, as that verb might be read. Nor is it clear whether he has somehow been ordained by God – *made* a priest – for this ministry or whether he is drawing a more metaphorical parallel (cf. NET). Either way, Paul has no compunction in applying the language to himself, and we can reasonably concur with Donald Robinson (1974: 231) that 'In this cult the god is Jesus Christ, and Paul is his *leitourgos* i.e., the priest.' As Hank Voss notes (2016: 8, 43), this should surprise us. As an avid student and teacher of Scripture, Paul from the tribe of Benjamin might be hesitant to associate himself with the cultic prerogatives of Levi's tribe, even in a metaphorical comparison. Perhaps, then, Paul like Hebrews is starting to realize that the old order of Levitical priesthood is coming to an end (Dunn 1988: 859–861). Although Paul does not spell out his precise priestly responsibilities, it is commonly understood – and consistent with his ministry in Romans and beyond – that he emphasizes the work of bringing outsiders closer to God, especially through a ministry of teaching or proclamation (e.g. NIV, NCV; Robinson 1974: 231–232; Kruse 2012: 538; Longenecker 2016: 1036). And if Paul has in mind here a passage such as Isaiah 66:20 (Dunn 1988: 860; Schreiner 1998: 767), this is both consistent with and an extension of those closing chapters of Isaiah. There the Gentiles would restore God's Israelite people to God, but now these Gentiles are themselves counted as gifts to God and thence servants of God! Romans joins Isaiah and 1 Peter and Revelation in using once-exclusive cultic imagery to celebrate the inclusion of Gentile worship.[27]

There are, of course, as many finer quibbles with this passage as with others. Few interpreters have followed Robinson (1974: 231) in thinking that Paul is helping the Gentiles to refine *their* offerings (as they glorify and obey God). Nor have many joined C. E. B. Cranfield (1979: 755) in seeing Paul not as an authorized priest but as a Levite aiding Christ the Priest. Even if either proved to be Paul's intent, it would hardly hamper the cultic imagery that he presents. The point is demonstrated by David Downs (e.g. 2006); even though Downs protests much of the traditional interpretation, he still acknowledges the cultic imagery that undergirds the passage.

What is especially interesting to us is the question of derivation. Does Paul consider himself to be an individualistic, vocational priest

---

[27] Further investigation might consider whether NT authors are exploiting fluid prepositions in the OT. Relevant examples in my present chapter largely concern the preposition *ek*. If Rom. 15:16 has in mind Isa. 66:20, then the phrase there (the Gentiles 'will bring your brothers and sisters *[rescued] out of* all the nations as a gift to the Lord') would move from being a locative source to something more partitive ('*[selected] from among* all the nations'). A similar transformation occurs if an exclusive sense of Exod. 19:5 ('*[chosen] instead of* [LXX *apo*] all the [other] nations') lies behind Rev. 5:9 ('*[selected] from* every tribe').

like his Levite cousins and his risen Lord? Or is Paul modelling himself on his national, corporate investiture? There is little to encourage us to think the former; we have noted that Paul would hardly identify himself with an exclusive (and potentially defunct) priestly caste, and there is little in his writings to suggest that he held a particularly priestly view of Jesus. Moreover, it would be much more natural for him to model his ministry after Israel's corporate commission. Such is the logic that leads many to conjoin that priestly language with Paul's prevalent focus on teaching (and that happens to be consistent with the cultic proclamatory language of acceptable spiritual sacrifices in 1 Pet. 2:4–10). Those who turn their mind to the question concur: 'In his ministry Paul fulfills the call of Israel to be a "royal priesthood" by whom the knowledge of God is conveyed to Gentiles' (Schreiner 1998: 766; cf. Breshears 1994: 18–19).

The missiological implications of the passage are not lost on Wright (2006: 525–526). He agrees that Paul's priestly identity possibly derives from Exodus 19:5–6; Paul is another member of Israel working hard to bless the wider nations. Wright wonders alternatively if Paul has Isaiah 66:20 in mind – applied to himself as much as to his Gentile worshippers. If so, this is a remarkable reversal of roles, with Paul (the archetypal Israelite, Phil. 3:4–6) casting himself as an unlikely 'Gentile' priest who brings God's 'Israelites' to him! This would match Paul's humble surprise at God's vocational grace to him (esp. 1 Cor. 15:8–10; 1 Tim. 1:12–17) and would emulate other New Testament examples where Jews are treated as Gentiles (e.g. Acts 4:23–28) and Gentiles attain the status of God's holy people (esp. 1 Pet. 2:4–10).

This brief passage in Romans thus reinforces what we have seen about the transformation of priestly service to God. Douglas Moo (1996: 890–891) helpfully compiles several key themes and texts and is worth citing at length as I draw towards the conclusion of my own New Testament survey:

In keeping with the rest of the NT, Paul assumes an eschatological transformation of the OT cultic ministry, in which animal sacrifices are replaced by obedient Christians (cf. 12:1) and the praise they offer God (Heb. 13:15), the temple by the community of believers (e.g., John 2:21; 1 Cor. 6:19; 1 Pet. 2:5), and the priest by Christians (1 Pet. 2:5, 9) or Christian ministers. But one thing has not changed: to be 'pleasing to God,' sacrifices must still be 'sanctified.' And so, Paul acknowledges, it is ultimately God himself, by his

Holy Spirit, who 'sanctifies' Gentiles, turning them from unclean and sinful creatures to 'holy' offerings fit for the service and praise of a holy God.

Other New Testament passages

Our study of Romans 15 should remind us that Paul also uses sacrificial language in Romans 12. Although my survey is all but complete, we should notice that other cultic hints are scattered throughout the New Testament.

At the very turning point of his long missive, in Romans 12:1 Paul uses cultic terms to summarize his call to transformed living. The Roman believers are 'to present your bodies as a living sacrifice, holy [and] acceptable to God, your considered worship'. The cultic language here is transparent and, as with 15:16, commentators marvel at Paul's willingness to extend narrow Jewish terms to everyday Christian living (e.g. Schreiner 1998: 646). The connection here between 'holiness' and 'pleasing to God' occurs in the central instructions for general living in Hebrews (esp. 12:14, 28) and in 1 Peter (esp. 2:5, 9; cf. 1:13–16), and Paul again places them together in Romans 15:16. Strictly speaking, though, there is no allusion to priesthood in 12:1. At best we might wonder if the idea is implicit in the notion of believers 'presenting' their bodies as sacrifices. But, akin to my caution about Scholer and Hebrews, the language here has a fairly broad sense of a *worshipper's* presentations and ought not to be pinned down more narrowly to a priestly role.[28]

Similar cultic images trickle through Paul's writings. Again, they move in an orbit related to the environment of cultic priests, but little about priesthood can be drawn from them. Paul praises the Philippians for 'the sacrifice and service of your faith' (Phil. 2:17). At best this might hint at a priestly offering. Even that possibility is

---

[28] Thus, while there is much to commend Voss's study (2016: 43–45 and beyond), he may end up passing off worshippers as priests in the same way as does Scholer (1991). In terms of our parallelogram, it may be that Voss and Scholer are too hasty to model new-covenant believers directly on the Aaronic priests, when many of the NT parallels seem to derive any such connection via Israel's corporate and worshipful priesthood. Certainly we should want to highlight the NT's call for Christian worshippers to be as 'holy' and 'purified' as the OT nation indwelt by God; see the calls exemplified in Matt. 5:48; 2 Cor. 7:1; Phil. 2:15; 1 Thess. 3:13; 4:7; 5:23; Heb. 12:14; 1 Pet. 1:16; 2 Pet. 3:14; 1 John 3:3. It is thus little surprise that the NT regularly addresses God's people as his 'holy ones', his 'saints' (e.g. Acts 9:13, 32, 41; Rom. 1:7; 8:27; 1 Cor. 1:2; 6:1–2; 14:33; 2 Cor. 1:1; 13:13; Phil. 1:1; 4:22; Col. 1:2, 4, 12, 26; 2 Thess. 1:10; 1 Tim. 5:10; Heb. 3:1; 13:24; Jude 3; Rev. 5:8; 8:3–4).

overshadowed by Paul's own 'drink offering' of himself in addition to theirs. The focus is squarely on the various offerings and not on the identity of those offering them. If anything, the description of Epaphroditus as 'your messenger and *minister* to my need' (2:25) appears to revert to the idea of an individual representative who stands in place of others who cannot themselves approach and minister (2:30). The Philippians certainly 'worship' God (3:3), and their gifts through Epaphroditus to Paul are 'a fragrant offering, an acceptable sacrifice, pleasing to God' (4:18), but I would not turn to Philippians to seek any deeper insights into specifically *priestly* elements of Christian identity and service.

Other cultic images appear for illustration and comparison (e.g. 1 Cor. 9:13–14; 2 Cor. 6:17; Eph. 5:2; 2 Tim. 4:6), but priestly connections are again fleeting at best. Likewise, if we could establish their veracity, some maximalist interpretations of Jesus as (high) priest in the Gospels could hint at Jesus' disciples as his authorized priests (e.g. Fletcher-Louis 2007: 75–77).

It is occasionally suggested that the letter greetings from Paul (also in 1 and 2 Peter and Revelation) might resemble the priestly blessing of Numbers 6:22–27 (e.g. Hoehner 2002: 150; Longenecker 2016: 88). There is little evidence to evaluate such a suggestion, and any theological weight is sometimes dismissed (Jobes 2005: 73–74) or a salutation altogether uncommented (Moo 1996). The study of Judith Lieu (1985) mentions the Aaronic blessing only to observe most New Testament salutations' *divergence*.

The concentrated bursts of 'reconciliation' language in 2 Corinthians 5:18–21 and Romans 5:10–11 (cf. 11:15) sound enticing but offer no additional clarity. The language is largely absent from the Old Testament and beyond Paul, although it clearly echoes the conciliatory mediation we have studied in both testaments. Several potential layers of priestly application might be discerned. Of primary importance, both these Pauline letters join Hebrews in highlighting Christ as the agent effecting this God-driven reconciliation (cf. Col. 1:19–20, 22; Eph. 2:15–16; 1 Tim. 2:3–6). The proclamation of this reconciliation is extended to human assistants in 2 Corinthians, although there is much debate about who composes the 'we' and 'you' involved. Certainly Paul sees himself (and probably also his apostolic colleagues) as serving a role not dissimilar to some of Moses' responsibilities (e.g. Scott 1998: 137–138), and further connections with Moses and with Israel's whole cultic system can be divined (e.g. Thrall 1994: 435–436; Hafemann 2000: 245–248). In turn, various commentators believe that Paul in principle expects his apostolic service to be extended to all believers (e.g. Hafemann 2000: 257, 263–264; Seifrid 2014: 189, 220, 230). Given that the object of 'we beg *you*' in 5:20 can justifiably be omitted (so CSB, NLT[2]; Moore 2003), Paul could even be directly describing Christian ministry towards all outsiders (e.g. Harris 2005: 447–448). Thus all beneficiaries of reconciliation might be counted among God's new heralds; 'a reference to all believers cannot be excluded' (Harris 2008: 481). However, whether we insist that Paul here extends or attributes such a ministry to all believers or that he speaks only of an apostolic minority, we must recognize that this again has limited connection with priestly service. Reconciliation is effected by Jesus alone: he is the active mediator. Akin to 1 Peter 2:4–10, Jesus' servants are oral echoes of 'the message of reconciliation' that originates from God and Christ (2 Cor. 5:19–20).[29]

Beyond the New Testament

It is not my quest in a biblical theology to investigate much the trajectories that extend beyond the scriptural record. There is much merit in such a project, and a few pertinent studies and implications are outlined shortly in the concluding chapter.

Post-biblical use of scriptural words is sometimes pursued in commentaries and lexicons. For example, Gottlob Schrenk (1965: 283) offers a dense page showing that 'priest' and 'high priest' language progressed into the early church much along the lines that we have investigated in recent chapters. Hebrews is echoed by church fathers proclaiming Jesus' superior ministry. The corporate ministry of God's believer-priests is extolled, and only occasionally are the terms applied in a hierarchical sense to Christian leaders. The distinction between 'priest' and 'high priest' remains fluid such that, modelled on Joshua in Zechariah 3 and using the eschatological wording of Malachi 1:11 for reforming the priesthood, Justin Martyr (*Dialogue with Trypho* 116) describes all Christian believers as 'the true high-priestly race of God', God's priests through whom 'in

---

[29] To be sure, there is more in 2 Cor. 5:18–21 to be mined. What connections spring from the apostolic leaders 'being ambassadors' – the verbal form (*presbeuō*) of the term for 'elders' used elsewhere (e.g. Acts 14:23; 15:2; 21:18; 1 Tim. 5:17; Titus 1:5; Jas 5:14; 1 Pet. 5:1)? And if Isa. 43:20–21 has a linguistic impact on the priestly goal in 1 Pet. 2:9–10, is there any significance in the influence of Isa. 43:18–19 on 2 Cor. 5:17?

every place among the Gentiles they are offering sacrifices pleasing to him and pure'.[30]

Summary

The New Testament transparently picks up the priestly identity of Israel from Exodus 19:5–6 and extends it wholesale to God's new-covenant people. This is not supersessionism in the sense of God abandoning his promises to Israel. As in Romans and Hebrews and Revelation and elsewhere, believing Gentiles are incorporated alongside believing Israelites into 'one new humanity' (Eph. 2:15), and God's new-covenant people inherit God's expectations for his old-covenant nation. Indeed, we have seen that God has always received praise from non-Israelites and had long planned for Gentiles to be counted among his corporate priests.

One of the grand rewards of the exercise of the discipline of biblical theology, and not least a biblical theology of (corporate) priest-hood, is that we can gain great insights into how God's history-wide strategies unfold across the canon. His concern to reconcile the world to himself, by the services of a priestly nation, teaches us about the election of Abraham and his people, about God's covenant purposes for that nation, and about the commissions and expectations that God placed upon them. We can thus better locate the (largely negative) appraisals of the Old Testament history books and prophets. And such details are not only valuable background context for the drama of the New Testament. The New Testament *continues and extends* God's commissions and expectations, calling his new-covenant people to the same goal and the same general means. The new-covenant people of God are to *be* and to *behave* in such a holy – God-worthy – fashion that the wider nations are brought to join the worship of the universe's creator.

---

[30] Justin's outright transfer of legitimate 'priests' from (some) Jews to (all) Christians becomes clearer in his next chapter (*Dialogue with Trypho* 117). There he turns to his Jewish interlocutor, Trypho, and insists that the sacrifices offered 'by Christians' are attested by God as 'pleasing', while those offered 'by you and through those priests of yours, he disowns, saying, "I will not accept your sacrifices from your hands" [Mal. 1:10]'.

Chapter Eight

Concluding reflections

Our survey of the biblical threads concerning individual priests and corporate priesthoods should be the starting point for many individual and corporate applications. Aspirants thinking of vocational church leadership need to consider the various models of church polity and how biblical concepts of priest and priesthood contribute (if at all). Gentile readers of the New Testament will benefit from grasping more of the Old Testament background that lies behind the narratives of the Gospels and Acts and various epistles. All believers will gain further clarity on the identity and work of Jesus and the identity and work of Christians as they delve into the various priests and priesthoods presented in Scripture. Let us consider a number of these starting points and the directions in which they might further be explored and applied.

Biblical insights

A summary of the two parts of my survey leads already to some immediate matters of status and function. Ordained or not, and supportive of priestly ordination or not, all Christian believers have much to learn and apply directly from the biblical insights.

Individual priests

We have considered the way in which God has nominated select individuals to mediate between his extreme holiness and humans who fall short of the 'Godness' it denotes.

Such priestly mediators have a guarding function, keeping unready people from encroaching, to their detriment, on God's sacred space. Yet God is not merely some introverted dignitary, fending off unworthy supplicants by posting a cordon of prophylactic lackeys. One of the praiseworthy distinctives of the biblical God is his interest in drawing near to humanity and his facilitation of such safe proximity. The biblical priests are thus tasked with explaining this to God's people, teaching what makes for higher degrees of holiness and approach and when it is less appropriate and more dangerous to blunder unprepared into God's presence. The priests even facilitate this graded holiness, pronouncing judgment on matters of clean and unclean and directing the sacrificial system whereby supplicants can 'upgrade' their holiness, their God-readiness. Other sacrifices simply celebrate this special status, with God and worshippers delighting in the heightened proximity.

Already, a good grasp of the Bible's cultic system – and especially the often unfamiliar Sinai chapters (Exod. 19 – Num. 10) – drives believing readers to a better theology: a more accurate comprehension of God and his personality. We encounter a personal deity, a missional Yahweh, a gregarious God who wants to meet with the humanity created in his image. This then inspires further clarification of our anthropology: people are the most valuable pinnacle of creation, and not some accident or afterthought to be tolerated alongside other elements of flora and fauna. The intersection of these divine and human identities then births a range of other theological investigations including the nature of such relationships and their covenants, the sin that impedes communion, the cultic system that accompanies and facilitates and celebrates successful proximity, and the missional goals that seek to disseminate blessing and reconciliation.

The old-covenant cultus presages a superior system with a better hope and a better covenant constituted through better promises and resulting in clean consciences and more confident access into God's presence. Such is the message of Hebrews (e.g. 6:19–20; 7:18–19; 8:6; 9:13–15; 10:19–22), a book formally part of the New Testament but whose Old Testament overtones and imagery see it often studied no more than Leviticus. The superior new-covenant system is overseen and enacted by a superior priest – a son, Jesus – appointed and made perfect for this ministry (esp. 7:26–28).

A biblical theology of priesthood thus makes an essential contribution to our Christology. Without tracing this particular developing thread through the biblical tapestry, any passion for the person and work of Jesus Christ is incomplete. To phrase matters as a confident challenge, those seeking to be a 'New Testament follower' and 'Jesus person' can enhance their standing greatly by embarking on a tour of biblical priesthood. They cannot disdain the Old Testament and the allegedly impenetrable chapters of the Pentateuch; they cannot defer study of the similarly difficult chapters of Hebrews; a Marcionite Bible or Bible-reading programme produces an imperfect portrait of the Lord they acclaim. To phrase matters more enticingly, anyone who includes a biblical theology of priesthood in their balanced biblical diet can only find their doxology enhanced as they marvel at the self-sacrifice of the Great High Priest who, through the eternal Spirit, brings purified worshippers to the living God (9:14)! The missionary God has always envisaged his name being worshipped in every place and in every language. It is in only one sense that, as God's worshippers grow in number and in variety, the number of vocational priests needs to expand to accommodate this worship. Far more prominent in a biblical theology of priesthood is the inverse observation that, at the key nexus where the new covenant greatly extends the races invited to worship and eases their entry into the people of God, the number of vocational priests necessary to facilitate this is reduced to one.[1]

Corporate priesthoods

A biblical theology of priesthood assures us that God has never relied exclusively on vocational priests to be his evangelists and to facilitate entry into his chosen number. We discover that God's corporate priesthoods have always played a role. We do well to articulate theologies of mission and evangelism that incorporate the place of God's corporate priests and their holiness.

Under the old covenant, God's treasured nation earns a priestly title ('a kingdom of priests', Exod. 19:5–6). This title further clarifies their holy *status* as they celebrate their unparalleled proximity to Yahweh. Yet we have seen that with great privilege comes great responsibility. The people of Israel are expected to leverage their special priestly status towards a special priestly *function*. They are to live as a holy, godly nation (and perhaps even to adopt activities of verbal proclamation) so that other nations are drawn to their God. Like their vocational cousins, all Israelites are to guard Yahweh's holiness and to advertise the privilege of being counted as his chosen attendants.

The same status and function are extended to those who join old-covenant Israel. When Yahweh's new covenant is implemented and the wider nations even more readily embraced, the same status and function are conferred also upon these 'Gentile Israelites'. Those who join the people of God without racial adoption into Israel are

---

[1] There are, of course, many other discontinuities attending the change of covenants. For example, Nelson (1993: 169–171) efficiently catalogues issues like the demise of sacred space (or, at least, its transference to something other than a geospatial model) and the transformation of external clean/unclean categories. Many of the Aaronic priests' physical duties are thus rendered unnecessary under the new covenant.

themselves incorporated into 'a royal priesthood' and are tasked with spiritual sacrifices: declaring God's praiseworthy acts (1 Pet. 2:4–10).

Thus a biblical theology of priesthood not only abets 'active' doctrines of mission and evangelism but also enhances more 'passive' doctrines of Christian identity and ecclesiology. Using these long-prepared old-covenant titles and images, God's new-covenant people are summoned to guard God's holiness and to advertise the privilege of being counted as his chosen attendants.

The intersection of individual and corporate priesthoods

My synthesis has focused around four different elements within its biblical theology: individual priests versus corporate priesthoods, and how these each appear under the old covenant and after new-covenant transformation. Aided by the visualization of a parallelogram, we have started to consider how these four elements interact with each other.

Within part I and part II and the foregoing summary, the transformations themselves are readily articulated. The Aaronic priests are squarely surpassed by the incarnate Jesus' sinless and eternal mediation. Hebrews 7:12 unashamedly uses the language of the Aaronic order being 'changed' or 'transferred' to our Lord. While there remain substantial continuities, the discontinuities are to the fore, especially in the pastoral rhetoric of Hebrews. The status and function of corporate Israel, however, are not effectively altered but are extended just as the identity of God's covenant people is extended. While recognizing some discontinuities, the continuities are to the fore, especially in the pastoral assurances of 1 Peter and Revelation.

Our parallelogram is thus helpful but potentially misleading. The transformation of the role of individual priests (the upper arrow in fig. 8.1) is one of significant change and discontinuity, even while the passage of corporate priesthood (the lower arrow) is largely continuous.

Aaronic priest ————————➤ *Jesus*

corporate Israel ————————➤ *corporate Christians*

Figure 8.1

The two horizontal arrows here both move from the old covenant to the new covenant, but the transitions represented by the arrows are not identical.

Apart from appealing to the visually inclined, the diagram serves one more immediate purpose. It invites further reflection on the connections between the vertical terms. This is of special value when it is sometimes intimated or asserted that corporate Christian priesthood is derived from Jesus' vocational priesthood. This is in the background of Roger Beckwith's (1989) investigation into one element of 'The Relation Between Christ's Sacrifice and Priesthood and Those of the Church', and it is certainly foregrounded by those (such as Scholer [1991]) who want to find a sense of corporate Christian priesthood in Hebrews with Christians inheriting their priestly role from their elder brother. When we turn soon to consider issues of contemporary church leadership, it is not hard to find older and newer examples whereby that same connection is made (e.g. Feuillet 1975; Chryssavgis 1987; O'Collins and Jones 2010). If Jesus is a priest, then some or all of his followers ought to be recognized as priests.

The uncertainty with this priestly connection is that the Scriptures themselves do not forge such a derivation with any transparency. We have seen that the New Testament teaches unambiguously about Jesus as a vocational priest and his followers as a corporate priesthood; it is the dependence of one upon the other that I query. The dilemma is explored by two further enhancements to our parallelogram.

As in chapter 6, we can be confident that there is a connection between the old-covenant priestly images. Exodus 19 introduces us to Israel's corporate priesthood, bare chapters and days before God introduces the idea of individual Aaronic priests in Exodus 28. We have noted parallels in their ordination ceremonies and it is rarely disputed that these priesthoods are intentionally juxtaposed. Admittedly, we have seen uncertainty about the order of dependence. Historical reconstructions typically assume that the nation's corporate identity was based upon the existence of a vocational caste within the nation. But we have seen that the opposite suggestion is equally plausible and theologically tantalizing: perhaps God instituted a class of priests in order to illustrate what the nation's corporate identity might look like (e.g. Davies 2004; Lightfoot 1869: 180–181). So we should confidently draw a vertical arrow between the leftmost, Old Testament elements. The arrow added shortly in figure 8.2 is double-ended to show the possibility of either derivation.

The assumed vertical arrow between the rightmost, New Testament elements is far less assured. I have already asserted that I do not find such a link transparently forged. We have seen that attempts at a link in Hebrews have not proved convincing. And much the same reasoning found for Hebrews obtains for our Scripture-wide parallelogram. Even as the Bible unfolds and the diagram transitions from the left to the right, the discontinuous transformation of individual priests is not the same as the continuous transfer of corporate priesthood. Something of this asymmetry is lost in a two-dimensional representation (and more creative artists and media could explore the use of different arrows or dimensions, perhaps producing a tetrahedron rather than a parallelogram).

In short, the asymmetrical transformation along the horizontal axis does *not* make the assured vertical connection in the Old Testament an equally assured connection in the New Testament. Certainly Jesus' individual priesthood and Christians' corporate priesthood are derived from closely related Old Testament antecedents, *but they are not derived in the same fashion.* There is thus little confidence that we should link the two rightmost priesthoods. For all the ways in which the New Testament celebrates the similarities between Jesus and his sisters and brothers (e.g. Heb. 2:10–18; Rom. 8:1–4), and notwithstanding the expectation that Christians will be conformed to his likeness even in this life (e.g. Rom. 8:29; 1 Cor. 11:1; 2 Cor. 3:18; Phil. 3:17–21; 1 Pet. 2:21–25; 1 John 2:3–6), there is little reason to see similarities between his priesthood and ours. As with distant cousins in a family tree there is some shared history but no real present connection.

The diagram might thus be finalized and enhanced as in figure 8.2. It remains a visualization only and deficient in what it might not clarify. But it ought to serve as a mnemonic of the various elements raised in my study as well as a schematic of their interrelated dependencies.

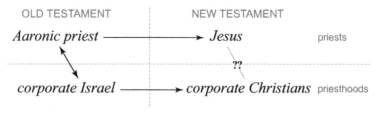

Figure 8.2

The language of 'finalized' may be optimistic. In particular, if we determine that Israel's *corporate* priesthood is primary and that the Aaronic priests were a localized illustration, we could promote the corporate priesthoods to the top tier of the diagram. This would further highlight the prominence of the people of God in mediating God to the world, though it could have the unfortunate side effect of making Jesus' priestly ministry look like the most derivative or least important element.

Vocational contributions?

Several studies of biblical priesthood have been written to influence the thinking of vocational church leaders. Studies can be found each way: promoting a more congregationalist 'flatness' or defending the more 'pointy' models of various episcopal structures. Similar studies explore or champion such polities themselves.

It is admirable that the Bible's teaching is surveyed in such vocational and ecclesiastical assessments. A biblical theology of priesthood should contribute to these, alongside biblical theologies of the people of God and of their leadership (and of many related elements). It is not the purpose of this volume to provide that broader exploration. Yet it is appropriate that we reflect briefly on some of the trajectories to which my current survey of priesthood might contribute.

The complications of basis

On what might contemporary vocational 'priests' be based? What are responsible starting points and trajectories within the biblical models we have been considering? In terms of the current book's structure, should vocational priests today consider themselves standing within the line of other individual priests (part I) or among God's corporate priesthood (part II)?

Little mileage is gained from a study of the Bible's corporate priesthoods. If all of God's people together function as a priesthood, then the model provides few additional insights. Any individual leaders serve *among* God's collective priesthood rather than somehow *in place of* them.[2]

We have seen that the example of Jesus is incomparable. While Aaronic individuals helped prepare God's people (past and present) to comprehend what Jesus would do, Jesus' priestly ministries (past

---

[2] Scholars of both testaments are adamant that the corporate priesthoods intend a collective that *as a whole* functions as a priest. It is easy to hear phrases such as 'a kingdom of priests' or 'the priesthood of all believers' and conjure an image of a collection of individual priests. But we are warned against this misunderstanding by the likes of Wells (2000: 52) on Exod. 19, by Achtemeier (1996: 156–157) and Jobes (2005: 160–161) on 1 Peter 2, and by Nelson (1993: 167–168) on a biblical theology of priesthood. To paraphrase Nelson's helpful differentiation of nuances (160, 168), Christian believers do not each have a personal priestly commission but are admitted to a corporate priestly guild.

and present) have clearly surpassed Aaron's. We have already observed in chapter 7 that the early church was hesitant to adopt 'priest' language for Christian leaders. Richard Nelson (1993: 172–173) affirms such hesitance, noting that sustained 'priest' language took more than two centuries to develop for individual leaders and agreeing that 'The New Testament gives us no hint that the earliest church turned to priestly paradigms from the Old Testament as it sought to conceptualize its evolving ministry.' The same is observed by J. B. Lightfoot (1869: 182–184); *all* believers were priests, and no biblical list of roles singles out a subset of church officers as 'priests'. (The historical transition in the roles and titles of church leaders is especially studied by Bulley [2000].) So it is difficult to defend much of a comparison with Old Testament priests, who, along with their sacrifices and sacred buildings, have been rendered cultically redundant. It is equally futile to draw close parallels with Jesus, whose superior ministry it is that renders all such earthly cultic ritual no longer necessary.

It is sometimes protested that God's holy nation (Israel) was still to be led by a class of holy priests (Aaron and his sons). This is then transferred to new-covenant settings, arguing that God's holy people (the church) can thus accommodate a class of special leaders (priests). We do well to contemplate if this transfer is valid. In cultic contexts, it seems to me that the language of 'holy' functions as a relative measure. National Israel was holier – closer to Yahweh – than the surrounding nations, yet Israel's priests were holier and closer to God than the average Israelite. It is not at all clear that such graded holiness still obtains under the new covenant. It is not apparent that Christian believers need holier mediators (other than Jesus) to facilitate their access to God.

The complications of language

Any contemporary sense of 'priest' is further complicated by the fact that the very word under inspection has a fluid history and application. What one believer or denomination grasps of the term may be at odds with another.

The crux of the problem is that our English word 'priest' is forced to describe a range of disparate roles. Introducing a lengthy dissertation on Christian ministry, Lightfoot (1869: 184) spells out the two major and distinct categories:

1. A biblical 'priest' (Hebr. *kōhēn*; Gk *hiereus*; Lat. *sacerdos*) is the special religious worker who offers sacrifices, mediating the gap

between God and humanity. These are the individual priests we have been examining.

2. Most contemporary 'priests' use the same English word but for a different end. The formal etymology of the English is considered to derive from Greek and Latin forms of *presbyter*, commonly translated 'elder'.

Lightfoot warns that 'On no subject has more serious error arisen from the confusion of language.' And we can readily see examples of how such confusion might arise. Does a particular denomination or ordination candidate lean more towards the second category? If so, then an episcopal 'priest' is effectively a congregational 'elder' by another title. Despite the difference in titles, both understand their roles to revolve around the concept of *presbyter*, a nominated representative from among equals and a role that enjoys biblical precedent (e.g. Acts 14:23; 1 Tim. 5:17–20; Titus 1:5; and OT exemplars).

The bigger pitfall is when we fail to recognize the first category. In essence, we might confuse a contemporary 'priest' (in the sense of *presbyter*) with the biblical 'priest' (in the sense of *sacerdos*). The common English word belies the two different senses. So a denomination or its clergy or its worshippers might look to its priests and expect them to function like the biblical priests. We have seen that there is limited, if any, warrant for this connection. The notion of a sacerdotal, vocational priest has certainly been resurrected in traditions that see in the Eucharist some kind of ongoing or repeated sacrifice, or that reserve for priestly individuals other functions or sacraments such as the pronouncing of blessings. The validity of the comparison turns on the accurate analysis of these ministries. The present volume is not the place for such an evaluation, although I would expect to find significant discontinuities between the ministries of biblical priests and of church leaders.

This ultimately becomes a question of what to call the two different kinds of priests. The English term 'priest' is firmly entrenched both for the biblical specialists and for contemporary church leaders in certain ecclesiastical traditions. Neither use is likely to be replaced with any ease. So we are required to remain alert to which sense of 'priest' we intend when we employ it. Like many other biblical words there is danger in its familiarity.[3]

---

[3] Scholars bear some responsibility for promulgating clarity or confusion. Bulley (2000) works from his second page to distinguish 'priest' from 'presbyter', while O'Collins and Jones (2010) generally oblige the word 'priest' to do double duty. Studies such as Bulley's and Lightfoot's investigate how the words and concepts have become so

The complications of structures

Church polities and their leadership structures remain points of differentiation – often markedly and even violently so. The impression I have is that, where the church is in decline (as in the post-Christendom West), denominational distinctives are being surrendered as believers are forced to defend the more foundational and agreeable elements of the faith. Although hardly exclusively so, quibbling over matters of denominational identity would seem more the luxury of times and places where the church is settled and in the ascendancy.

For church traditions that wish to align their practices and their language with the Bible, the concept of vocational 'priests' will remain difficult. Unbelievers, along with the substantial majority of believers, will naturally resonate with the mystical use of the word. Just as in the ANE context of the Old Testament and the Mediterranean context of the New Testament, a 'priest' is a special individual – even a magical one – with special access to deity. The Bible itself readily acknowledges such individuals in the service of other gods (e.g. Gen. 41:45, 50; 47:22, 26; 1 Sam. 5:5; Acts 14:13). Persisting with the language of 'priest' risks perpetuating this misunderstanding, which is all the more awkward if the English sense of Christian 'priests' was never intended to bear this connotation. Other factors also give the label a potentially limited lifespan.[4]

By querying the appropriateness of the title 'priests' I do not intend to challenge the usefulness of setting apart church leaders at local and denominational levels. It is simply that the title 'priest' is a label whose contemporary English currency is limited and one that has very limited alignment with the biblical concept it also connotes. We might concur with Manson (1958: 69), who, being judicious with his terms, captures the Bible's point succinctly: 'In a word, while all believers are priests, all believers are not [vocational] ministers.'[5]

(note 3 *cont.*) enmeshed in the history of the church. Manson (1958: 35–42) is among those who ask very practical questions about how different leaders in different traditions who bear different titles might regard each other.

[4] The second decade of the twenty-first century continues to see increased outrage at the abuses of power by organized clergy, among the most heinous of which is sexual predation. Based partly on their demographic dominance (and sometimes on their expectations of celibacy), church traditions with an episcopal structure such as Roman Catholic, Anglican and Orthodox face the ignominious condemnation of some who bear the title 'priest'.

[5] We should, of course, query whether Manson is then fair in constraining the language of 'ministers' to those who are paid vocationally to lead congregations. My

Missional contributions

Misapprehension of the term works both ways. We have seen that the superior and permanent priestly ministry of Jesus renders no need for further individual mediators between God and humanity. Again, there might be articulate leaders who explain God's ways and gifted administrators who organize God's people, but such ministries hardly overlap with the biblical sacerdotal priests. Contemporary leaders might sometimes be *communicative* mediators, heralding news of God's reconciliation, but they are not specialist *conciliation* mediators who themselves broker a peace accord and cajole God and individuals to accede to the agreed terms.

Rather, it is Jesus who warrants primary recognition of such a title. Based on the common antecedent of Israel's individual priests and corporate priesthood, we can see also the way in which corporate Christianity contributes to the announcement of this reconciliation. Just as we might unhelpfully constrain the title 'priest' to a select group of religious specialists, we might fail to extend it to include every believer as part of the church.

There are plenty of consequences for Christian living. Israel's individual priests were called to especially holy lives (e.g. Lev. 21 – 22), as was the nation as a whole (esp. Lev. 17 – 27). We know the famous command, addressed to 'the whole community of the people of Israel', to 'Be holy, because I, Yahweh your God, am holy' (Lev. 19:2). We have seen that the purpose of this visible holiness was to attract the attention of the wider nations. And this element continues for the new-covenant people of God; the same epistle that applies Exodus 19 to the increasingly Gentile church also applies Leviticus 19 (Lev. 19:2 ← 1 Pet. 1:13–16). Missional ethics remains a fruitful and biblical discipline (e.g. Wright 2004; Draycott and Rowe 2012) and the particular missional basis is rightly tied to God's commission of his people as a 'priestly' community (e.g. Wright 2006: 357–392; Haydock 2015; Anizor and Voss 2016). Where personal and corporate holiness is in decline, studies such as these explore some of the obedient applications of being God's priestly people among the wider nations. While God's 'ordaining' of his people as a priesthood may start with their status, a functional response is required.

study of corporate priesthood is one tool with which we might critique other helpful and unhelpful terminology.

My survey has demonstrated several of the complexities when it comes to understanding the personnel involved in bringing human beings into the presence of the holy God to worship him. There are several discontinuities as God's whole-Bible plan transforms over time from the introductory models of the Old Testament through to their realization in the New, and we must never minimize them (as can be readily done in a discussion of 'priests'). Yet there are many continuities as well. These, especially, should lead us to better comprehend and praise God for the priestly work accomplished and continued by Jesus, and to value and execute the priestly behaviour and ministry conferred upon corporate Christian believers.

Bibliography

Abernethy, A. T. (2016), *The Book of Isaiah and God's Kingdom: A Thematic-Theological Approach*, NSBT 40, London: Apollos.

Achenbach, R. (1999), 'Levitische Priester und Leviten im Deuteronomium: Überlegungen zur sog. "Levitisierung" des Priestertums', *ZABR* 5: 285–309.

Achtemeier, P. J. (1996), *1 Peter*, Hermeneia, Minneapolis: Fortress.

Alexander, T. D. (2008), *From Eden to the New Jerusalem: An Introduction to Biblical Theology*, Grand Rapids: Kregel.

——— (2012), *From Paradise to the Promised Land: An Introduction to the Pentateuch*, 3rd ed., Grand Rapids: Baker.

——— with D. W. Baker and B. K. Waltke (1988), *Obadiah, Jonah and Micah*, TOTC 23A, Leicester: Inter-Varsity Press.

Allen, L. C. (1976), *The Books of Joel, Obadiah, Jonah, and Micah*, NICOT, Grand Rapids: Eerdmans.

——— (1997), '*zkr* (2349)', *NIDOTTE* 1: 1100–1106.

——— (2008), *Jeremiah: A Commentary*, OTL, Louisville: Westminster John Knox.

Anizor, U., and H. J. Voss (2016), *Representing Christ: A Vision for the Priesthood of All Believers*, Downers Grove: InterVarsity Press.

Armerding, C. E. (1975), 'Were David's Sons Really Priests?', in G. F. Hawthorne (ed.), *Current Issues in Biblical and Patristic Interpretation*, Grand Rapids: Eerdmans, 75–86.

Ashley, T. R. (1993), *The Book of Numbers*, NICOT, Grand Rapids: Eerdmans.

Attridge, H. W. (2013), 'How Priestly Is the "High Priestly Prayer" of John 17?', *CBQ* 75: 1–14.

——— (2016), 'Jesus the Incarnate High Priest: Intracanonical Readings of Hebrews and John', in G. Gelardini and H. W. Attridge (eds.), *Hebrews in Contexts*, Leiden: Brill, 283–298.

Aune, D. E. (1997), *Revelation 1–5*, WBC 52A, Dallas: Word.

Averbeck, R. E. (1996), 'Priest, Priesthood', *EDBT* 632–638.

——— (1997a), '*ṭāhēr* (3197)', *NIDOTTE* 2: 338–353.

—— (1997b), '*mizbēaḥ* (4640)', *NIDOTTE* 2: 888–908.

—— (1997c), '*ma'ăśēr* (5130)', *NIDOTTE* 2: 1035–1055.

—— (1997d), 'Offerings and Sacrifices', *NIDOTTE* 4: 996–1022.

—— (2015), 'The Lost World of Adam and Eve: A Review Essay', *Them* 40: 226–239.

Baigent, J. W. (1981), 'Jesus as Priest: An Examination of the Claim that the Concept of Jesus as Priest May Be Found in the New Testament Outside the Epistle to the Hebrews', *VE* 12: 34–44.

Baldwin, J. G. (1964), '*Ṣemaḥ* as a Technical Term in the Prophets', *VT* 14: 93–97.

—— (1972), *Haggai, Zechariah and Malachi*, TOTC 24, Leicester: Inter-Varsity Press.

—— (1988), *1 and 2 Samuel*, TOTC 8, Leicester: Inter-Varsity Press.

Ballentine, S. E. (2002), 'Job as Priest to the Priests', *ExAud* 18: 29–52.

Bandstra, A. J. (1992), ' "A Kingship and Priests": Inaugurated Eschatology in the Apocalypse', *CTJ* 27: 10–25.

Barker, P. A. (2004), *The Triumph of Grace in Deuteronomy: Faithless Israel, Faithful Yahweh in Deuteronomy*, Paternoster Biblical Monographs, Carlisle: Paternoster.

Basser, H. W. (2000), 'Priests and Priesthood, Jewish', *DNTB* 824–827.

Bauckham, R. J. (1993), *The Climax of Prophecy: Studies on the Book of Revelation*, Edinburgh: T&T Clark.

Beale, G. K. (1999), *The Book of Revelation*, NIGTC, Grand Rapids: Eerdmans.

—— (2004), *The Temple and the Church's Mission: A Biblical Theology of the Dwelling Place of God*, NSBT 17, Leicester: Apollos.

—— (2005), 'Eden, the Temple, and the Church's Mission in the New Creation', *JETS* 48: 5–31.

—— (2011), *A New Testament Biblical Theology: The Unfolding of the Old Testament in the New*, Grand Rapids: Baker Academic.

—— and M. Kim (2014), *God Dwells Among Us: Expanding Eden to the Ends of the Earth*, Downers Grove: InterVarsity Press; Nottingham: Inter-Varsity Press.

Beckwith, R. T. (1989), 'The Relation Between Christ's Sacrifice and Priesthood and Those of the Church: An Attempt at a Summary Statement', *Chm* 103: 231–239.

Begg, C. T. (1999), 'The Peoples and the Worship of Yahweh in the Book of Isaiah', in M. P. Graham, R. R. Marrs and S. L. McKenzie (eds.), *Worship and the Hebrew Bible*, JSOTSup 284, Sheffield: Sheffield Academic Press, 35–55.

Bergen, R. D. (1996), *1, 2 Samuel*, NAC 7, Nashville: Broadman & Holman.

Bird, M. F. (2009), *Are You the One Who Is to Come? The Historical Jesus and the Messianic Question*, Grand Rapids: Baker Academic.

—— (2010), *Crossing Over Sea and Land: Jewish Missionary Activity in the Second Temple Period*, Peabody: Hendrickson.

Blauw, J. (1962), *The Missionary Nature of the Church: A Survey of the Biblical Theology of Mission*, London: Lutterworth.

Blaylock, R. M. (2016), 'My Messenger, the LORD, and the Messenger of the Covenant: Malachi 3:1 Revisited', *SBJT* 20: 69–95.

Block, D. I. (1997), *The Book of Ezekiel Chapters 1–24*, NICOT, Grand Rapids: Eerdmans.

—— (1998), *The Book of Ezekiel Chapters 25–48*, NICOT, Grand Rapids: Eerdmans.

—— (1999), *Judges, Ruth*, NAC 6, Nashville: Broadman & Holman.

—— (2010), 'To Serve and to Keep: Toward a Biblical Understanding of Humanity's Responsibility in the Face of the Biodiversity Crisis', in N. J. Toly and D. I. Block (eds.), *Keeping God's Earth: The Global Environment in Biblical Perspective*, Downers Grove: InterVarsity Press; Nottingham: Apollos, 116–140.

—— (2012), *Deuteronomy*, NIVAC, Grand Rapids: Zondervan.

—— (2013), 'Eden: A Temple? A Reassessment of the Biblical Evidence', in D. M. Gurtner and B. L. Gladd (eds.), *From Creation to New Creation: Biblical Theology and Exegesis*, Peabody: Hendrickson, 3–29.

—— (2014), *For the Glory of God: Recovering a Biblical Theology of Worship*, Grand Rapids: Baker Academic.

Blomberg, C. L. (2000), 'The Unity and Diversity of Scripture', *NDBT* 64–72.

Bock, D. L. (2013), 'Son of Man', *DJG* 894–900.

Boda, M. J. (2001), 'Oil, Crowns and Thrones: Prophet, Priest and King in Zechariah 1:7–6:15', *JHebS* 3: Article 10.

—— (2004), *Haggai, Zechariah*, NIVAC, Grand Rapids: Zondervan.

—— (2012), 'Perspectives on Priests in Haggai–Malachi', in J. Penner, K. M. Penner and C. Wassen (eds.), *Prayer and Poetry in the Dead Sea Scrolls and Related Literature*, STDJ 98, Leiden: Brill, 13–33.

—— (2016), *The Book of Zechariah*, NICOT, Grand Rapids: Eerdmans.

Bond, H. K. (2007), 'Discarding the Seamless Robe: The High Priesthood of Jesus in John's Gospel', in D. B. Capes, A. D. DeConick, H. K. Bond and T. A. Miller (eds.), *Israel's God and Rebecca's Children: Christology and Community in Early Judaism*, Waco: Baylor University Press, 183–194.

Booth, S. M. (2015), *The Tabernacling Presence of God: Mission and Gospel Witness*, Eugene: Wipf & Stock.

Boxall, I. (2006), *The Revelation of Saint John*, BNTC 18, London: A&C Black.

Breshears, G. (1994), 'The Body of Christ: Prophet, Priest, or King?', *JETS* 37: 3–26.

Bruce, F. F. (1990), *The Epistle to the Hebrews*, rev. ed., NICNT, Grand Rapids: Eerdmans.

Bruckner, J. K. (2004), *Jonah, Nahum, Habakkuk, Zephaniah*, NIVAC, Grand Rapids: Zondervan.

Brunson, A. C. (2003), *Psalm 118 in the Gospel of John: An Intertextual Study on the New Exodus Pattern in the Theology of John*, WUNT 2.158, Tübingen: Mohr Siebeck.

Bulley, C. J. (2000), *The Priesthood of Some Believers: Developments from the General to the Special Priesthood in the Christian Literature of the First Three Centuries*, Paternoster Biblical and Theological Monographs, Milton Keynes: Paternoster.

Butler, T. C. (2009), *Judges*, WBC 8, Nashville: Thomas Nelson.

Caird, G. B. (1984), *A Commentary on the Revelation of St. John the Divine*, 2nd ed., BNTC, London: A&C Black.

Carpenter, E. (1997), '*sĕgullâ* (6035)', *NIDOTTE* 3: 224.

Carson, D. A. (2000), 'Systematic Theology and Biblical Theology', *NDBT* 89–104.

——— (2007), '1 Peter', in G. K. Beale and D. A. Carson (eds.), *Commentary on the New Testament Use of the Old Testament*, Grand Rapids: Baker Academic, 1015–1045.

Chapman, S. B. (2016), *1 Samuel as Christian Scripture*, Grand Rapids: Eerdmans.

Chester, T. (2016), *Exodus for You*, Epsom: The Good Book Company.

Cheung, A. T. M. (1986), 'The Priest as the Redeemed Man: A Biblical-Theological Study of the Priesthood', *JETS* 29: 265–275.

Childs, B. S. (1974), *The Book of Exodus*, OTL, Philadelphia: Westminster.

——— (2001), *Isaiah: A Commentary*, OTL, Louisville: Westminster John Knox.

Chisholm Jr, R. B. (2013), *A Commentary on Judges and Ruth*, Kregel Exegetical Library, Grand Rapids: Kregel Academic.

Chryssavgis, J. (1987), 'The Royal Priesthood (Peter 2.9)', *GOTR* 32: 373–377.

Clark, R. (1935), 'The Imperial Priesthood of the Believer (Revelation 1:6; 1 Peter 2:5, 9)', *BSac* 92: 442–449.

Cockerill, G. L. (1993), review of *Proleptic Priests*, by J. M. Scholer, *JBL* 112: 171–173.

—— (2012), *The Epistle to the Hebrews*, NICNT, Grand Rapids: Eerdmans.

Cody, A. (1969), *A History of Old Testament Priesthood*, AnBib 35, Rome: Pontifical Biblical Institute.

Cole, G. A. (2007), *He Who Gives Life: The Doctrine of the Holy Spirit*, Foundations of Evangelical Theology, Wheaton: Crossway.

—— (2009), *God the Peacemaker: How Atonement Brings Shalom*, NSBT 25, Nottingham: Apollos.

Cole, R. D. (2000), *Numbers*, NAC 3B, Nashville: Broadman & Holman.

Craigie, P. C., P. H. Kelley and J. F. Drinkard Jr (1991), *Jeremiah 1–25*, WBC 26, Dallas: Word.

Cranfield, C. E. B. (1979), *Romans IX–XVI*, ICC, Edinburgh: T&T Clark.

Crocker, L. K. (2013), 'A Holy Nation', *RTR* 73: 185–201.

Davids, P. H. (1990), *The First Epistle of Peter*, NICNT, Grand Rapids: Eerdmans.

Davidson, R. M. (2015), 'Earth's First Sanctuary: Genesis 1–3 and Parallel Creation Accounts', *AUSS* 53: 65–89.

Davies, J. A. (2004), *A Royal Priesthood: Literary and Intertextual Perspectives on an Image of Israel in Exodus 19.6*, JSOTSup 395, London: T&T Clark International.

Dearman, J. A. (2002), *Jeremiah, Lamentations*, NIVAC, Grand Rapids: Zondervan.

—— (2010), *The Book of Hosea*, NICOT, Grand Rapids: Eerdmans.

Deenick, K. (2011), 'Priest and King or Priest-King in 1 Samuel 2:35', *WTJ* 73: 325–339.

Delcor, M. (1997), '*ml'* to be full, fill', *TLOT* 2: 664–666.

Dempster, S. G. (2003), *Dominion and Dynasty: A Biblical Theology of the Hebrew Bible*, NSBT 15, Leicester: Apollos.

deSilva, D. A. (2000), *Perseverance in Gratitude: A Socio-Rhetorical Commentary on the Epistle 'to the Hebrews'*, Grand Rapids: Eerdmans.

—— (2006), 'The Invention and Argumentative Function of Priestly Discourse in the Epistle to the Hebrews', *BBR* 16: 295–323.

Dickson, J. P. (2003), *Mission-Commitment in Ancient Judaism and in the Pauline Communities: The Shape, Extent and Background of Early Christian Mission*, WUNT 2.159, Tübingen: Mohr Siebeck.

Diffey, D. S. (2013), 'David and the Fulfilment of 1 Samuel 2:35: Faithful Priest, Sure House, and a Man after God's Own Heart', *EvQ* 85: 99–104.

Dillard, R. B. (1987), *2 Chronicles*, WBC 15, Waco: Word.

—— (1992), 'Joel', in T. E. McComiskey (ed.), *The Minor Prophets*, 3 vols., Grand Rapids: Baker, 1: 239–313.

Downs, D. J. (2006), '"The Offering of the Gentiles" in Romans 15.16', *JSNT* 29: 173–186.

Dozeman, T. B. (2009), *Commentary on Exodus*, ECC, Grand Rapids: Eerdmans.

—— (2015), *Joshua 1–12*, AYB 6B, New Haven: Yale University Press.

Draycott, A., and J. Y. Rowe (eds.) (2012), *Living Witness: Explorations in Missional Ethics*, Nottingham: Apollos.

Duguid, I. M. (1994), *Ezekiel and the Leaders of Israel*, VTSup 56, Leiden: Brill.

—— (1999), *Ezekiel*, NIVAC, Grand Rapids: Zondervan.

Duke, R. K. (2003), 'Priests, Priesthood', *DOTP* 646–655.

Dumbrell, W. J. (2002), 'Genesis 2:1–17: A Foreshadowing of the New Creation', in S. J. Hafemann (ed.), *Biblical Theology: Retrospect and Prospect*, Downers Grove: InterVarsity Press; Leicester: Apollos, 53–65.

Dunn, J. D. G. (1988), *Romans*, 2 vols., WBC 38, Waco: Word.

Durham, J. I. (1987), *Exodus*, WBC 3, Waco: Word.

Edwards, J. R. (2002), *The Gospel According to Mark*, PNTC, Grand Rapids: Eerdmans.

Elgvin, T. (2009), 'Priests on Earth as in Heaven: Jewish Light on the Book of Revelation', in F. García Martínez (ed.), *Echoes from the Caves: Qumran and the New Testament*, Leiden: Brill, 257–278.

Ellingworth, P. (1993), *The Epistle to the Hebrews*, NIGTC, Grand Rapids: Eerdmans.

—— (2000), 'Priests', *NDBT* 696–701.

Elwell, W. A. (ed.) (1996), *Evangelical Dictionary of Biblical Theology*, Grand Rapids: Baker.

Enns, P. (2000), *Exodus*, NIVAC, Grand Rapids: Zondervan.

Evans, C. A. (2001), *Mark 8:27–16:20*, WBC 34B, Nashville: Thomas Nelson.

Evans, M. J. (2005), 'Samuel', *DOTHB* 863–866.

Fee, G. D., and D. K. Stuart (2014), *How to Read the Bible for All Its Worth*, 4th ed., Grand Rapids: Zondervan.

Feinberg, J. S. (ed.) (1988), *Continuity and Discontinuity: Perspectives on the Relationship Between the Old and New Testaments*, Westchester: Crossway.

Feuillet, A. (1975), *The Priesthood of Christ and His Ministers*, tr. M. J. O'Connell, Garden City: Doubleday.

Firth, D. G. (2009), *1 & 2 Samuel*, AOTC 8, Nottingham: Apollos.

Fishbane, M. A. (1975), 'Composition and Structure in the Jacob Cycle (Gen. 25:19–35:22)', *JJS* 26: 15–38; repr. in *Text and Texture*, New York: Schocken, 1979, 40–62.

Fletcher-Louis, C. H. T. (2006), 'Jesus as the High Priestly Messiah (Part 1)', *JSHJ* 4: 155–175.

——— (2007), 'Jesus as the High Priestly Messiah (Part 2)', *JSHJ* 5: 57–79.

——— (2013), 'Priests and Priesthood', *DJG* 696–705.

Forbes, G. W. (2014), *1 Peter*, EGGNT, Nashville: Broadman & Holman Academic.

France, R. T. (1998), 'First Century Bible Study: Old Testament Motifs in 1 Peter 2:4–10', *Journal of the European Pentecostal Theological Association* 18: 26–48.

——— (2002), *The Gospel of Mark*, NIGTC, Grand Rapids: Eerdmans.

Fretheim, T. E. (1991), *Exodus*, IBC, Louisville: John Knox.

——— (1997), '*šrt* (9250)', *NIDOTTE* 4: 256–257.

Gage, W. A., and S. P. Carpenter (2014), *A Literary Guide to the Life of Christ in Matthew, Mark, and Luke–Acts: How the Synoptic Evangelists Tell the Story of Jesus*, Fort Lauderdale: St Andrews House.

Garr, W. R. (2000), '"Image" and "Likeness" in the Inscription from Tell Fakhariyeh', *IEJ* 50: 227–234.

Garrett, D. A. (2003), 'Levi, Levites', *DOTP* 519–522.

——— (2014), *A Commentary on Exodus*, Kregel Exegetical Library, Grand Rapids: Kregel.

Gentry, P. J. (2008), 'The Covenant at Sinai', *SBJT* 12: 38–63.

——— and S. J. Wellum (2012), *Kingdom Through Covenant: A Biblical-Theological Understanding of the Covenants*, Wheaton: Crossway.

Glazier-McDonald, B. (1987), *Malachi: The Divine Messenger*, SBLDS 98, Atlanta: Scholars Press.

Goheen, M. W. (2011), *A Light to the Nations: The Missional Church and the Biblical Story*, Grand Rapids: Baker Academic.

Goldingay, J. E. (2003), *Old Testament Theology*, vol. 1: *Israel's Gospel*, Downers Grove: InterVarsity Press.

——— (2008), *Psalms*, vol. 3: *Psalms 90–150*, BCOTWP, Grand Rapids: Baker Academic.

Gordon, R. P. (1986), *I & II Samuel*, Library of Biblical Interpretation, Grand Rapids: Regency.

Goswell, G. R. (2011), 'David in the Prophecy of Amos', *VT* 61: 243–257.

Grabbe, L. L. (2004), 'A Priest Is Without Honor in His Own Prophet: Priests and Other Religious Specialists in the Latter Prophets', in L. L. Grabbe and A. O. Bellis (eds.), *The Priests in the Prophets: The Portrayal of Priests, Prophets and Other Religious Specialists in the Latter Prophets*, London: T&T Clark International, 79–97.

Gray, G. B. (1925), *Sacrifice in the Old Testament: Its Theory and Practice*, Oxford: Clarendon.

Grisanti, M. A. (2001), 'Inspiration, Inerrancy, and the OT Canon: The Place of Textual Updating in an Inerrant View of Scripture', *JETS* 44: 577–598.

Gupta, N. K. (2009), 'A Spiritual House of Royal Priests, Chosen and Honored: The Presence and Function of Cultic Imagery in 1 Peter', *PRSt* 36: 61–76.

Guthrie, G. H. (1994), *The Structure of Hebrews: A Text-Linguistic Analysis*, NovTSup 73, Leiden: Brill.

——— (2007), 'Hebrews', in G. K. Beale and D. A. Carson (eds.), *Commentary on the New Testament Use of the Old Testament*, Grand Rapids: Baker Academic, 919–995.

Habel, N. C. (1985), *The Book of Job*, OTL, Philadelphia: Westminster.

Hafemann, S. J. (2000), *2 Corinthians*, NIVAC, Grand Rapids: Zondervan.

Hagner, D. A. (2005), 'The Son of God as Unique High Priest: The Christology of the Epistle to the Hebrews', in R. N. Longenecker (ed.), *Contours of Christology in the New Testament*, Grand Rapids: Eerdmans, 247–267.

Hamilton Jr, J. M. (2006), *God's Indwelling Presence: The Holy Spirit in the Old and New Testaments*, NAC Studies in Biblical Theology 1, Nashville: Broadman & Holman Academic.

—— (2010), *God's Glory in Salvation Through Judgment: A Biblical Theology*, Wheaton: Crossway.

—— (2014a), *What Is Biblical Theology? A Guide to the Bible's Story, Symbolism, and Patterns*, Wheaton: Crossway.

—— (2014b), *With the Clouds of Heaven: The Book of Daniel in Biblical Theology*, NSBT 32, Downers Grove: IVP Academic; Nottingham: Apollos.

Hamilton, V. P. (1990), *The Book of Genesis: Chapters 1–17*, NICOT, Grand Rapids: Eerdmans.

—— (1995), *The Book of Genesis: Chapters 18–50*, NICOT, Grand Rapids: Eerdmans.

—— (2011), *Exodus: An Exegetical Commentary*, Grand Rapids: Baker Academic.

Harrington, W. J. (1993), *Revelation*, SP 16, Collegeville: Liturgical Press.

Harris, M. J. (2005), *The Second Epistle to the Corinthians*, NIGTC, Grand Rapids: Eerdmans.

—— (2008), '2 Corinthians', *EBC*[2] 11: 415–545.

Hartley, J. E. (1992), *Leviticus*, WBC 4, Dallas: Word.

—— (2000), *Genesis*, NIBCOT 1, Peabody: Hendrickson.

—— (2003), 'Atonement, Day of', *DOTP* 54–61.

Haydock, N. (2015), *The Theology of the Levitical Priesthood: Assisting God's People in Their Mission to the Nations*, Eugene: Wipf & Stock.

Hays, J. D. (2016), *The Temple and the Tabernacle: A Study of God's Dwelling Places from Genesis to Revelation*, Grand Rapids: Baker.

Heil, J. P. (1997), 'The Narrative Strategy and Pragmatics of the Temple Theme in Mark', *CBQ* 59: 76–100.

Hendel, R. S. (1998), *The Text of Genesis 1–11: Textual Studies and Critical Edition*, New York: Oxford University Press.

Herring, S. L. (2012), 'Moses as Divine Substitute in Exodus', *CTR* 9.2: 53–68.

Hieke, T., and T. Nicklas (eds.) (2012), *The Day of Atonement: Its Interpretations in Early Jewish and Christian Traditions*, TBN 15, Leiden: Brill.

Hill, A. E. (1998), *Malachi*, AB 25D, New York: Doubleday.

—— (2003), *1 & 2 Chronicles*, NIVAC, Grand Rapids: Zondervan.

—— (2012), *Haggai, Zechariah and Malachi*, TOTC 28, Nottingham: Inter-Varsity Press.

Hoehner, H. W. (2002), *Ephesians*, Grand Rapids: Baker Academic.

Holladay, W. L. (1986), *Jeremiah 1: A Commentary on the Book of the Prophet Jeremiah Chapters 1–25*, Hermeneia, Minneapolis: Fortress.

Homan, M. M. (2000), 'The Divine Warrior in His Tent: A Military Model for Yahweh's Tabernacle', *BRev* 16.6: 22–34, 55.

Horton, M. S. (2011), *The Christian Faith: A Systematic Theology for Pilgrims on the Way*, Grand Rapids: Zondervan.

Hostetter, E. C. (1997), 'ṣûṣ (7437)', *NIDOTTE* 3: 784–786.

Houtman, C. (2000), *Exodus*, vol. 3: *Chapters 20–40*, tr. S. Woudstra, HCOT, Leuven: Peeters.

Hubbard, D. A. (1989), *Joel and Amos*, TOTC 22B, Leicester: Inter-Varsity Press.

—— (1996), 'Priests and Levites', *NBD*³ 956–962.

Hubbard, R. L. (2009), *Joshua*, NIVAC, Grand Rapids: Zondervan.

Hudson, D. M. (1994), 'Living in a Land of Epithets: Anonymity in Judges 19–21', *JSOT* 62: 49–66.

Hughes, Paul E. (2003), 'Jethro', *DOTP* 467–469.

Hughes, Philip E. (1973–4), 'The Blood of Jesus and His Heavenly Priesthood in Hebrews', *BSac* 130: 99–109, 195–212, 305–314; *BSac* 131: 26–33.

Japhet, S. (1982), 'Seshbazzar and Zerubbabel – Against the Background of the Historical and Religious Tendencies of Ezra-Nehemiah', *ZAW* 94: 66–98.

Jenson, P. P. (1992), *Graded Holiness: A Key to the Priestly Conception of the World*, JSOTSup 106, Sheffield: JSOT Press.

—— (1997), 'khn (3912)', *NIDOTTE* 2: 600–605.

—— (2012), 'Temple', *DOTPr* 767–775.

Jobes, K. H. (2005), *1 Peter*, BECNT 16, Grand Rapids: Baker Academic.

Joslin, B. C. (2007), 'Can Hebrews Be Structured? An Assessment of Eight Approaches', *CurBR* 6: 99–129.

Kaiser Jr, W. C. (1978), *Toward an Old Testament Theology*, Grand Rapids: Zondervan.

—— (2008), *The Promise-Plan of God: A Biblical Theology of the Old and New Testaments*, Grand Rapids: Zondervan.

—— (2012), *Mission in the Old Testament: Israel as a Light to the Nations*, 2nd ed., Grand Rapids: Baker Academic.

Keener, C. S. (2012–15), *Acts*, 4 vols., Grand Rapids: Baker Academic.

Keil, C. F., and F. Delitzsch (1996), *Commentary on the Old Testament*, tr. J. Martin et al., 10 vols., Peabody: Hendrickson; update of Edinburgh: T&T Clark, 1866–91.

Kilmartin, E. J. (1975), review of *The Priesthood of Christ and His Ministers*, by A. Feuillet, *TS* 36: 516–518.

Kiuchi, N. (1987), *The Purification Offering in the Priestly Literature: Its Meaning and Function*, JSOTSup 56, Sheffield: JSOT Press.

—— (2007), *Leviticus*, AOTC 3, Nottingham: Apollos.

Klein, G. L. (2008), *Zechariah*, NAC 21B, Nashville: Broadman & Holman.

Kline, M. G. (1980), *Images of the Spirit*, Grand Rapids: Baker.

Klingbeil, G. A. (2005), 'Priests and Levites', *DOTHB* 811–819.

Koester, C. R. (2001), *Hebrews*, AB 36, New York: Doubleday.

—— (2014), *Revelation*, AYB 38A, New Haven: Yale University Press.

Kooij, A. van der (2006), 'A Kingdom of Priests: Comment on Exodus 19:6', in R. Roukema (ed.), *The Interpretation of Exodus*, CBET 44, Leuven: Peeters, 171–179.

Kruse, C. G. (2012), *Paul's Letter to the Romans*, PNTC, Grand Rapids: Eerdmans.

Kugler, R. A. (2010), 'Priests', in J. J. Collins and D. C. Harlow (eds.), *The Eerdmans Dictionary of Early Judaism*, Grand Rapids: Eerdmans, 1096–1099.

Kühlewein, J. (1997), '*qrb* to approach', *TLOT* 3: 1164–1169.

Kwakkel, G. (2011), 'Paronomasia, Ambiguities and Shifts in Hos 5:1–2', *VT* 61: 603–615.

Lane, W. L. (1991), *Hebrews*, 2 vols., WBC 47, Dallas: Word.

Leithart, P. J. (1999), 'Attendants of Yahweh's House: Priesthood in the Old Testament', *JSOT* 85: 3–24.

—— (2000), 'Womb of the World: Baptism and the Priesthood of the New Covenant in Hebrews 10.19–22', *JSNT* 78: 49–65.

—— (2003), *The Priesthood of the Plebs: A Theology of Baptism*, Eugene: Wipf & Stock.

Lessing, R. R. (2014), *Isaiah 56–66*, ConcC, St Louis: Concordia.

Leuchter, M. (2007), '"The Levite in Your Gates": The Deuteronomic Redefinition of Levitical Authority', *JBL* 126: 417–436.

—— (2013), 'Samuel: A Prophet Like Moses or a Priest Like Moses?', in M. R. Jacobs and R. F. Person Jr (eds.), *Israelite Prophecy and the Deuteronomistic History: Portrait, Reality, and the Formation of a History*, AIL, Atlanta: Society of Biblical Literature, 147–168.

Levenson, J. D. (1993), *The Death and Resurrection of the Beloved Son: The Transformation of Child Sacrifice in Judaism and Christianity*, New Haven: Yale University Press.

Levine, B. A. (1989), *Leviticus*, JPSTC, Philadelphia: Jewish Publication Society.

Lieu, J. M. (1985), '"Grace to You and Peace": The Apostolic Greeting', *BJRL* 68: 161–178.

Lightfoot, J. B. (1869), *St Paul's Epistle to the Philippians*, 2nd ed., London: Macmillan.

Lints, R. (2015), *Identity and Idolatry: The Image of God and Its Inversion*, NSBT 36, Nottingham: Apollos.

Lister, J. R. (2015), *The Presence of God: Its Place in the Storyline of Scripture and the Story of Our Lives*, Wheaton: Crossway.

Long, V. P. (2009), '2 Samuel', in J. H. Walton (ed.), *Zondervan Illustrated Bible Backgrounds Commentary: Old Testament*, 5 vols., Grand Rapids: Zondervan, 2: 412–491.

Longenecker, R. N. (2007), 'Acts', *EBC*² 10: 663–1102.

——— (2016), *The Epistle to the Romans*, NIGTC, Grand Rapids: Eerdmans.

McCann, J. C. (2002), *Judges*, IBC, Louisville: John Knox.

McCarter Jr, P. K. (1980), *I Samuel*, AB 8, New York: Doubleday.

McComiskey, T. E. (1992), 'Hosea', in T. E. McComiskey (ed.), *The Minor Prophets*, 3 vols., Grand Rapids: Baker, 1: 1–237.

McConville, J. G. (1999), 'Priesthood in Joshua to Kings', *VT* 49: 73–87.

——— (2002), *Deuteronomy*, AOTC 5, Leicester: Apollos.

McKelvey, R. J. (2013), *Pioneer and Priest: Jesus Christ in the Epistle to the Hebrews*, Eugene: Wipf & Stock.

McKeown, J. (2008), *Genesis*, THOTC, Grand Rapids: Eerdmans.

Malone, A. S. (2007), 'The Invisibility of God: A Survey of a Misunderstood Phenomenon', *EvQ* 79: 311–329.

——— (2009), 'God the Illeist: Third-Person Self-References and Trinitarian Hints in the Old Testament', *JETS* 52: 499–518.

——— (2011), 'Distinguishing the Angel of the Lord', *BBR* 21: 297–314.

——— (2014), 'Disputing Old Testament Indwelling', in J. T. K. Lim (ed.), *Holy Spirit: Unfinished Agenda*, Singapore: Genesis/Word N Works, 81–85.

——— (2015), *Knowing Jesus in the Old Testament? A Fresh Look at Christophanies*, Nottingham: Inter-Varsity Press.

——— (2016), 'Acceptable Anachronism in Biblical Studies', *BT* 67: 351–364.

Manson, T. W. (1958), *Ministry and Priesthood: Christ's and Ours*, London: Epworth.

Marcus, J. (1992), *The Way of the Lord: Christological Exegesis of the Old Testament in the Gospel of Mark*, Louisville: Westminster John Knox.

────── (2009), *Mark 8–16: A New Translation with Introduction and Commentary*, AYB 27A, New Haven: Yale University Press.

Marx, A. (1995), 'La généalogie d'Exode vi 14–25: sa forme, sa fonction', *VT* 45: 318–336.

Mascarenhas, T. (2005), *The Missionary Function of Israel in Psalms 67, 96, and 117*, Lanham: University Press of America.

Mason, E. F. (2008), *'You Are a Priest Forever': Second Temple Jewish Messianism and the Priestly Christology of the Epistle to the Hebrews*, STDJ 74, Leiden: Brill.

Matera, F. J. (2007), *New Testament Theology: Exploring Diversity and Unity*, Louisville: Westminster John Knox.

Mathews, K. A. (1996), *Genesis 1–11:26*, NAC 1A, Nashville: Broadman & Holman.

────── (2005), *Genesis 11:27–50:26*, NAC 1B, Nashville: Broadman & Holman.

Merrill, E. H. (1993), 'Royal Priesthood: An Old Testament Messianic Motif', *BSac* 150: 50–61.

────── (1994), *Haggai, Zechariah, Malachi*, Chicago: Moody.

Meyers, C. L. (2005), *Exodus*, New Cambridge Bible Commentary, Cambridge: Cambridge University Press.

────── (2008), 'Framing Aaron: Incense Altar and Lamp Oil in the Tabernacle Texts', in S. Dolansky (ed.), *Sacred History, Sacred Literature: Essays on Ancient Israel, the Bible, and Religion*, Winona Lake: Eisenbrauns, 13–21.

Michaels, J. R. (1988), *1 Peter*, WBC 49, Waco: Word.

────── (2010), *The Gospel of John*, NICNT, Grand Rapids: Eerdmans.

Middleton, J. R. (2005), *The Liberating Image: The* Imago Dei *in Genesis 1*, Grand Rapids: Brazos.

────── (2014), *A New Heaven and a New Earth: Reclaiming Biblical Eschatology*, Grand Rapids: Baker Academic.

Milgrom, J. (1970), *Studies in Levitical Terminology: The Encroacher and the Levite, The Term ʿAboda*, Near Eastern Studies 14, Berkeley: University of California Press.

────── (1990), *Numbers*, JPSTC, Philadelphia: Jewish Publication Society.

────── (1991), *Leviticus 1–16*, AB 3, New York: Doubleday.

────── and D. I. Block (2012), *Ezekiel's Hope: A Commentary on Ezekiel 38–48*, Eugene: Cascade.

Millar, J. G. (1998), *Now Choose Life: Theology and Ethics in Deuteronomy*, NSBT 6, Leicester: Apollos.

Milstein, S. J. (2016), 'Saul the Levite and His Concubine: The "Allusive" Quality of Judges 19', *VT* 66: 95–116.

Moberly, R. W. L. (1983), *At The Mountain of God: Story and Theology in Exodus 32–34*, JSOTSup 22, Sheffield: JSOT Press.

—— (2008), 'Exodus', in K. J. Vanhoozer (ed.), *Theological Interpretation of the Old Testament: A Book-by-Book Survey*, Grand Rapids: Baker Academic, 42–51.

Moffatt, J. (1924), *A Critical and Exegetical Commentary on the Epistle to the Hebrews*, ICC, Edinburgh: T&T Clark.

Moo, D. J. (1996), *The Epistle to the Romans*, NICNT, Grand Rapids: Eerdmans.

Moore, R. K. (2003), '2 Corinthians 5.20b in the English Bible in the Light of Paul's Doctrine of Reconciliation', *BT* 54: 146–155.

Morales, L. M. (2015), *Who Shall Ascend the Mountain of the Lord? A Biblical Theology of the Book of Leviticus*, NSBT 37, Nottingham: Apollos.

Morales, R. J. (2010), *The Spirit and the Restoraton of Israel: New Exodus and New Creation Motifs in Galatians*, WUNT 2.282, Tübingen: Mohr Siebeck.

Mosis, R. (1978), 'Ex 19,5b.6a: Syntaktischer Aufbau und lexikalische Semantik', *BZ* 22: 1–25.

Moster, D. Z. (2014), 'The Levite of Judges 17–18', *JBL* 133: 729–737.

—— (2015), 'The Levite of Judges 19–21', *JBL* 134: 721–730.

Moṭ, L. F. (2015), *Morphological and Syntactical Irregularities in the Book of Revelation: A Greek Hypothesis*, Linguistic Biblical Studies 11, Leiden: Brill.

Mueller, E. A. (2001), *The Micah Story: A Morality Tale in the Book of Judges*, StBibLit 34, New York: Peter Lang.

Naselli, A. D., and P. R. Gons (2011), 'Prooftexting the Personality of the Holy Spirit: An Analysis of the Masculine Demonstrative Pronouns in John 14:26, 15:26, and 16:13–14', *Detroit Baptist Seminary Journal* 16: 65–89.

Nelson, R. D. (1993), *Raising up a Faithful Priest: Community and Priesthood in Biblical Theology*, Louisville: Westminster John Knox.

Niehaus, J. J. (1995), *God at Sinai: Covenant and Theophany in the Bible and Ancient Near East*, Studies in Old Testament Biblical Theology, Carlisle: Paternoster.

Nongbri, B. (2010), 'Greek Authors on Jews and Judaism', in J. J. Collins and D. C. Harlow (eds.), *The Eerdmans Dictionary of Early Judaism*, Grand Rapids: Eerdmans, 692–696.

O'Collins, G., and M. K. Jones (2010), *Jesus Our Priest: A Christian Approach to the Priesthood of Christ*, Oxford: Oxford University Press.

O'Kennedy, D. F. (1997), '*ḥll* (2725)', *NIDOTTE* 2: 145–150.

Olson, D. T. (1985), *The Death of the Old and the Birth of the New: The Framework of the Book of Numbers and the Pentateuch*, BJS 71, Chico: Scholars Press.

—— (1996), *Numbers*, IBC, Louisville: Westminster John Knox.

Organ, B. E. (2001), 'Pursuing Phinehas: A Synchronic Reading', *CBQ* 63: 203–218.

Osborne, G. R. (2002), *Revelation*, BECNT 19, Grand Rapids: Baker Academic.

Oswalt, J. N. (1986), *The Book of Isaiah: Chapters 1–39*, NICOT, Grand Rapids: Eerdmans.

—— (1998), *The Book of Isaiah: Chapters 40–66*, NICOT, Grand Rapids: Eerdmans.

—— (2003), *Isaiah*, NIVAC, Grand Rapids: Zondervan.

Pagolu, A. (1998), *The Religion of the Patriarchs*, JSOTSup 277, Sheffield: Sheffield Academic Press.

Pao, D. W. (2000), *Acts and the Isaianic New Exodus*, WUNT 2.130, Tübingen: Mohr Siebeck.

Parsons, M. C. (1988), 'Son and High Priest: A Study in the Christology of Hebrews', *EvQ* 60: 195–216.

Paul, M. J. (1997), 'Melchizedek', *NIDOTTE* 4: 934–936.

Perrin, N. (2010), *Jesus the Temple*, London: SPCK.

—— (2013), 'The Temple, a Davidic Messiah, and a Case of Mistaken Priestly Identity (Mark 2:26)', in D. M. Gurtner and B. L. Gladd (eds.), *From Creation to New Creation: Biblical Theology and Exegesis*, Peabody: Hendrickson, 163–177.

—— (2014), *Finding Jesus in the Exodus: Christ in Israel's Journey from Slavery to the Promised Land*, New York: Faith Words.

Peterson, D. G. (1995), *Possessed by God: A New Testament Theology of Sanctification and Holiness*, NSBT 1, Leicester: Apollos.

—— (2009), *The Acts of the Apostles*, PNTC, Grand Rapids: Eerdmans.

Petterson, A. R. (2009), *Behold Your King: The Hope for the House of David in the Book of Zechariah*, LHBOTS 513, New York: T&T Clark.

———— (2015), *Haggai, Zechariah & Malachi*, AOTC 25, Nottingham: Apollos.

Piotrowski, N. G., and D. S. Schrock (2016), '"You Can Make Me Clean": The Matthean Jesus as Priest and the Biblical-Theological Results', *CTR* 14.1: 3–13.

Propp, W. H. C. (2006), *Exodus 19–40*, AB 2A, New York: Doubleday.

Provan, I. W. (1995), *1 and 2 Kings*, NIBCOT 7, Peabody: Hendrickson.

Reid, A. S. (2013), *Exodus: Saved for Service*, Reading the Bible Today, Sydney South: Aquila.

Reymond, R. L. (2002), *A New Systematic Theology of the Christian Faith*, 2nd ed. rev., Nashville: Thomas Nelson.

Richards, E. R. (2000), 'Silvanus Was Not Peter's Secretary: Theological Bias in Interpreting *dia Silouanou egrapsa* in 1 Peter 5:12', *JETS* 43: 417–432.

Roberts, J. J. M. (1991), *Nahum, Habakkuk, and Zephaniah*, OTL, Louisville: Westminster John Knox.

Robinson, D. W. B. (1974), 'The Priesthood of Paul in the Gospel of Hope', in R. J. Banks (ed.), *Reconciliation and Hope: New Testament Essays on Atonement and Eschatology*, Exeter: Paternoster, 231–245.

Rooke, D. W. (1998), 'Kingship as Priesthood: The Relationship Between the High Priesthood and the Monarchy', in J. Day (ed.), *King and Messiah in Israel and the Ancient Near East*, JSOTSup 270, Sheffield: Sheffield Academic Press, 187–208.

———— (2000), *Zadok's Heirs: The Role and Development of the High Priesthood in Ancient Israel*, Oxford: Oxford University Press.

———— (ed.) (2009), *Embroidered Garments: Priests and Gender in Biblical Israel*, Sheffield: Sheffield Phoenix.

Rooker, M. F. (2000), *Leviticus*, NAC 3A, Nashville: Broadman & Holman.

Rose, W. H. (2005), 'Zerubbabel', *DOTHB* 1016–1019.

Rosner, B. S. (2013), *Paul and the Law: Keeping the Commandments of God*, NSBT 31, Nottingham: Apollos.

Ross, A. P. (1988), *Creation and Blessing: A Guide to the Study and Exposition of the Book of Genesis*, Grand Rapids: Baker.

———— (2002), *Holiness to the LORD: A Guide to the Exposition of the Book of Leviticus*, Grand Rapids: Baker Academic.

Sailhamer, J. H. (2008), 'Genesis', *EBC*² 1: 21–331.

Salters, R. B. (2010), *A Critical and Exegetical Commentary on Lamentations*, ICC, London: T&T Clark.

Sarna, N. M. (1989), *Genesis*, JPSTC, Philadelphia: Jewish Publication Society.

—— (1991), *Exodus*, JPSTC, Philadelphia: Jewish Publication Society.

Schnabel, E. J. (2004), *Early Christian Mission*, 2 vols., Leicester: Apollos.

—— (2012), *Acts*, ZECNT 5, Grand Rapids: Zondervan.

Schniedewind, W. M. (1994), 'King and Priest in the Book of Chronicles and the Duality of Qumran Messianism', *JJS* 45: 71–78.

Scholer, J. M. (1991), *Proleptic Priests: Priesthood in the Epistle to the Hebrews*, JSNTSup 49, Sheffield: Sheffield Academic Press.

Schreiner, T. R. (1998), *Romans*, BECNT 6, Grand Rapids: Baker.

—— (2003), *1, 2 Peter, Jude*, NAC 37, Nashville: Broadman & Holman.

Schrenk, G. (1965), '*hieros*, etc.', *TDNT* 3: 221–283.

Schrock, D. S. (2013), 'A Biblical-Theological Investigation of Christ's Priesthood and Covenant Mediation with Respect to the Extent of the Atonement', PhD diss., Southern Baptist Theological Seminary.

Schultz, R. (1997), 'Servant, Slave', *NIDOTTE* 4: 1183–1198.

Schüssler Fiorenza, E. (1972), *Priester für Gott: Studien zum Herrschafts- und Priestermotiv in der Apokalypse*, NTAbh 7, Münster: Aschendorff.

—— (1998), *The Book of Revelation: Justice and Judgment*, 2nd ed., Minneapolis: Fortress.

Scobie, C. H. H. (2003), *The Ways of Our God: An Approach to Biblical Theology*, Grand Rapids: Eerdmans.

Scott, J. M. (1998), *2 Corinthians*, NIBCNT 8, Peabody: Hendrickson.

Seifrid, M. A. (2014), *The Second Letter to the Corinthians*, PNTC, Grand Rapids: Eerdmans; Nottingham: Apollos.

Sheldon, L. J. (2014), 'Images of Power and a Kingdom of Priests', *AUSS* 52: 161–172.

Sklar, J. (2013), *Leviticus*, TOTC 3, Nottingham: Inter-Varsity Press.

Small, B. C. (2014), *The Characterization of Jesus in the Book of Hebrews*, BibInt 128, Leiden: Brill.

Smalley, S. S. (1961), 'The Imitation of Christ in I Peter', *Chm* 75: 172–178.

Smith, D. L. (2016), 'The Uses of "New Exodus" in New Testament Scholarship: Preparing a Way Through the Wilderness', *CurBR* 14: 207–243.

Smith, G. V. (1998), *Amos*, rev. ed., Mentor Commentary, Fearn: Christian Focus.

—— (2001), *Hosea, Amos, Micah*, NIVAC, Grand Rapids: Zondervan.

—— (2009), *Isaiah 40–66*, NAC 15B, Nashville: Broadman & Holman.

Spina, F. A. (1994), 'Eli's Seat: The Transition from Priest to Prophet in 1 Samuel 1–4', *JSOT* 62: 67–75.

Sprinkle, J. M. (1994), *'The Book of the Covenant': A Literary Approach*, JSOTSup 174, Sheffield: JSOT.

Stevenson, G. (2001), *Power and Place: Temple and Identity in the Book of Revelation*, BZNW 107, Berlin: de Gruyter.

Strong, A. H. (1907), *Systematic Theology*, 8th ed., London: Pickering & Inglis.

Stuart, D. K. (1987), *Hosea–Jonah*, WBC 31, Waco: Word.

—— (1989), *Ezekiel*, Communicator's Commentary 18, Dallas: Word.

—— (1998), 'Malachi', in T. E. McComiskey (ed.), *The Minor Prophets*, 3 vols., Grand Rapids: Baker, 3: 1245–1396.

—— (2006), *Exodus*, NAC 2, Nashville: Broadman & Holman.

Sweeney, M. A. (2003), *Zephaniah*, Hermeneia, Minneapolis: Fortress.

Tait, M. B. (2010), 'The Search for Valid Orders: The Melchizedek Christology in Hebrews', *Chm* 124: 127–142.

Tate, M. E. (1990), *Psalms 51–100*, WBC 20, Dallas: Word.

Thellman, G. S. (2013), 'Scribes', *DJG* 840–845.

Thompson, J. A. (1980), *The Book of Jeremiah*, NICOT, Grand Rapids: Eerdmans.

Thomson, C. A. (1961), 'Samuel, the Ark, and the Priesthood', *BSac* 118: 259–263.

Thrall, M. E. (1994), *A Critical and Exegetical Commentary on the Second Epistle to the Corinthians*, vol. 1: *II Corinthians I–VII*, ICC, Edinburgh: T&T Clark.

Tsumura, D. T. (2007), *The First Book of Samuel*, NICOT, Grand Rapids: Eerdmans.

Übelacker, W. G. (1995), review of *Proleptic Priests*, by J. M. Scholer, *STK* 71: 89–90.

Utzschneider, H. (2014), 'Tabernacle', in T. B. Dozeman, C. A. Evans and J. N. Lohr (eds.), *The Book of Exodus: Composition, Reception, and Interpretation*, VTSup 164, Leiden: Brill, 267–301.

VanderKam, J. C. (2004), *From Joshua to Caiaphas: High Priests After the Exile*, Minneapolis: Fortress.

VanGemeren, W. A. (2008), 'Psalms', *EBC*² 5: 21–1011.

Verhoef, P. A. (1987), *The Books of Haggai and Malachi*, NICOT, Grand Rapids: Eerdmans.

Vos, G. (1907), 'The Priesthood of Christ in the Epistle to the Hebrews', *PTR* 5: 423–447, 479–604.

Voss, H. J. (2016), *The Priesthood of All Believers and the* Missio Dei: *A Canonical, Catholic, and Contextual Perspective*, Princeton Theological Monograph Series 223, Eugene: Pickwick.

Walsh, J. T. (2001), *Style and Structure in Biblical Hebrew Narrative*, Collegeville: Liturgical Press.

Walton, J. H. (2001), *Genesis*, NIVAC, Grand Rapids: Zondervan.

——— (2003a), 'Creation', *DOTP* 155–168.

——— (2003b), 'Eden, Garden of', *DOTP* 202–207.

——— (2009), *The Lost World of Genesis One: Ancient Cosmology and the Origins Debate*, Downers Grove: IVP Academic.

——— (2011), *Genesis 1 as Ancient Cosmology*, Winona Lake: Eisenbrauns.

——— (2015a), *The Lost World of Adam and Eve: Genesis 2–3 and the Human Origins Debate*, Downers Grove: InterVarsity Press.

——— (2015b), 'Response to Richard Averbeck', *Them* 40: 240–242.

Watts, R. E. (1997), *Isaiah's New Exodus and Mark*, WUNT 2.88, Tübingen: Mohr Siebeck.

Webb, B. G. (2012), *The Book of Judges*, NICOT, Grand Rapids: Eerdmans.

Wells, J. B. (2000), *God's Holy People: A Theme in Biblical Theology*, JSOTSup 305, Sheffield: Sheffield Academic Press.

Wenham, G. J. (1975), 'Were David's Sons Priests?', *ZAW* 87: 79–82.

——— (1979), *The Book of Leviticus*, NICOT, Grand Rapids: Eerdmans.

——— (1981), *Numbers: An Introduction and Commentary*, TOTC 4, Leicester: Inter-Varsity Press.

——— (1986), 'Sanctuary Symbolism in the Garden of Eden Story', in *Proceedings of the Ninth World Congress of Jewish Studies*, Jerusalem: World Union of Jewish Studies, 19–25; repr. in Richard S. Hess and David Toshio Tsumura (eds.), *'I Studied Inscriptions from before the Flood': Ancient Near Eastern, Literary, and Linguistic Approaches to Genesis 1–11*, Sources for Biblical and Theological Study 4, Winona Lake: Eisenbrauns, 1994, 399–404.

——— (1987), *Genesis 1–15*, WBC 1, Waco: Word.

——— (1994), *Genesis 16–50*, WBC 2, Dallas: Word.

——— (1995), 'The Theology of Old Testament Sacrifice', in R. T. Beckwith and M. J. Selman (eds.), *Sacrifice in the Bible*, Carlisle: Paternoster, 75–87.

——— (1996), 'Clean and Unclean', *NBD*[3] 209–212.

——— (1997), *Numbers*, OTG, Sheffield: Sheffield Academic Press.

—— (2003), *Exploring the Old Testament*, vol. 1: *The Pentateuch*, London: SPCK.

Wenkel, D. H. (2014), 'Jesus at Age 30: Further Evidence for Luke's Portrait of a Priestly Jesus?', *BTB* 44: 195–201.

Weyde, K. W. (2015), 'The Priests and the Descendants of Levi in the Book of Malachi', *AcT* 35: 238–253.

Williams, D. A. (1998), ' "Then They Will Know That I Am the Lord": The Missiological Significance of Ezekiel's Concern for the Nations as Evident in the Use of the Recognition Formula', MA diss., All Nations Christian College.

Williamson, P. R. (2003), 'Covenant', *DOTP* 139–155.

—— (2007), *Sealed with an Oath: Covenant in God's Unfolding Purpose*, NSBT 23, Nottingham: Apollos.

—— (2008), 'Promises with Strings Attached: Covenant and Law in Exodus 19–24', in B. S. Rosner and P. R. Williamson (eds.), *Exploring Exodus: Literary, Theological and Contemporary Approaches*, Nottingham: Apollos, 89–122.

Wilson, A. J. (2015), 'When Jesus Got the Bible Wrong', *Christianity Today* 59.7: 28.

Winkle, R. E. (2012), ' "Clothes Make the (One Like a Son of) Man": Dress Imagery in Revelation 1 as an Indicator of High Priestly Status', PhD diss., Andrews University.

Wise, M. O., with B. D. Chilton and P. W. Comfort (2000), 'Temple, Jewish', *DNTB* 1167–1183.

Witherington III, B. (1998), *The Acts of the Apostles*, Grand Rapids: Eerdmans.

—— (2007), *Letters and Homilies for Jewish Christians*, Downers Grove: IVP Academic; Nottingham: Apollos.

Wood, L. J. (1976), *The Holy Spirit in the Old Testament*, Grand Rapids: Zondervan.

Woudstra, M. H. (1981), *The Book of Joshua*, NICOT, Grand Rapids: Eerdmans.

Wright, C. J. H. (1997), '*nḥl* (5706)', *NIDOTTE* 3: 77–81.

—— (2001), *The Message of Ezekiel: A New Heart and a New Spirit*, BST, Leicester: Inter-Varsity Press.

—— (2004), *Old Testament Ethics for the People of God*, Leicester: Inter-Varsity Press.

—— (2006), *The Mission of God: Unlocking the Bible's Grand Narrative*, Nottingham: Inter-Varsity Press.

Younger Jr, K. L. (2002), *Judges, Ruth*, NIVAC, Grand Rapids: Zondervan.

Index of authors

Index of Scripture references

Note: Primary discussions of a passage are often indicated in **bold**.

Titles in this series:

229

An index of Scripture references for all the volumes may be found at
http://www.thegospelcoalition.org/resources/nsbt

Printed and bound by CPI Group (UK) Ltd, Croydon, CR0 4YY

13/04/2025

14656474-0001